Contents

Foreword v
Preface ix
Acknowledgements xi

Chapter 1: An Early Diet of Love and Faith 1
Chapter 2: The Promise and Piety of Youth 17
Chapter 3: Getting Ready to Take on the World 31
Chapter 4: Realising a Dream 53
Chapter 5: Cracks Appearing 75
Chapter 6: Hermeneutical Humps 107
Chapter 7: Fearful Fundamentalism 131
Chapter 8: Vocational Bumps 169
Chapter 9: New Horizons Opening 199
Chapter 10: Where to from Here? 227

Appendices 235
Index 295

In loving memory of
Douglas Haig and Audrey Evelyn Mascord

Foreword

Keith Mascord has written first about the pain then the exhilaration of self-discovery. The book traces the stages of his transformation from what St Paul once called 'one degree of glory to another'. I chose the phrase carefully because there is no hint here of dismissal of past experience, simply the progressive stages of Keith's opening to a sense of wonder at the meaning of his own life journey.

Keith's first chapters grip the reader with his sensitive recollections of childhood and youth. His family played an immense role in shaping the man who today offers challenge to that very past. He writes in these opening chapters with beauty and imagination; this reader at least was reading a gentle and perceptive journey though a childhood nurtured in the heart of American fundamentalism. The imagery and sensitivity here are an essential aspect of the rest of the book. Keith may have shifted his theological and hermeneutical interests, but he places value on his beginnings: they are the mainstay of the man's passion for life.

Chapters five and six take you by surprise. And this is not because you have been unprepared for theological and philosophical engagement. This was implicit from the opening chapter. In that sense, the book has defined its primary readership. The title alone, *A Restless Faith: Leaving Fundamentalism in a Quest for God*, locates the book in that growing body of evangelical self-critique. It reminds me of Doug Frank's recent book *A Gentler God*: you meet the evangelical greats, you engage their theological energy, and, with growing misgiving, you face the commentators' uncertainties. There is a deep sense of inner chasm in these opening chapters.

I met again many people whose lives have intersected with my own—the spokespersons of conservative religion. Keith dressed them in fresh clothes, not the dreary apparel of some of my own personal recollections. How exciting to read Keith's encounters with Alvin Plantinga. In recent years, I have corresponded with a Professor emeritus from Calvin College MI about the conclusions drawn by Plantinga, former Director of the Center for Philosophy of Religion, University of Notre Dame, on 'evidentialism' and 'probability'. Keith, who knows Plantinga personally, as well as through his publications and presentations, focused on these two issues.

Keith takes us to the heart of this philosophy through his own sense of the man's presence and dignity. Keith speaks about Plantinga's South Bend Christian Reformed Church as a dynamic meeting place for 'ancient historians, biologists, and specialists of all sorts'. He found the preaching relevant and engaging within a church 'that was openly and honestly wrestling with issues of faith and life, without censoring alternative points of view' (p.82). Now that took me quite by surprise: I hadn't expected such a glowing affirmation.

Keith's presentation of Plantinga's philosophy will take time for careful reading, but it is essential to the incisive themes that follow. Platinga engages evolutionary rationalism in a way that has placed him at the centre of debates about neuroscience and the evolution of religion and the evolution of 'God'. In that conversation, many see his arguments about neurophysiology to be out of step with current cognitive science conclusions. The debate is open and critical to the large world of controversy over the strident claims of atheism and the equally strident claims of fundamentalism.

Keith did his doctoral studies on this philosophy which makes these two chapters all the more fundamental to the coherence of this book. They are essential reading. The way Keith writes in this section suggests another audience altogether for his reflections and conclusions. Those who will journey out of fundamentalism will need to hone their own position through careful analysis of the alternatives and willingness for genuine dialogue.

As I read to this point, I paused to recall the generations of young men and women who like Keith had entered Moore Theological College from non-Anglican conservative backgrounds to train for Anglican ministry. The denomination, at least in Sydney, gathers academically and professionally skilled people around central dominant figures. These theological guides offer a rationalistic method for Bible interpretation and ministry expression, and they gather students as disciples to their opinions.

Keith offered in return his understanding of how myth and event from the past might be explored through careful and critical study (hermeneutics). In the process he embraced 'atheism' (p.98), a staging post on the way to a fresh understanding of God. The reader might well pause to consider the many times in this book that the words 'atheist' and 'atheism' occur: on my counting nineteen times in the actual text. This is today's issue: the faith we have inherited needs a more powerful apologetic than the self-protective theology that fundamentalism offers.

And then, almost as a universal connecting theme in the book, we meet Noah, the man of flood and rainbow and dove of acceptance. Noah's epic punctuates the whole book as a catalyst for its many contemporary sub-themes—homosexuality, people of other religions, women's ministry and teaching about hell. Keith unveils conservative catch-cries on each of these issues, and then re-visions them for contemporary Australians.

In chapter seven, the themes suddenly change, and again the book moves onto familiar territory: once more I know all the personae. Keith here is gentle, but perceptive—well, you do see his nemesis in Phillip Jensen, and to some extent in Phillip's brother, Peter, the present Anglican Archbishop of Sydney. These men are leaders in Sydney Anglican conservative theology. Keith shows them locked into a way of understanding the Bible that has and will continue to have an impact on the way generations of clergy understand the Bible, the church—and most important the mission of Christianity to a multi-ethnic, multi-faith, secular Australian community. And here is a third audience. Social historians will value this book as, with the end of the Jensen ascendancy, analysis of the changing fortunes of Anglicanism in Australia will enter its next phase.

In the introduction to his 2007 doctoral thesis, 'A Mediating Tradition: The Anglican Vocation in Australian Society', Randal Nolan makes this observation:

> Anglicanism has, in fact, been part of the Australian story from the beginning of European settlement. It must not retreat into a private religious world... It needs to be part of the ongoing debate about Australia—what Australia is and what it stands for. The Anglican tradition must both engage in the conversation about Australia and act as a prophetic and mediating presence, especially at the points of tension which cause fractures in national life.

Keith has another book to write for that audience. It will address the essential dialogical spirit of Anglicanism. For generations, we have lived in tension with each other, and from within our ranks we have offered alternate views on every possible theme. Andrew McGowan has described this as 'conversation and persuasion' where 'orthodoxy is determined not by decree but by concrete participation in a Church where the historic creeds, sacraments, and scripture itself are likely to generate debate at the same time as being touchstones of unity' (*Eureka Street*, 21 March 2012).

With the 'evidences' of Christianity under such close scrutiny, nothing less than a fresh look at Christology will help the Anglican Church to face the challenges of Australian indifference to formal religion. All the hints are here in the present volume, and they are already under consideration in the way Keith currently shapes his understanding of ministry and hermeneutics. This is a book that challenges the fundamentalist past with the ethics of relationship; at its heart is a captivating insight into Jesus the man for others.

Bill Lawton
26 March 2012

> Bill Lawton completed his research degree at the University of NSW on the theme of utopian attitudes to social change among Sydney Anglicans in the late 19th and early 20th centuries; published under the title *The Better Time to Be*. He was a lecturer and Dean of Students at Moore College from 1959, with a couple of parish breaks till 1989. He has worked in Sydney parishes, including most recently St John's Darlinghurst; has been a chaplain with SCEGGS Anglican School for Girls, and National Chaplain for Mission Australia. Currently, he explores links between spirituality, phenomenology and pastoral ministry. See further: *www.keysensitivy.com*

Preface

The idea of writing this book originated in the immediate aftermath of a game of table tennis with my second eldest son, Jon. He asked me whether I had plans to write another book. I had written one previously, a published version of my Th.D. thesis on Alvin Plantinga.[1] There were certainly things that had emerged from that research which could usefully occasion another venture into writing.

Jon's question came at a time of uncertainty in our family life. A year earlier, I had begun a new career, the fourth career change of my life. After years of working in churches and para-church organizations, I returned to secular work as a Probation and Parole Officer. This represented something of a sea change in my life. It also invited questions, not always asked, by those who knew of my long involvement in church life. Had I lost my faith? Was I disillusioned or cranky? Most were relieved to discover I hadn't and wasn't. Still, the questions were reasonable. Why had Keith left full-time Christian ministry? Was he intending to return to it? These were questions I myself had not answered. Faced with such questions, I wondered whether it might be helpful to reflect more deeply on where I had come from, and where I might go into the future. This seemed as good a time as any to do some reflective writing.

As it has turned out, I have very much enjoyed getting back in touch with my past and with many of the characters who inhabited that past. What quickly struck me as I started writing was that my story is not intrinsically

---

[1] Keith Mascord, *Alvin Plantinga and Christian Apologetics*, (Bletchley: Paternoster Theological Monographs, 2006).

more interesting than any other's. The thing that might extend its appeal beyond my immediate family and friends is my lifelong interest in epistemology, the study of knowledge. My whole life has been an incessant and sometimes urgent journey of discovery and learning, a continual wrestling with questions, many of which I still have no answer to. It is this continuing quest to understand and to know that provides the shape and much of the content of this life history. My hope is that people asking similar questions will find something of benefit for their own life's story.

Acknowledgements

I am indebted to a host people for the inspiration, encouragement, suggestions, and gentle critique that each contributed to bringing this book to its final form. Chief among them are my family. I simply could not have written this book without the warm support of Judy, Damien, Sinyee, Jon, Daniel, Jared, and Kieran. Details of my life story would still be muddled or misleading had it not been for Judy's patient attention to detail and superior memory. My mum had a small part to play in the early editing process. The book is dedicated to her and Dad. It seeks to honour them and to express gratitude for the wonderful heritage they bequeathed to me and my siblings, Alan, Dorothy, and Joyce. I am hugely grateful for their constructive feedback, as I am for comments offered by Mum's brother, Paul Furseth.

I also benefitted greatly from the suggestions of many friends and former colleagues who have read all or some of the book. I would like to acknowledge the following: Brian Tucker, Vic Branson, James Brierley, Angus Brook, Ruth McCall, John McIntyre, David Watkins, Dave Smith, Giselle Mawer and Simon Mawer. A number of present and former faculty of Moore Theological College also provided valuable input in areas of their expertise.

I am especially indebted to Joanne Tuscano whose expert and painstakingly detailed editing of the book has eliminated many, if not all, of its typos and stylistic deficiencies. Her creative input has been invaluable. Judy and good friend Alex Livingston also spent hours trawling through the manuscript to bring it up to scratch. I am so thankful for them, and for all those, named and unnamed, who have jointly contributed to my life's story and to its telling in this book.

CHAPTER 1

An Early Diet of Love and Faith

A puff of wind. A drop of rain. An eerie stillness as birds fall silent. Children pause to stare. Parents come out to look as large clouds grow and grow to fill the sky and block the sun. Lightning strikes and thunder booms as children start to run, and parents call out, anxious, as the rain begins to fall, ever thicker and harder, cascading from the sky. Puddles become streams, and soon become rivers, breaking their banks to send people and livestock in search of higher ground. And still it rains and rains, and does not stop, nor even pause to give frightened families time to collect their belongings to flee encroaching waters. Lakes become seas, joining oceans to submerge the earth. Noah looks on as the world is swallowed below him.

I was only three, maybe four, when I first heard the story of Noah's flood. It fascinated and frightened me. As with generations of children before me, I was captivated by picture-book images of the world's animals assembling to walk two by two onto Noah's gigantic ark. But I was also filled with early-childhood dread as I imagined the horror of families like mine scrambling to stay ahead of rising floodwaters, of mums and dads carrying infants up hills, and then mountains, in futile efforts to avoid being swept away by nightmarishly deep waters, of getting to the top and waiting for the inevitable. What would it be like to drown? What had these people done to make God so angry?

Perhaps I didn't wonder about those questions on my first encounter with this story, but more than once as this story was re-told and re-read in Sunday school and family devotional cycles, I did. The story of Noah's flood disturbed me as a child. It continued to disturb me as I grew older. It raised questions, harder and harder questions, about the goodness and justice of God, for example, that in time would reshape my faith. Like no other biblical story, it became pivotal in a lifelong dialogue with God, a dialogue that became a quest to understand the truth about God.

The story of this quest, which is the story of this book, has its deep origins in two earlier stories. Over sixty years ago, the widely separated life stories of Douglas Haig Mascord and Audrey Evelyn Furseth collided in a romance that determined not only the DNA of my physical existence, it also gave direction and shape to the spiritual path I would take.

Douglas Haig Mascord was born on 14 March 1917, a year before the end of World War I. Dad grew up with a deep sense of the fragility and wonder of life. As a young boy, growing up in the coastal coal-mining town of Catherine Hill Bay, just south of Newcastle in New South Wales, he heard stories not only about the Great War, but also of the worldwide flu epidemic that killed somewhere in the vicinity of 50 million people, more than three times as many as were killed in World War I. His elder brother, Allan, was one of those victims.

Dad grew up a Methodist. His dad was an organist and Circuit Steward, his mum an influential and highly respected matriarch of that tiny coastal town. Dad was earnest and sincere in his faith, a faith nurtured by frequent excursions to Bethshan Holiness Mission at Wyee, not far from Wyong on the Central Coast. Bethshan had its origins in the 1907 visit to Australia of a female evangelist, Rev. R. L. Wartheim of the Methodist Episcopal Church in Denver. She preached that a Christian could become perfect (or sinless) in this life. So impressed by her preaching was Elliot John Rien that he organized a Holiness Convention at his property, which was the birthing of Bethshan Holiness Mission. Not too many years later, a young Douglas Mascord would have his faith enlivened by this form of earnest, pietistic preaching. Dad recalls returning from Bethshan as a fired up eighteen-year-old, with his equally fervent younger brother, Tom, and preaching the gospel on a roadside corner, until someone politely—or perhaps not so politely—asked them to move along.

Dad grew up feeling that he was different to others because of his increasingly earnest Christian faith. He was uncomfortable with the vulgarity and down-to-earth worldliness of many of his non-churchgoing neighbours. He was saved from being a social outcast by the respectability of his family and by his own growing prowess as a cricketer. In later years, Dad would bemoan the fact that some perceptive talent scout hadn't spotted and nurtured his considerable talent. 'Had they done so, [he] would surely have played cricket for Australia.' Perhaps he might have. At age eighteen, Dad was chosen to play on the Sydney Cricket Ground during Country week. At age sixty, he was still topping the averages in his local cricket competition, so sharp was his eye, so correct his technique. Alas, neither of these was passed on to his second or eldest son, despite keen efforts to not let us miss the opportunity of timely coaching—by Dad himself.

Catherine Hill Bay left a deep mark on Dad. He would often tell us stories, some embellished for effect, about the Bay and his early life there. But more influential still was the life that opened up beyond the Bay. It was leaving the Bay that would make Dad the man he became. His first major leaving was by bus to Newcastle Boys High, to the bigger world of the industrial, but still largely working-class city of Newcastle. Dad was not only a talented cricketer, he was talented academically and thrived on the opportunity to match his skills with some of the cream of the Newcastle district.

Dad's next major leaving came with the onset of World War II. When fighting broke out, he had finished school and was working, like his father, in the coal mine. Working locally put a ceiling on his ambitions and prospects for a life beyond the Bay. World War II changed all that. Dad joined the Army, became a signaller in the Artillery, and saw action in the Middle East and New Guinea.

His world got bigger. Rubbing shoulders and doing battle with soldiers of all classes, backgrounds, and nationalities helped to bring Dad out of himself. He was shy, but also able and ambitious. While in New Guinea fighting the Japanese, he became captivated by the deadly power at the disposal of American fighter pilots, and got the idea that he would like to be a pilot. So obsessed did he become with this idea that he bugged and bugged his commanding officer to let him transfer to the RAAF (the Royal Australian Air Force), until he eventually relented. I for one am glad he did, because Dad was soon sailing for Canada where, just outside of the little town of Claresholm, Alberta, he would meet his future wife and my mother.

Mum was the daughter of a pioneering family. Her grandfather, Albert Fenton, arrived in Claresholm from Boone County, Missouri, in 1913. Claresholm had only been established as a township ten years earlier to service the surrounding winter-wheat and prime-beef growing region, not far from the foothills of the Rocky Mountains. Albert rented a farm east of Claresholm, then sent for his wife and family, including Stella Mae, my mum's mum.

Mum's father, Andrew Furseth (Anglicized from Furuseth) had already been living in and around Claresholm since 1902, having emigrated from Norway at the age of seventeen. Andrew met Mae in 1924 and married a year later. Nine months from then, on 7 March 1926, Audrey (mum) was born, followed by Dorothy and Paul.

Mum had her own early encounters with the Holiness Movement. She remembers attending revivalist-type meetings in a large tent at a spot on the Red Deer River north of Claresholm. People travelled from all over Alberta for an annual pilgrimage to hear preachers—mostly American—calling for conversion and holiness of living. Mum heeded that call and was baptized in a nearby river. From her earliest days, she had a heart for God, and, like Dad, was earnestly and devoutly Christian. She remembers her Aunt Lola giving her a Bible and telling her to read a verse a day. She wasn't content with this and decided instead to read a chapter a day, beginning a lifelong habit of Bible reading.

Mum and Dad's early experience of faith was remarkably similar, as was their small-town origins. Dad had to leave Catherine Hill Bay to encounter the wider world. In Mum's case, the wider world came to her. Claresholm doubled, even trebled in size during World War II, as trainee airmen from all over the Commonwealth arrived to learn to fly at a specially built airfield southwest of Claresholm. Mum's church quickly swelled with New Zealanders, South Africans, English, and Australians.

The war was all but over when a tall, dark, and handsome Australian airman arrived at church one Sunday. The year was 1944. Mum had just turned eighteen and had no thoughts of marriage, or even of romance. Australians were known for being hard to understand, for speaking too fast, and for not opening their mouths widely enough (adaptively useful for keeping out swarming flies). Dad was remarkable for being able to be understood and for his fine tenor voice and untrained ability on the piano. Dad caught

Mum's attention, and on a walk across a golf course one day, proposed to her, inviting her to leave her home and family and follow him to the other side of the world. He admitted upfront that this was a big ask, but Mum took the risk and married him, on 16 March 1945. At war's end, she sailed for Sydney along with a shipload of other war-brides.

The Journeys Begin

My parents' marriage began as an invitation to a journey, and journey they did: to Australia, then back to Canada, then back to Australia, then back to Canada, and then back to Australia, all in the space of twenty-three years. Dad was never fully at home, was always ready to move on to something new. Audrey was mostly content to voyage in his wake, figuring rightly that this would introduce her to a smorgasbord of new experiences. Her children were mostly content as well. We were the beneficiaries of Dad's wander lust, each of us accompanying our parents across the Pacific three times. For me, at ages seven, nine, and eleven, this meant three long weeks of uninhibited fun on the high seas, with memorable visits to Hawaii, Fiji, and New Zealand along the way.

It certainly wasn't easy for Mum to move that often, and to move so far, not knowing whether she would ever see her Canadian (or Australian) loved ones again. On the final voyage back to Australia, my nineteen-year-old brother Alan didn't join us. He was by then tired of the tripping. Even as an eleven-year-old, I had some sense of the pathos of that departure. For me, moving was almost always an adventure. The only negative of that final trip was that I had to miss out on an upcoming ice-hockey season. Otherwise, moving was OK. It has been a pattern of my life to happily move on—both literally and metaphorically.

Prairie Bible Institute Days

Even as a baby, I was quickly on the move. Mum and Dad returned from Australia in early 1949 with Alan (then four) to take up work in the beautiful city of Victoria, British Columbia. Alan was joined by Dorothy in May 1951 and by me in May 1953. Two months later, the family left Vancouver Island to travel by truck and train over the Rockies to Three Hills, Alberta, where Dad had secured a job as a bookkeeper on the staff of Prairie Bible Institute (PBI).

Although I have no memories of my birthplace (it was forty-two years before I got back to Victoria), I do have early and vivid memories of my second home, a three-storey duplex on the edge of a then dirt road that led out of town to three small bumps called hills on an otherwise flat prairie landscape. In the basement of our small half-house was a coal-fired furnace to heat the home and dry clothes in winter. The living area, kitchen, and lounge room were above the basement, and up a further narrow flight of stairs were three bedrooms, one of which I shared with Dorothy. Outside was a fenced-in yard and wooden sidewalks that it would soon be my joy to bump along on a little blue tricycle.

I have the happiest of memories of these early days. Out the back of our house was a large field (or paddock—depending on which side of the Pacific you come from). Every spring, its black fertile soil was dug up and planted out with peas and beans, corn and lettuce, spinach and potatoes. Out beyond the field was an outdoor ice-hockey rink where Alan first taught me to skate, pulling me along behind a snow plough. My all-time best Christmas present, at age three or four, was a brand new pair of red and black ice skates. Skating was fun, but just as fun was building tunnels and forts in the snow that piled up along the outside walls of the rink. Winter, for us kids, was magic.

Memories compete with each other to claim the title of 'earliest', but certainly among those contestants are memories of being introduced to the faith of my parents, conveyed at first through illustrated Bible story books, nightly prayers, Sunday school, and church. An early memory is of walking at night along snow-lined streets to the nearby Tabernacle, an enormous 4,300-seat auditorium, to attend a Christmas Eve service. It was not quite filled that night, many of the students having gone home for Christmas, but there were still plenty there, including a small orchestra and choir leading us in the singing of Christmas Carols. We children were given netted bags of nuts, candy, and fruit as we left for home to our inevitably fruitless efforts to stay awake to see Santa.

PBI was the brainchild of local farmer, J. Fergus Kirk, who, in 1922, invited a recent graduate of the Christian and Missionary Alliance Bible Institute in Kansas, L. E. Maxwell (1895-1984), to teach the Bible to the young people of Three Hills. The first class of eight met in a small abandoned farmhouse. Over time, the College grew and grew, especially in the years immediately after World War II. When our family arrived there in 1953, over 900 students were enrolled. The institute had grown to become the largest Bible College in Canada and a major North American supplier of Christian missionaries to all parts of the world.

It is hard to imagine a better place within which to become a Christian and to have one's faith nurtured. Not only did I have parents who were passionately Christian, whose lives at home matched their lives in church, whose integrity of life and faith was impressive and lifelong, I also grew up within a community of similarly zealous and committed people. And I was made to feel a part of that community. I can remember as a young boy being noticed at church by some of the preachers and elders, some of whom remembered my name and would say 'hi' to me, which was quite impressive in a church of that size. Dad and Mum would often have students over for lunch after church to enjoy Mum's Shanty Man sandwiches (a Canadian version of salad sandwiches) and to engage in lively theological discussion with Dad who just loved having people around.

Living at PBI was community living at its best, certainly from the vantage point of my first seven years. Every summer, we would pack our bags and get on board a PBI bus to travel 40 miles to the institute's own campsite on the shores of Pine Lake. This was holiday heaven; living in simple cabins lit by kerosene lamps, with distinctively smelly pit toilets nearby, but not too nearby. The lake itself had a distinctive odour, as did the surrounding vegetation. Years later, after having been away from Canada for thirty years, I returned to Pine Lake with my wife Judy, our five sons, and Judy's mum. They couldn't believe that after all those years I could still remember those smells. I could and I had.

I grew up with a Christianity that sanctified the whole of life, including holidays at Pine Lake. God was the benevolent Creator of all things—including work and leisure. Mum and Dad excelled at both. Holidays at Pine Lake were filled with swimming, exploring, relaxing, reading, blue and boysenberry hunting (and eating), hot-dog roasting (on big bonfires), and fishing. Dad was renowned for his ability with the hand-line, having learnt his skills along the unspoiled coastline of his own early youth. It wasn't unusual for us to come back from an afternoon's fishing expedition with as many as twenty or more perch and pike, the snaring of a big pike being the most exciting.

The Christianity I grew up with was also about all of history and all of time. The Bible begins with the words, 'In the beginning, God created the heavens and the earth.' It ends with the expectant prospect of the return of Jesus to wrap up history and to usher in a new heaven and a new earth. Between these two book-ends are all of history (and prehistory) and all of our earthly futures. Although some of the details might be sketchy, the Christian Bible is the source of a grand and comprehensive meta-narrative. The beginning and end is there. So also is the beginning of the end, the story of Jesus, the fulcrum on which the Christian Bible turns. His is *the* story to make sense of all stories.

The Christianity I grew up with was also, therefore, a religion for the whole world. My first seven years were spent in the company of people from all over the world preparing to go back to every part of the world with the message of this comprehensive Christian gospel. It wasn't at all hard as a young boy to embrace this message. It made sense of life. It made sense of my life. Very quickly, it was hard or soft-wired into my consciousness, stubbornly persuasive in its hold, as belief systems like this are, especially when formed in childhood. Beliefs formed this early take deep root. In my case, the soil was rich and well watered. So influential are the early years of belief formation that people seldom stray or stray far from their early formed beliefs. When they do stray—except during the healthily rebellious teenage years—it creates discomfort.

Years after my time at PBI, I came to work at a Bible College, Moore Theological College, in Sydney. Among the subjects I taught was philosophy. Every year throughout fifteen years of teaching (10 full time and 5 part-time), I would raise the issue of doubt. I developed a questionnaire that I would ask my third-level Philosophy students to fill in. It asked when they had come to faith, with three possible answers: during childhood, during adolescence, and in adulthood. I asked if their parent or parents were Christian, allowing them space to nuance their answers. I also asked them whether and to what extent they doubted their Christian beliefs.

The results were remarkably similar in every year that I conducted this survey (with classes of between 30 and 60). Students who had come to faith or been nurtured into faith as children were least likely to doubt. I was amazed at how many said they had never doubted. Those most likely to doubt were those who had come to faith in their adulthood or during adolescence, especially if their parents or significant others were not of Christian faith. Those whose early experience of Christian faith was like mine were least likely to doubt and were therefore most likely to keep the faith.

Most people don't change their core beliefs and values. They may tinker with them and refine them and appropriate them in new ways, but they do not normally jettison them. As a young boy growing up, I was not aware of any reason to question my beliefs. I was, however, aware that not everyone was like me or my parents. The campus of PBI covered about a third of the area of Three Hills. On the other side of the main road coming into Three Hills was what we called 'downtown,' where those who weren't Christian, or who weren't Christians like us, lived. The wider world to which the graduates of PBI would be sent was just a short walk away.

And there were things about the faith that made me uncomfortable even as a boy. One was the story of Noah's flood, already mentioned, with its description of God's decision to wipe out every living creature, human, and animal, with the exception of Noah, his wife, and sons. Even more disturbing for me was going to see a play—at the age of seven—about not being ready when Jesus returns. There was a belief, shared by my parents, that Jesus would come back to the earth twice. His first second coming was to take all Christians out of the world. This was known as the Rapture, based on an interpretation of some words of Jesus recorded in the Gospel of Matthew. Note the allusion to Noah's flood:

> 'But about that day and hour no-one knows, neither the angels of heaven, nor the Son, but only the Father. For as the days of Noah were, so will be the coming of the Son of Man. For as in those days before the flood they were eating and drinking, marrying and giving in marriage, until the day that Noah entered the ark, and they knew nothing until the flood came and swept them all away, so too will be the coming of the Son of Man. Then two will be in the field, one will be taken and the other left. Two women will be grinding meal together, one will be taken and one will be left.' (Matt. 24: 36-41, NRSV)

I grew up believing that the Rapture was imminent; that Christians all over the world would suddenly be taken to heaven. We therefore needed to be ready at all times; needed to be sure we were Christians, or we'd miss this upward call. As a seven-year-old, I surely wanted to be ready, especially after seeing that play. Being left behind would have meant being suddenly without my parents, and probably brother and sisters as well. At that stage, I still hadn't grown out of being afraid of the dark. It was a nightmarish prospect to think I might be left behind, not just by family, but by all other Christians as well. I do remember earnestly asking Jesus to forgive and accept me as I was going off to sleep that night.

Scary and disturbing beliefs like these don't, in themselves, undermine a belief system. In my case, they reinforced them. However, over time, they can, and in my case did, eat away at the edges and even at the foundations of that belief system. I wasn't aware back then where PBI located itself on the spectrum of theological positions. It was, in fact, very much aligned to North American fundamentalism. Fundamentalism began in the United States as a movement to safeguard Christian faith from the corrosive impact of critical biblical and historical studies that were increasingly calling into question traditional Christian beliefs. The institute's current website claims that it has shed its associations with 'strict Christian fundamentalism,' and is better identified as 'evangelical . . . with roots in Christian orthodoxy.' Nevertheless, its current Doctrinal Statement (below) suggests it hasn't strayed far from its fundamentalist roots.[2]

> **PRAIRIE'S DOCTRINAL STATEMENT**[3]
>
> **The Scriptures**
> We believe the Old and New Testament Scriptures as originally given by God are divinely inspired, inerrant, trustworthy, and constitute the only supreme authority in all matters of doctrine and conduct.

---

[2] In seeking to understand PBI's fundamentalist roots, I have been greatly helped by reading Timothy Wray Callaway's doctoral thesis: 'Training Disciplined Soldiers for Christ: the influence of American Fundamentalism on Prairie Bible Institute during the L. E. Maxwell Era (1922-1980).

[3] Taken from Prairie Bible Institute's website: www.prairie.edu

The Godhead

We believe there is one living and true God, eternally existing in three persons, Father, Son and Holy Spirit, the same in essence and co-equal in power and glory.

Jesus Christ

We believe in the full deity and full humanity of our Lord Jesus Christ, we affirm His virgin birth, sinless life, divine miracles, vicarious and atoning death, bodily resurrection, ascension, ongoing mediatorial work, and personal return in power and glory.

The Holy Spirit

We believe in the Holy Spirit by whose regenerating power and ongoing ministry the believer is enabled to live a holy life, to witness and work for the Lord Jesus Christ.

Creation

We believe in the direct creative acts of God as recorded in Genesis.

Satan

We believe in the personality of Satan, a fallen angel, who, with other angelic beings rebelled against God and was cast out of Heaven. Although he was defeated at the cross and his final destiny shall be the lake of fire, he continues to be the archenemy of God, angels and humanity.

Humanity and Sin

We believe humanity was created in the image of God. In Adam all humankind fell and incurred eternal separation from God. As a consequence, all humans are declared by God to be inherently depraved and in need of salvation.

Salvation

We believe the grace of God provides salvation from sin for all humanity only through personal repentance and faith in Jesus Christ and His atoning work.

> **The Church**
> We believe the Church, the Body of Christ, constitutes all true believers and with Christ as head, the church exists in local expression to glorify Him, edifying believers, and evangelizing lost humanity.
>
> **Christ's Return**
> We believe in the literal, physical, imminent return of the Lord Jesus Christ
>
> **Future State of the Dead**
> We believe in the bodily resurrection of both the saved and the lost, those who are saved unto the resurrection of eternal life and those who are lost unto the resurrection of eternal conscious punishment.

The beliefs articulated in this Doctrinal Statement are beliefs I once held—each and every one of them at some stage in my life. However, even from my earliest days, there were factors at work that would call these beliefs into question.[4] A first step towards that questioning happened when I first left PBI.

Living Down Under

Just over seven years after we arrived in Three Hills, we were on the move again as a family, back to Australia. We'd expanded our numbers to four children with the birth of Joyce in September 1958. She had just turned two when we set off in a blue car of some sort to travel over the Rockies via Seattle to Vancouver. It was on this trip that we saw our very first television at the home of a relative in Calgary, with *Tom and Jerry* introducing us to the delights of the small screen. I remember lots from that trip across the prairies and over the Rockies, including waving goodbye and throwing streamers to my grandma from the decks of the *SS Iberia* before it sailed out to sea and over the ocean to Australia.[5]

---

[4] All, or at least many, of these beliefs have come under threat over time for me. Some have been jettisoned. Others have been re-configured or re-cast in light of what I have come to see as better ways of understanding my faith.

[5] September 1960.

Travelling to the place of Dad's birth and growing up years was exciting. He would have loved taking us out to the Bay,[6] and further up the coast to one of his favourite places, the Bogey Hole, which for us was a scarily deep rock pool filled with fish and crabs and slimy seaweed. We were introduced to his brother, Tom, and Aunty Joan and cousins, Ken, Geoff, and Ros, Dad's sister Lorna and Uncle Cliff and cousins Velma, Graham, Margaret, and John. We didn't need to be introduced to the ubiquitous flies or encroaching summer heat, or to the sounds of crickets, cicadas, magpies, kookaburras, and galahs. We didn't want to be introduced to poisonous snakes and deadly spiders, or even to not-deadly-at-all snakes and spiders. Taking a nightly trip to the outside toilet (or dunny as we learnt to call it, with its smelly dunny can) was not something we took to quickly, for all sorts of good reasons, including the prospect of disturbing some nocturnally active creature.

Coming to Australia introduced me to a lot that was new. School the Australian way was new. I'd started school at PBI Grade School, a very Christian school in every way. Swansea Public was secular, with time out for Scripture. I was no longer living in a Christian community. Our neighbours and most of my school friends didn't go to church, or, if they did, I was unlikely to know about it. They didn't go to church with us.

Australia in 1960 was still a nominally Christian country, but churchgoing had never been a majority pursuit, nor did it figure, except negatively, in Australia's national mythology. Going to church was for women and children who have always predominated, not for men, who in Australia were better known for drinking and playing hard while avoiding the twin topics of religion and politics. Our little wooden Methodist Church, just down the road from us in Wood Street, had a friendly, active, but small congregation, nothing like the gigantic Tabernacle at Prairie. Coming to Australia introduced me to a Western world fast becoming post-Christian. The sixties would see church numbers plummet, so much so that many churches were closed or refurbished for other use, our little Methodist church soon to be one of those.

---

[6] Catherine Hill Bay.

There is a lot more I could write about my first trip to Australia. I have lots of memories, almost all of them good, of this short stay. And it was short. Just twenty months after arriving in Australia, we were boarding another ship, the *SS Oronsay*, bound for Vancouver, en route to Three Hills.

Living Downtown

The year was 1962, the month of our arrival, July—at the beginning of the Canadian summer holidays. I am not sure that we got out to Pine Lake that year because Dad was busy beginning a new job with Japan Evangelical Mission. Its offices were on the edge of PBI. The implication for us of Dad no longer working at PBI was that we had to find a place to live outside of its campus. I'm not sure what instinct it was that guided him, perhaps it was his taste for novelty and being different, but Dad decided to build a cedar log house for us to live in, the first of its kind in Three Hills, and maybe the last. It was fun watching it being built, fun to meet our future neighbours, including an ultra-rich—compared to us—family who lived in a three-storeyed mansion across the street.

I had already begun to have some experience of living outside of a Christian community, but this new living arrangement heightened the contrast because the two realities were now side-by-side. We were living downtown, towards the far end of town, but every Sunday we would walk all the way back to PBI for church. I don't know what downtown people thought of PBI or of us. My guess is that there would have been some ambivalence, but I do remember one day deciding to walk to church by myself to avoid being seen with my big-black-Bible-carrying parents all dressed up in their Sunday best.

As I had done briefly in Australia, I quickly picked up the ways of my new friends, was quick to shed my recently acquired Aussie accent for the lingo of my new neighbours and school friends. Fitting in was something I would need to become adept at, and I did quickly learn to fit in. I even learnt to swear. I don't remember all the words, but I do remember being aware of how much I was swearing, and of how much I enjoyed it, until one day I shocked myself by adding to an already full repertoire the words, '*Jesus Christ* . . .' The words were barely out of my mouth when I decided to stop swearing altogether. I did from that day on.

What stopped me was not the idea that swearing was wrong. I was certainly well enough aware of that to avoid swearing within earshot of my parents. Rather, what stopped me was the instant thought that the person whose name I had just used as a swear word was someone I had grown to love. It felt like a betrayal. Swearing itself was now doubly wrong, I figured, for precipitating such thoughtless profanity.

Living downtown did not erase the deep impact of having lived at PBI and the continuing deep impact of having ardently Christian parents. Although I adapted well to downtime life, I was never entirely comfortable. I was always, to some extent, an outsider. I was an outsider to that downtown world, but I was also, simultaneously and progressively, an outsider to the world of PBI. I was both an insider and an outsider, beginning a pattern that would recur more than once in the years that followed.

Moving gave me practice at being an outsider. After just over two years back in Canada, my dad was again struck by the impulse to move. None of the rest of us felt it, but move we did. I am glad we did, looking back. Another hugely formative period of my life was about to begin.

CHAPTER 2

The Promise and Piety of Youth

I had all sorts of good reasons not to want to go back to Australia. We had only just resettled into Canada. We were living in a brand new cedar log house. We liked our neighbours. I had good friends. I had even come close to having my first girlfriend—until I got a crew cut and she dumped me! I was going to have to leave behind gridiron, baseball, and ice hockey, and, just as bad for an eleven-year-old, Australia didn't yet have hot dogs—only saveloys and frankfurters.

As some compensation, we did get to have another three-week holiday on the *SS Oronsay*, the same ship that we had come back to Canada on. As *Tom and Jerry* had introduced us to the small screen, the Beatles first movie, *A Hard Day's Night,* introduced us to the big screen, and to rock music. Our parents were not the least bit concerned, at that stage, by the obviously subversive intent of such music.

Sailing back into Sydney Harbour[7] was exciting, as was being reunited with our cousins. A custom quickly developed of driving to their place on Friday nights to have tea (the Australian equivalent of Canada's supper) and to watch *Bonanza*, a now ancient American cowboy show. Another treat was to go on holidays all the way up the north coast of New South Wales to Maclean, and out from Maclean to Brooms Head where our Uncle Cliff had a holiday cottage just over a sand hill from the beach. Aussie beaches

---

[7] On 28 November 1964.

were already legendary in our family's folklore, and we took to the water like the porpoises we'd sometimes find ourselves bodysurfing with.

It is not easy trying to recreate what was going on in my head all those years ago, but I do remember turning up for my first day at school at the tail end of fifth class and deciding, 'I'm going to be popular!' I can't quite remember why I thought that. Perhaps these were the early stirrings of my native optimism, or, just as likely, a brave attempt to suppress my nerves. Whatever the reason, being popular was to become something of a theme of the next few years, not just me being popular, but wanting my Christian faith to be popular.

High School

Sixth class passed quickly and happily. I was sick on the first day of High School, nerves I think, but for no good reason. I already knew a number of fellow starters from Swansea Public. I had also met and become best friends with Kenny Fraser, who with his family and mine attended Pelican Baptist Church, not far from our Swansea home. Kenny (now Ken) was among the funniest people I have ever met. An early English class was spent uncontrollably laughing, with every attempt not to look at each other thwarted by the merest glance and renewed hilarity.

Ken and I egged each other on in our increasingly fervent Christian faith. The foundations for me had already been set within the supportive warmth of a family not fanatical in its faith, but certainly devout and consistent. As for many church families at that time, Sunday was sacred. We didn't work on Sunday. We didn't play sport or go to the beach or do anything much, except go to church and sit around reading or 'resting'. This was the Sabbath, or the Christian equivalent. There were times that I resented the strictness of this regime, but I now look back fondly to the weekly chance to slow down and be reflective, and to read. I loved to read and, for variation, would listen to tapes of sermons.

I'm not sure where we got the tapes, but I do remember an American preacher—a woman—an evangelist maybe, but very impressive. I didn't think twice about the appropriateness of listening to a woman preach, despite being raised in a very traditional male-dominated household. I had learnt from my father's (and mother's) knee that women were not normally preachers, nor pastors, and certainly not leaders of men. Men were created to lead. Dad definitely was the leader in our home. But he was also as gentle and loving a father and husband as one could hope for. In later years, I would hear stories of abusive male dominance, of often cruel disregard for the feelings, talents, and opinions of wives and daughters by men and boys who could justify their actions from Scripture. I also came to see that Mum herself was sinned against by such interpretations, quietly and submissively believing that she had to go along with Dad's often impulsive decisions.

While growing up, I saw nothing of this dynamic, or, perhaps more accurately, had inherited enough of my dad's chauvinism not to notice. I certainly inherited my dad's passion for the Christian faith, and even followed his footsteps in making excursions to Bethshan Holiness Mission to have my faith stirred. Sometimes we would go to weekend camps there. An early memory is of hearing another evangelist, Norm Hunter,[8] attempt to scare us into Christian faith. I'd been scared before, as a youngster, feeling that I would miss out on the Rapture, but this was seriously deliberate scaring. I don't remember anything of what Norm Hunter preached; nothing of the early content of his sermons. He wasn't the most engaging of preachers. Or perhaps he was at the tail end of his career. Norm had wispy greying hair, longish for those times, a bit like Doc Brown in the *Back to the Future* movies. But what Norm Hunter lacked in preaching ability he made up for in his passionate and frightening appeals.

At the end of his evangelistic sermons, he would have us singing hymns like 'Just As I Am,' a many-versed hymn designed to evoke or express a commitment to follow Jesus. Each verse concluded with the words, 'O Lamb of God, I come, I come!' Norm would interrupt, and then interrupt again and again the singing of this final hymn to plead with us to accept Jesus, or face the grisly prospect of going to hell—forever! Not to heed the call, then and there, would mean risking becoming hardened or, worse still, dying unexpectedly and unprepared. Nothing at all could be worse than that because we would then suffer eternal conscious torment, the agony of never-ending physical and spiritual pain.

---

[8] Not his actual name.

I remember going to a Youth for Christ rally in Newcastle some time during these years and hearing a preacher tell us of a deep geological dig that had unearthed subterranean sounds eerily and scarily like the sounds of human wailing. I remember at the time being just a little sceptical, but talk of hell did frighten me. PBI's Doctrinal Statement is explicit in declaring that the eternal conscious punishment of the lost will be physical as well as spiritual. This was a frightening doctrine to grow up with.

I am quite claustrophobic. There is nothing more terrifying for me—even to this day—than being underground; under mountains or even a few tonnes of rock. Just the thought of it frightens me, and I grew up thinking that hell was like this, in fact much worse, with not even the prospect of death to soften the torment. I know that my dad was troubled by thoughts of hell. His own extended family was not all Christian. He had a number of close relatives who were avowed atheists. When some of them were facing the prospect of death, we the family would hear Dad pleading with God to have mercy or, when they died, crying tears of anguish for their now irreversible state. Dad was tender-hearted, and a noisy prayer!

The prospect of hell gave weight and seriousness to the evangelistic appeals of preachers like Norm Hunter. It certainly impacted both me and Ken. United by the seriousness and joy of our faith, we quickly became inseparable. Though he lived at Pelican, we were often at each other's homes or enjoying the surf at Caves or Blacksmiths Beach. These were the early years of our adolescence. Our heads had begun to be turned by some of our new female classmates at Swansea High. At that stage, we mostly admired them from a shy distance, though there were some early games of spin the bottle[9] to embolden our clumsy attempts to win over the opposite gender.

This was a time when our bodies were changing, our horizons broadening. I remember the thrill of skinny-dipping at the deserted end of Caves Beach with a group of other boys—of various ages—and coming back to find that someone had taken our clothes and hidden them. Fortunately for us, the sudden panic of this discovery was soon followed by the welcome relief of finding them discarded not too far away.

---

9   A game where the spinner of a bottle has to kiss the person of the opposite gender closest to where the bottle ends up pointing.

These were enjoyable and exciting years in lots of ways. But always it was my inherited faith that inspired and excited me the most. It was during these years that I discovered Billy Graham, the American evangelist. Billy Graham was a Southern Baptist who as a sixteen-year-old responded to the evangelistic preaching of an earlier, older style evangelist, Dr Mordecai Ham. As he would later ask many others to do, the young Graham walked forward to publically declare his decision to follow Jesus as his Lord and Saviour.

By the time I became aware of Billy Graham, he had already embarked on an international preaching career that in 1959 brought him to Australia. I missed seeing him by a year, but soon learnt of the amazing impact of that first visit 'down under.' During his four months of preaching in Australia and New Zealand, attendance figures almost reached 3½ million, with 146,734 people coming forward to commit, or re-commit their lives to Jesus. Included among those was a future boss of mine and the present Archbishop of Sydney, Peter Jensen.

What impressed me most as a young and impressionable teenager was the size of the crowds Billy Graham attracted. People flocked to hear him preach. Never has there been a preacher who has attracted more people to hear the Christian gospel. Stadiums designed to accommodate large crowds were filled to overflowing. The Melbourne Cricket Ground, Australia's biggest in 1959, had 143,000 people crammed into it for Billy Graham's final meeting, with 4,000 outside listening in on hastily rigged-up speakers. The final meeting in Sydney was even bigger with 150,000 people cramming into the sports and adjoining cricket grounds.

I am not sure when I first heard Billy Graham preach. It was probably on the radio, perhaps listening at home to one of his weekly broadcasts of the *Hour of Decision*. Sometimes a portion of one of his Crusade sermons would be broadcast. I was instantly mesmerized by this confident, southern-accented preacher who spoke with such authority and passion. I just loved listening to him and began to devour books about him including Jack Pollock's uncritically favourable biography. I wanted to be like this man, so much so that, after church on Sunday nights, I'd re-preach the sermon our local Baptist pastor had done such a poor job of—or so I thought—to my best friend, Ken. How he put up with me, I don't know. How anyone could put up with such youthful arrogance is beyond me. But I was young and I was keen. I also believed that Billy Graham could and would convert my 'non-Christian' friends if only I could get them along to hear him.

During the weeks leading up to the 1968 Sydney Crusade, I plastered an advertising poster onto my school bag of Billy Graham preaching to a capacity crowd of 90,000 at the Los Angeles Memorial Coliseum—inviting not a few sceptical comments that a preacher couldn't possibly attract that many people, or that *surely* the picture must have been doctored. None of this deterred me in the slightest. Somehow, Ken and I managed to persuade a busload of our fellow classmates to travel to Sydney to hear Dr Graham preach.

One of the all-time great moments of my life, after all the months of expectation, was to finally walk into the Sydney Show Ground to the sounds of 'To God be the glory, great things he has done' being sung by a choir of 5,000. I had never been happier, never more euphoric than on that day. To see so many people—60,000 of them—coming to a Sunday afternoon evangelistic rally, and to hear their voices lifted in praise of God was pure pleasure, as was the anticipation of waiting for Billy Graham to walk up to the pulpit to preach. The sermon didn't disappoint, but it wasn't quite the climax. The real climax was the appeal by Billy Graham, an appeal punctuated by the singing of the same hymn that Norm Hunter had so skilfully employed: 'Just as I am without one plea, but that thy blood was shed for me, and that thou bidst me come to thee, O Lamb of God, I come, I come.' And people did come, in their thousands, including six or seven of the school friends Ken and I had invited to join us that day.

The following Sunday, we were all in church, a row of young disciples, all keen to learn more about what it meant to be a follower of Jesus. These were thrilling days to be a Christian, although, as Bob Dylan had begun to sing, 'The Times, They Are-A-Changing.' This was 1968. Only nine years had passed since 1959, but it could just as easily have been thirty years. A profound and (at that stage) irresistible sea change was underway. The tide had begun to run out for traditional forms of Christian faith and practice. The sixties and seventies would see a dramatic fall off in church attendance in Australia and right throughout the Western world. Included in this exodus from Christian faith and practice was that row-full of school friends, except for Ken and me.

My hope had been that Billy Graham and others like him (myself even) could turn the tide, or, at least, stem it, by offering a credible and countercultural alternative. Though time has disappointed this hope, I have never lost my admiration for Billy Graham. Looking back, I am sure that what attracted me first was his apparent success. He seemed to be a winner, and I liked winners. He was popular. He could outdraw anyone, and that impressed me. But there were other things about Billy Graham that I sensed as a youngster, but would come to appreciate more as an adult. He seemed always to have a bigger vision than those who criticized him, including Christians of more conservative persuasion. From his earliest days, he was vilified for involving Roman Catholics and liberal Protestant churches in his Crusades. Such was his confidence in the message he proclaimed that he overlooked these differences in the cause of preaching to as many people as he could. There was a generosity of spirit about Billy Graham. He was also surprisingly progressive in many ways, being one of the first evangelists in America to insist on non-segregated meetings. At one early Crusade, he even walked around the stadium where organizers had set up barriers to keep blacks and whites apart, and threw them down, not unlike his temple-disrupting Lord. When Martin Luther King was imprisoned in the early stages of the Civil Rights campaign, Billy Graham paid bail to get him out. There is much to admire about Billy Graham. He certainly made an impact on me.

The Second Half of High School

Within weeks of the Billy Graham Crusade,[10] the Mascords were on the move again, this time up the coast of New South Wales to what had earlier been a holiday destination, Maclean. Dad, always restless, had been offered the chance to buy a Funeral Director's business, and, thinking this might be a nice step-down towards retirement, took it. We, his long-suffering family, again came along for the ride.

I am not sure why we moved house in May. My brother Alan remembers the exact date, 18 May, the day of his marriage to Donna Tetz back in Alberta. It is not hard to imagine the feelings my mum must have had, moving again (bad enough), and on the day of her eldest son's wedding.

---

[10] In Sydney, April 20-28.

Dad would also have felt the sadness of being so far away on such a special day. But, once again, I was oblivious to any such feelings.

I can't remember being sad to move, despite having to leave good friends behind. Moving, as it had been before, was an adventure; always more positive and hopeful than negative. I arrived in Maclean in time for the school's athletic carnival. Having already begun to distinguish myself as a sprinter in Swansea, I surprised a few of my new classmates by shading the previous year's 100-yards champion into third place (someone else beat us both). I then took out the 200-yard sprint and created a school record in the discus; a feat also achieved by my sister Dorothy at the same carnival.

Being good at sport is definitely a social advantage, certainly in Australia, but probably in most places. An interest in sport, particularly in the then tribal sports of rugby league and cricket was a potent key to social acceptability. You didn't have to be academically bright to speak the languages of sport. For Australians, it was, and still is, an equalizer in a country that prides itself on being egalitarian. I was good at sport. I loved sport, and I loved the way it opened doors to treating all people as of equal value.

I was also reasonably good at school work and had benefitted from all the informal preaching I had been doing before coming to Maclean. I entered and won a public speaking contest in Newcastle and was also normally third speaker in my year's debating team. News of my success at public speaking travelled north. Perhaps my sister dobbed me in, because, not long after arriving at Maclean High School, the principal lined me up to do a speech in front of the whole school. I do remember this vividly. I carefully wrote out the speech on palm cards as I had been taught. It was a talk about UNICEF. I was happy enough with the final product and not too nervous about giving it until part way through I realized I had mixed up the cards. There seemed to be a card missing. Dorothy's comment afterwards: 'You were going so well!' Not knowing what to do in such a calamitous circumstance, I simply turned around and walked off the stage in utter embarrassment, the embarrassment of that day having permanent effect: I now always go through any speech or sermon I am about to give and check that every single page is there and in order.

I think maybe I was something of a nerd. I am fairly sure I was. I was certainly naïve and idealistic. Not long after arriving in Maclean, I was escorted home by a very nice and very nice-looking person from the year above. She lived a block or two away, and I found out later that she was 'interested' in this new Canadian from down south. I wasn't aware of that at the time, though probably enjoyed the attention, brief though it was. I spent most of the walk home enthusing to her about the Billy Graham Crusade. Possibly I was also sounding her out about the strength of her Christian commitment. She was an occasional attender at our local Methodist church. Strange, but that was the first and only time she walked me home.

Typical of youthful relationships, and perhaps of my confidence, I wasn't too put off by the rebuff, and soon became romantically attracted to another girl, Jenny Page, from First Form (Year 7). Jenny and her family also attended Maclean's Methodist Church, which our family did as well. It had an active Sunday school and youth group called Christian Endeavour (CE). I threw myself into involvement in all aspects of church life, often attending camps, some local, at Brooms Head, others up and down the coast. A highlight of those camps was to have Jenny there as well. At the core of our friendship was a shared enthusiasm for the Christian faith.

I made other really good friends at Maclean High including Doug Towner and Geoff Kearns. Doug, a talented musician, went on to become school captain. I became his captain-of-vice (vice captain). Geoff was a quiet achiever, vying for first place in most exams. He and I went on to become close mates at university. We were keenly Christian and seemed to have the respect of those who were not of that persuasion in our class.

In terms of religions, there wasn't much else that someone could be at that time and in that place. I don't think I had ever seen a Muslim, a Hindu, a Buddhist, or a Sikh. The closest to unusual were Seventh-Day Adventists, Mormons, or Jehovah's Witnesses. Even if people weren't churchgoing Christians, they would have seen themselves as of that general persuasion, and people like Doug, Geoff, and I were reasonably persuasive advocates for a keener form of Christian faith. One of the reasons for that, I think, was that we were in every other respect normal fun-loving teenagers.

There were lots of new things to begin to enjoy in life—including driving. This was the time that we all got our licenses. Learning to drive was fun; learning how to drive fast was even more fun. There was any number of suitably winding dirt roads around Maclean to take our parents' cars out on, to see how well we could slide them around corners. Being Christian didn't inhibit us at all—possibly the opposite. I once had a carload of my friends squealing out, 'You might know where you are going when you die, but we don't. Slow down!' I am now embarrassed to tell this story, frightened by memories of how stupid we sometimes were.

Youth and responsibility are often strangers. Impetuosity and risk are its better friends, but there was a lot to like about this time of our lives. The late sixties and early seventies saw male hairstyles getting longer and scruffier under the influence of the hippie and rock music movements. Progressive class photos saw our hair creep down onto and below our shoulders. By the time I got to uni, mine was well down my back, with a beard added for good measure. My parents didn't much like the long hair, nor did an impatient barber who scooted me out of his shop one day saying, 'If you want to wear your hair like a woman, look after it like a woman does!' But what is interesting, looking back, is that, for me at least, the long hair was not a statement of rebellion against the ways of my parents or their generation. I don't think I ever really did rebel, except in the mildest of ways.

And the reason for that, I am sure, is my Christian faith. I shared the faith of my father, mother, and siblings. I saw the world the way they saw the world. I read the Bible the way they read the Bible. I also think that my parents were great parents. They never seemed to overreact to my youthful irresponsibility. Perhaps they were grateful that my passage through these years wasn't as turbulent as it was for others my age.

Also contributing to a smoother transition into adulthood was the fact that I had so much in common with my dad, with mum also, but as a teenager I had more to do with Dad. For a start, he dreamed of turning me into a top-notch cricketer. One of the first things he did at our new home in Maclean was to build a seventeen-yard cement cricket pitch with nets. There wasn't room for the normal twenty-two-yard length pitch. The very best feature of this pitch was that Dad had sloped the front end of the pitch to avoid a right-angular edge. This had the unintended, but joyful, consequence of producing bouncers if the bowler could hit that front-end lip. Dad was an enormously talented defender, but even he had trouble getting his head out of the way of such rearing bouncers.[11]

Just as fun as playing cricket in the backyard was playing theology. Dad loved the Bible and spent his life trying to unearth its meaning and patterns. He was never content to just accept what he heard from preachers or pastors or 'so-called experts' as he called them. He had to find out for himself. I loved to take Dad on, whatever the topic. He wasn't the easiest person to have a discussion with. He was more inclined to lecture, and, for variation, ask you what you thought. For most people, this meant being put on the spot, a nerve-wracking experience if you didn't know the topic or lacked confidence. I loved the challenge to at least try to match it with Dad, and was young and brash enough to interrupt him to put my point of view across. I didn't come away bloodied too often.

What we had in common was a hermeneutic; our way of reading the Scriptures. Dad had inherited from his fundamentalist background the belief that the Scriptures, Old and New Testament, were the divinely inspired, inerrant, and entirely trustworthy words or Word of God. What the Bible says is what God says. Dad never questioned what he read in his Bible. The only challenge was to understand it. Dad would spend hours poring over the Scriptures. He knew hundreds of verses by heart, and he could bring them together from everywhere to back up his own carefully crafted and, he thought, fully justified doctrinal positions.

The Bible was like a mine out of which he would dig verses or passages to be laid side by side with others of similar theme. From these Scriptural nuggets, doctrines could be fashioned. It wasn't too important to take account of what layer of the biblical revelation the nuggets were extracted from, though Dad was aware of the two big layers of the Old and New Testaments—aware enough of the differences to recognize what was 'new' about the New Testament and 'old' about the Old. Generally speaking,

---

[11] A bouncer is a ball that rears up from the pitch, normally produced by fast bowlers bowling short so by the time it gets to the batsman, it is around their head and shoulders or even higher.

however, Dad wasn't one to make too much of the differences on the assumption that both Testaments had one Author.[12]

Armed with his hermeneutic, Dad went looking for verses from which he could build a defendable doctrine of the Second Coming of Jesus. The circles in which he had grown up, reaching back to his Bethshan days, were all keenly interested in this topic, and exploring it became one of Dad's lifelong preoccupations. Along the way, he was exposed to lots of theories including those of John Nelson Darby of the Brethren Movement. Dad's own version of this doctrine, over which he laboured for many years, was a refinement of what has come to be known as premillennialism. According to all versions of premillennialism,[13] Jesus will return to the earth before a final thousand-year period of history during which Christ will reign over all the earth with Jerusalem as his capital.

The way that Dad went about his work was to simply go looking, to scroll back and forth across the biblical landscape looking for relevant clues. What Dad did not do, ever I think, was to seriously question the assumptions that he brought with him to the text. He had a couple of working principles to guide his doctrine-building work. The first was that if a text could be taken literally, it should be; only when it was obvious that it was metaphorical or symbolical did he take it that way. The second working principle was that wherever there is a Scriptural promise, it will be fulfilled at some point. God doesn't lie, so if the text says that something will happen, it will. Dad was well enough aware that a lot of biblical promises hadn't been fulfilled, at least literally, and Dad did favour the literal. The way he and others before him could continue to maintain the literal fulfilment of biblical promises, such as that Jerusalem would be great again, was to dump all

---

[12] Dad was aware of and had largely rejected a school of thought called dispensationalism, according to which human history is divided into successive dispensations or periods of history in which God relates to human beings in significantly different ways.

[13] Postmillennialists believe that Jesus will return after the millennium, which often isn't interpreted as a literal thousand years. Amillennialists typically apply the relevant verses of the book of Revelation (chapter 20, verses 1-10) to the church age as a whole.

not-yet-fulfilled promises into the millennium. What hasn't yet been fulfilled will be fulfilled literally during the millennium.

Sharing with Dad the same hermeneutic and, at that stage, a similar interest in Christ's Second Coming, I read as many books as I could on the subject, including Hal Lindsey's *The Late Great Planet Earth* (1969). Lindsey argued that present-day events were literal fulfilments of biblical prophecies, and he set out to show the links. Particularly important was the foundation of modern Israel in 1948 because Jesus had predicted—at least according to Lindsey's interpretation of Matthew 22: 32-34—that he would return to earth within one generation of that event. This prediction, of course, has now had to be modified, and yet large numbers of Christians are still of the persuasion that we are living in the last days.

Reading books like Lindsey's gave me a strong sense of the immediate relevance of my faith. I believed I'd soon be seeing Jesus, maybe even before I left school, and possibly before I got married and had children. The idea of my being around to become a grandfather would have seemed far-fetched. I had already learnt to travel lightly and believed that the next major move would be upward.

Another influence that I at least experimented with during these years was Pentecostalism or, more particularly, the Charismatic Movement, a movement of Pentecostalism that had spread into more mainline churches during my school years.[14] This movement, at its best, contemporizes the faith and seeks to unleash or give space for a present-day experience of the spiritual dynamic described in the New Testament. It looked to revive practices such as speaking in tongues and to encourage the exercise of long-neglected spiritual gifts, including the gifts of healing and prophecy. This movement was certainly biblical even if also sometimes wacky in its interpretations of the Bible. But it was fresh and new and ever so contrasting with stodgier forms of Christianity, some of which have become so fixated on the Bible, and so scared of experience, that God has gotten squeezed out of the present to be entombed in the text.

---

[14] The movement is dated to around 1960 for Protestants and 1967 for Roman Catholics.

More could be said about these years. They were rich and wonderful in a host of ways. There is a wonderful optimism about youth, and I felt it. They say that your high school years are the best years of your life. For me, they were certainly great years with little that was negative or difficult to deal with. I knew that there were likely to be challenges to come, but I hadn't felt too many yet. I was as secure and committed in my inherited faith as I could be. The next stage of my life offered an opportunity to question and rethink that security and commitment.

CHAPTER 3

Getting Ready to Take on the World

The idea of becoming a pastor and preacher came to birth early in my high school years. In embryonic form, it reached back to PBI days and to a succession of impressive preachers and pastors, including Billy Graham, who came to define an ideal that would guide me into adulthood. When it came to choosing subjects for Fifth and Sixth Forms (Years eleven and twelve), I deliberately chose subjects that would prepare me to be a preacher and pastor. I even chose what I thought would be the best career to transition me into ministry—high school teaching. I chose to major in English and History, and to pull out of Science. Even though I enjoyed science and have retained a lifelong interest in its methods and subject matter, the Fifth Form Science teacher we were likely to get was, we thought, inept and uninspiring. This was reason enough to concentrate on the humanities.

University

I remember well my first day at university. I had managed to snare a Teachers Scholarship at a time when teachers were in short supply and the scholarships were generous. My grandmother was out from Canada and accompanied Mum, Dad, and me on the trip up to the New England Tablelands and across to Armidale. I felt so grown up, so ready for this new independence. The day we arrived in Armidale was sunny and warm. It was the tail end of summer. I had been accepted into Earle Page College, one of eight residential colleges built to house us students.

I was a little embarrassed to have my parents and grandma accompany me on my walk into the college and up the stairs to the top floor of C Block, what with me so obviously a new boy (freshman). But it was still seriously exciting to open the door to my very own room, room 207. It was not big, but big enough, with its desk, single bed, and built-in wardrobe.

My parents didn't say as much, but I'm sure they were apprehensive about what these next few years would mean. I was going to university at a time of social and spiritual upheaval. They may even have had an inkling of my unspoken intention to re-examine my inherited faith. I was aware that a big part of the reason I was a Christian was that my parents and siblings were Christian. I had often wondered how different it would have been had I been born into another family with very different socializing influences. I wondered if I was a Christian just because I'd been brought up that way, or whether a case could be made for Christianity that was strong enough to persuade me of its truth irrespective of my background. That was the question I wanted answered during my time at university.

I was aware that increasing numbers of people were questioning, and in many cases rejecting, the Christian message as not true. I figured that if I was going to be a preacher and pastor, if I was going to win people to the Christian faith, I needed to be fully conversant with the very best reasons for not embracing the faith. It was for that reason that I decided to study philosophy.

Someone has described philosophy as a particularly stubborn attempt to think clearly. I wanted to think clearly about my Christian beliefs. I also wanted to give myself time to think. I had a sense that were I to become as heavily involved in Christian activities as I had been while at high school I would have neither the time nor the critical distance to subject my faith to fair scrutiny. I felt I needed to take a step back and to tread lightly for a while. I also had the sense to realize that this process didn't give me license to act as if I wasn't a Christian—to become a prodigal simply to find out what it was like to live as if I didn't believe.

The truth is I didn't end up being anything like a prodigal. I was more like his older brother, who, while perhaps admiring the cheek of his younger brother, hadn't been game to stray himself. I did wonder, however, what it would be like to stray, what it would be like to smoke cannabis or experience the effects of psychedelic drugs or wear saffron robes and sit for hours and meditate. The Beatles' high-profile spiritual journey to the East began a conversation within the West (and with me) that continues to this day. The sixties, out of which we had just come, had produced or reinvigorated a proliferation of cultural alternatives, many of them refreshingly non-materialistic. Just up the road from my hometown of Maclean were hippy-like communities clustered around the tiny coastal fringe town of Nimbin. In my second year of uni, Nimbin was the site of an Aquarius Arts Festival organized and attended by university students from around Australia, our own mini-version of Woodstock. Though I didn't attend, I felt its lure, was intrigued by the stories that filtered back.

Sexual mores were changing rapidly. University residential colleges, including Earle Page in the year after I arrived there, were fast becoming co-ed with stories emerging of students taking full advantage of newly shared facilities, including shower rooms, for intimacies not always kept private.[15] Freedoms ushered in by the sixties and given opportunity by the loosening restraints of being away from home became for many an excuse for uninhibited hedonism. Earle Page College, when I arrived, was relatively restrained in the expression of such license, being better known for its hard drinking and hard playing, with rugby and rugby league being the major sports. Mostly, I stood at some distance from all this, although I did play rugby.

Making a larger and more profound impression on me in these early years of university was the recognition that many of those I went to class with had significantly different ways of understanding the world than I did. More often than not, these different understandings were antagonistic to, or dismissive of, the Christian faith I had grown up with. Karl Marx had persuaded some that religion was the opiate of the masses, which, in time, we would outgrow. Freud concurred, as did John Lennon in his provocative anthem, *Imagine,* released the year before I entered university. Its vision of a world without religion, private property, or nationalism struck a chord in many a young heart.

---

[15] Colleges becoming co-ed also contributed, it should be said, to greater mutual respect between the genders and, consequently, less irresponsible or predatory sexual expression.

Not very long into my first year, I decided to track down Bertrand Russell's much read tract, *Why I am not a Christian*. I remember looking for it and feeling a mixture of excitement and apprehension, wondering whether my faith would be robust enough to withstand the reasoning powers of one of Europe's best philosophers. It felt like I was about to bite into forbidden fruit and was careful about who might be watching. As it turned out, I didn't lose my faith. In fact, I found the book disappointing. It didn't seem that the Christianity that I had grown up with was at all damaged by Russell's critique.

Despite the disappointment of that early encounter with atheism, it did not in any way sate my appetite for exploring this obvious alternative to my inherited beliefs. Throughout all the years since, I have been quick to read and would often buy books written to cast doubt on the existence of God, and to expose the weaknesses and irrationalities of religious beliefs like mine. I have always been keen to listen to any such arguments, and to take on board criticisms that might be justified. On my shelves are books by Richard Dawkins, Sam Harris, Michel Onfray, and Christopher Hitchens. The natural instinct of many who share my faith is to dismiss and defend. My own instinct is otherwise. I have always wanted to listen, and not just to individual arguments, but to what might lie behind the vehemence and passion that appears to drive these writers. The truth is that many of their criticisms are justified, even if sometimes overstated, even if the forms of religion targeted are easy to hit.

The willingness to listen and to take on board fair criticism was nurtured for me in the home. My dad was always willing to accept, and even to mount, critiques of his own inherited traditions. He was open to being persuaded by better arguments than his. I had grown up in an argumentative household. My future wife, Judy, who I was just about to meet at university, was shocked by the vehemence of the arguments (mostly theological) that I had with Dad. She once asked me, after one such apparently bruising session, 'Don't you feel hurt by what he was saying to you?' I was amazed by the question. I had been having the best of fun.

Perhaps it was my dad's Protestantism that contributed to his willingness to critique and be critiqued. Whatever the source, I inherited from him a willingness to engage with and be guided by argument. My first ever course in philosophy (Philosophy 1) was a bird's-eye-view historical survey of

Western philosophy. There wasn't too much in what I learnt in that course to make me uncomfortable. I empathized with the originating impulse of Western philosophy, which was the desire to understand the universe in consistently rational terms, to look for patterns and principles, and to move beyond earlier understandings. I was attracted by the endless and essentially humble questioning of Socrates, and have increasingly come to appreciate the value of asking questions to expose inadequate understandings.

I was also pleasantly surprised to find that philosophers were not all atheists. In fact, most weren't, at least historically. In their quest to understand the world and our part in it, philosophers would often retain or arrive at some notion of deity. Plato, for example, suggested that the world may have been created by a Demiurge, a master craftsman employing pre-existing forms to fashion the material universe. Aristotle reasoned his way to an Unmoved Mover responsible for the fluid flux of perceived reality. Descartes, writing many years later, and in the wake of Christianity's by then long ascendency in the west, argued that the existence of God was the necessary guarantor of all rational and scientific endeavours. Not only did God exist, God needed to exist. We humans couldn't reasonably do without God.

Studying philosophy did not confirm or disconfirm my Christian faith for me, but it was comfortably consistent with my then rationalistic and exploratory approach to life. I was, however, aware that many contemporary philosophers, including most who lectured me, were not of Christian or of any religious faith. Moreover, some of these appeared to be persuaded by some powerful reasons for not believing in God or the truth of Christianity, foremost among these being problems created by evil and suffering. The existence of an all-powerful, all-knowing, and all-loving God was, one could argue, inconsistent with (or improbable given) the obvious existence and extent of evil and suffering. Giving extra credence to an atheistic understanding of the world was Darwin's theory of evolution. Although Darwin was not himself a convinced non-theist, his theory did allow for the reasonable possibility that God did not exist. Contra Descartes, God could be considered surplus to explanatory requirements.

I was aware of at least some of the challenging implications of Darwin's theory, but was still not overly concerned, for a number of reasons. For one, I was a non-scientist. I was happy and felt rationally justified in suspending judgment about whether and to what extent scientific explanations could be found that would render God redundant. I had a hunch that even if God was not required as a necessary link or first cause in the vast sequence of causes and effects that geological and biological research had unearthed, there might still be a crucial and unifying place for God as the one to make ultimate sense of all that is. I also felt that the beauty and wonder of nature was at least consistent with there being an ultimate source of that wonder and beauty. My father had bee-keeping as one of his hobbies. He was fascinated by the wonderful skills and fantastic organizing ability of bees, mysteriously hard-wired into them and their colonies. Dad was in awe of this amazing complexity and of nature in general, which he (and I) had no trouble attributing to God.

Helpful First Encounters with Evangelical Anglicanism

Many of the challenges to Christian faith that I would later wrestle with more seriously did not, at that stage, derail or even seriously buffet my inherited beliefs. One important reason for that was that at university I encountered a new (for me) and engagingly intellectual form of Christianity: evangelical Anglicanism.

The term evangelical, from the Greek word *euangelion*, meaning gospel or good news, was first used to describe churches at the time of the Protestant Reformation.[16] Evangelicalism has since become an essentially para-church movement with a number of key emphases including evangelism, biblical authority, and personal conversion. In its heyday, evangelicalism was noted for having an active social conscience. English evangelicals, led by William Wilberforce (1759-1833), were at the forefront of efforts to outlaw slavery.

In the early twentieth century, evangelical concern for the authority of the Bible found expression in efforts to articulate and defend the fundamentals of the faith, giving birth to fundamentalism. Before World War II, evangelicalism and fundamentalism were indistinguishable, certainly in the United States. However, after the war and under some influence from the evangelist Billy Graham, evangelicalism began to differentiate itself from a

---

[16] Lutheran and Reformed Churches in Germany were so described, for example.

fundamentalism that had increasingly become sectarian, anti-intellectual, and socially inactive. Evangelicals began to engage again with critical biblical scholarship, with renewed efforts to take on board the best of this scholarship. I was a beneficiary of this new engagement.

When I got to university, my first inclination was to find a Baptist or perhaps Methodist church, but a number of my new Earle Page College fellow boarders were attending a newly built Anglican Chapel (St Mark's) up on the university campus. I tagged along. I liked what I heard. I didn't much like the liturgy, or, more accurately, wasn't used to praying responsively or in unison with others. I needed, occasionally, to escape into town for some Baptist-style ecclesiastical sanity, but not for long, and I did return. The then Anglican Chaplain was Maurice Betteridge. What I remember of Maurice's preaching was that it was informed by what appeared to be up-to-date biblical and historical scholarship. It was intellectually engaging. I began to learn about the importance of genre, especially with respect to the early chapters of Genesis. If taken literally, these chapters were in obvious conflict with the findings of contemporary science. I was also introduced to historical and archaeological studies that helped to bring to life the biblical narratives. I decided to put up with the liturgy to keep hearing sermons like those preached by Maurice Betteridge.

In thinking about why I held on to Christian faith while many of my school friends did not, one of the major factors, no doubt, was the high quality of ministry enjoyed by those of us who attended St Mark's Chapel. I only benefitted from the tail end of Maurice Betteridge's tenure.[17] However, by the time Tony Doran arrived in 1973, my second year, I was already won over to this new style of Christianity. Tony was the most impressive person I have ever met. The chaplains who followed Tony were also impressive. The first of these, Michael Hill, was a philosopher by orientation and training, a great help for a baby philosopher like me. Kevin Giles, who followed Michael, was also very able—somewhat provocatively so—but certainly stimulating and stretching. I was here encountering a form of evangelical Christianity which had a place for mind and heart, allowing me to remain a Christian with integrity.

---

[17] He had been chaplain since 1965.

Almost as important an explanation for why I retained Christian faith while others in my earlier circles did not, were the friends I made at university. Although I arrived there vowing that I would take a step or two back to examine my faith, I also recognized the importance of having good friends. I even prayed that God would give me a best friend for this time in my life. God gave me two. The first, Michael Dasey, ended up being the best man at my wedding. The second, Judy Gibson, would be my bride.

When Michael Dasey was in year twelve, his brother gave him a New Testament to read. He read it through once and couldn't shake the impression that what he was reading was true. Michael, who, up to that stage, had had little exposure to the sort of personalized Christian faith he was about to embrace, asked God for some confirmation that what he was reading was true. He read through the New Testament a second time and became convinced that it was true, and he became a Christian. When Michael arrived at university, a year before me, he too eased his way into active Christian involvement. His tendency, which continues to this day, was to become friends and relate at all levels with those living around him. Michael loved sport, was a fine cricketer and handy footballer, and had no trouble connecting. He also had (and has) a great sense of humour.

Michael had a strong sense that his newly embraced Christian faith was not a retreat from life, but rather its full-blooded and full-bodied embrace. He became convinced that the God he had met in Jesus was in the business of restoring, rather than thwarting, human potential, was about life to the full, not its negation. I shared that conviction. Although I wasn't used to the drinking culture that thrives within university colleges, I quickly decided I wouldn't let my lack of alcoholic experience inhibit my enjoyment of any party I attended. I even reasoned that I enjoyed such parties more because I stayed alert, had less chance of embarrassing myself, and could wake up the next morning without a hangover. Michael was the best of allies in this approach to life.

A lifelong friendship was forged in those early days. We were friends, but also the keenest of competitors, especially on the touch rugby field. We'd play touch rugby almost every day, and for even longer hours around exam time—to the benefit of our results, we believed. Michael's influence was not all good, some would argue. He was a supporter of the Manly Sea Eagles, a then-wealthy northern suburbs (of Sydney) rugby league club. I ditched the then-struggling Souths (a poorer inner-city club) for the high flying Eagles. My sons and many others are not impressed by this act of disloyalty. I too have a tinge of regret. Thinking back, it was probably another example of my tendency to pick winners. Such a tendency didn't prepare me well for understanding those who aren't winners. Knowing what it was like to be a loser was something I was yet to learn.

I met my second best friend (second in chronology, but not priority) in my second year and her first. Judy was among Earle Page College's first intake of female boarders. My first instantly interested sight of her was when she was coming up the stairs of C block where I lived. Judy seemed a little nervous. She had her mum and dad with her as I had a year earlier. My first thought was, 'I hope she is coming up to our floor.' I wasn't disappointed.

The summer holiday before, Geoff Kearns (my friend from Maclean) and I had gone south to earn money fruit picking. I had recently had an operation to fix a shoulder that kept dislocating in heavy rugby tackles. Over the summer, I had re-strengthened the shoulder picking pears just outside of Shepparton in northern Victoria. I was fit and brown and a little brazen in turning up to uni in a new-scar-revealing singlet. My hair was as long and hippy-like as it would ever get. Up on Top C, the floor master had organized a supper to welcome newcomers. I was especially keen to be there, and especially interested in talking to the young brunette who had earlier caught my eye. Her diary account of that first official meeting and of the few days that followed:

> Had evening in common room . . . quite good . . . met everyone in floor . . . beer drinkers.
>
> (Two days later) Tonight watched *Two a Penny* and met a whole lot of Christians . . . (including) . . . Keith—Canadian (?)
>
> (Next day) Went to Fellowship tonight . . . Keith is a Christian!
>
> (Next day) Went to Chapel twice today with Keith. Don't think anything but friendship is going to come of it.
>
> (A few days later) Keith is a <u>close</u> friend . . . nothing more.

There were some other diary entries in the days that followed that suggested that something more than a close friendship had just begun, but we certainly did become close friends. We lived in nearby rooms. Many were the times we'd work and study together, enjoying coffees and *Music to Midnight*, a jazz-oriented radio program I'd have playing on my (by then deceased) granddad's cabinet radio. The initial romantic tinge of our first encounters quickly morphed into a brother-sister type relationship. It was only towards the end of our time at university that romance was reawakened, just before a trip to Indonesia to visit Tony and Gaye Doran.

Tony and Gaye met at the University of New England in 1968. Tony had returned from Germany where he had been progressing doctoral studies in physics (on electrical-spark development in hydrogen and nitrogen). Gaye, who was majoring in botany and geography, first met Tony at a Bible Study he was leading, and was impressed. A romance resulted, aided by their mutual desire to become missionaries. Tony entered Moore Theological College[18] in 1970 and was persuaded by the then Principal Broughton Knox to go on to ordination. Their plan was to go to Indonesia with the Church Missionary Society. This would have happened in 1973 had not Maurice Betteridge persuaded Tony to become his short-term chaplaincy successor. Those of us who attended during the eighteen months that Tony and Gaye were there are eternally grateful.

Tony was the best advertisement for Sydney evangelical Anglicanism that I have ever met.[19] What initially impressed me was his respectful and insightful handling of the Scriptures. Tony was a skilful exegete and fine preacher. As with Maurice Betteridge, issues of genre and context, literary and historical, were factored in to any exposition. Verses weren't pulled out of context and combined misleadingly with others, as was too often the practice among preachers I had grown up with. I was also introduced to a new (for me) eschatology or view of the end times. Moore College graduates like Tony were much more sensitive to the existence of metaphor and symbol, and to seeing that Judaic and Christian understandings about

---

[18] The Seminary of the Anglican Diocese of Sydney.
[19] It is worth saying, by way of qualification, that Tony was born in Armidale (April 1, 1942) and lived in Africa prior to his family coming to live in Sydney. While in Sydney, the family attended Brethren as well as Anglican churches.

the future could change over time in response to unfolding events. Earlier predictions were re-envisaged or recast often in highly metaphorical language. Sydney Anglicans, for this and other reasons, tended to be amillennialists. They did not take literally descriptions in the book of Revelation of the thousand-year banishment of Satan (Revelation chapter 20).

I was drawn to this new and seemingly more sophisticated approach to the Scriptures. I was drawn more strongly still to Tony Doran himself. As a child, Tony suffered from dislocated hips, a problem not entirely corrected by surgery. When we first met him, Tony still had a slight limp. He was a small man physically, but not in any other way. The word that most people use to describe Tony is humble. Tony was humble in the sense of being self-forgetful. When you were with him, he was 'all there' for you, gently attentive to what you were saying. With many people, with me too often, personal agendas intrude into conversations with others. We didn't feel that way with Tony. Tony had the most beautiful smile and infectious laugh. He seemed to be so himself, not hiding behind some self-protective façade. The warmth on the outside was an inner warmth fed by an obviously personal devotion to the Jesus he had dedicated his life to serving.

When I think back to the eighteen months that Tony and Gaye were with us at Armidale, I realize that for much of that time I wasn't fully engaged with the faith of my younger years, nor yet with this newer evangelicalism. I was still attempting to keep myself at some distance. I didn't attend the Evangelical Union (EU), for example. I didn't sign up for a trip to the Aquarius Arts Festival at Nimbin, despite my being interested for other reasons in this event. Tony organized that trip as an opportunity for us to express our faith in what he knew would be a challenging environment. Tony wasn't just gentle and humble; he was also courageous and willing to step outside his comfort zone.

Not long after arriving in Armidale, he applied to the Student Union to give a series of lectures each entitled, 'A Christian Mind on . . .' He chose a number of controversial subjects including abortion and homosexuality. It was a game thing for Tony to attempt, especially in the early seventies. He knew that the reaction of some would be hostile, as it was. I don't remember attending more than one of those lectures, but what I noticed then, and what I now notice as I read them through again, is how good they were, and not just in content, but in approach. Tony had the gift of empathy. He had a feel for the human dimension of what he was saying. This came through warmly in his words. But Tony also had strongly held convictions which he was willing to stand by, regardless of how they might be received.

Eighteen months was too short a time for us, but it did mean that Tony and Gaye and their young family could move on to missionary work in Sumatra. Some of us students had the privilege of visiting them in Indonesia in late 1975. They had become involved in student ministry, which flourished under their guidance until Tony was found to have cancer. While working to earn money to support himself through theological college, years earlier, Tony had worked for three weeks in an asbestos factory—long enough for the invisible fibres to do their deadly work. Tony came back to Australia where he died on 29 October 1983.

Some of the strongest objections to Christian faith can be devised by drawing attention to apparently needless suffering. Why does a good and all-powerful God allow suffering, especially given its prevalence and severity in the world? Why did God not protect Tony, especially given that his reason for working in that factory was to earn money to attend College to become a missionary in service of God, especially when you consider what a good advertisement Tony was for God? Those are hard questions to even attempt to answer.

Tony's replacement as chaplain was Michael Hill. Michael was a philosopher, and, as such, well aware of puzzles created by suffering and evil. He himself was to later face the terrible loss of his wife Christine who died suddenly from the effects of cardiomyopathy in November 1992. I have very fond memories of getting to know Christine and Michael. As with chaplaincy families before them, they were wonderfully hospitable in welcoming students into Rymbosa, the chaplaincy home just up the hill from Bishopscourt in Armidale proper. Many were the delicious meals we enjoyed there.

Michael had (and has) a dry and cheeky sense of humour. His time as chaplain wonderfully complemented Tony's and Maurice Betteridge's, certainly for us. He and Christine were both warmly approachable, their whole approach relational. Michael was also a handy cricketer with a love for sport that helped him connect with sports-mad people like myself. He was a thinker, a stimulating preacher, and a fine pastor. During Michael's time, Judy and I became progressively more involved in St Mark's Fellowship (formerly the Anglican Society). By the time Michael and Christine had left Armidale and were replaced by Kevin and Lynley Giles, Judy and I had become secretary and president—with our friends beginning to speculate about what turned out to be the future direction of our relationship.

My final year at university was unsettling. Kevin Giles came to chaplaincy from Germany where he had completed a master's degree in New Testament studies. There was a restlessness about Kevin that matched my own. He was a reformer by nature, happy to take on unpopular causes, and to make himself unpopular in the process. Early on in his time at UNE, he preached a series of sermons on women in ministry arguing that the church had misread New Testament passages that appear to permanently prohibit women from exercising authority over men, or from teaching or preaching to them.[20] I now agree with him, but, at the time, his arguments unsettled me and many others within the congregation at St Mark's Chapel, some of whom left to join other churches.

I wasn't then ready to consider this new approach. I was already beginning to alarm my father by my, he would say, too ready embrace of Anglican evangelicalism. I passed on copies of Kevin's papers which he responded to in detail. I was inclined to go with my dad on this one, and did so for quite some years to come.

Some of those who left the chapel community in quiet protest against Kevin's then radical views on women's ministry began to attend the Free Presbyterian church in Armidale. I attended a couple of times, but was put off by its hard line Calvinism. Evangelical Anglicanism, as I was coming to encounter it, was also Calvinistic. John Calvin (1509-1564) is well known for highlighting the doctrine of predestination, according to which God pre-chooses those he will save without regard for any choices they might make. The beauty of this doctrine, which Calvin believed he had drawn

---

[20] For example, 1 Timothy 2: 11-15.

directly from the Scriptures, was that it gave all the glory or credit to God, with no room left for human pride.

I had trouble with the doctrine of predestination. The version that I encountered most over the years can be traced back through Calvin to St Augustine of Hippo (354-430). It goes something along these lines:[21]

> Adam (the first human person) had a choice to obey and follow God, but he (and his wife Eve) chose to disobey. That one choice by, one man (and his wife), so affected Adam's offspring (us) that we now inevitably make similar choices to disobey and ignore God. Moreover, we have inherited Adam's post-choice sinful nature making us incorrigibly sinful. We sin by nature and by choice. Such is the character and seriousness of our sin that we deserve the punishment of everlasting punishment.
>
> God would be fully justified in sending every single child of Adam to hell to suffer there forever. However, such is the amazing grace of God that he has chosen to save some of his sinful creatures, and to do so by means of the sacrificial and substitutionary death of Jesus, his Son. By his Spirit, God irresistibly draws to himself those he has pre-chosen, creating persevering faith. No-one who is truly elect irretrievably falls from grace. All are saved and enjoy heaven with God forever.

The doctrine, as spelt out here, was neat and logical, but it still didn't seem right. I didn't like the idea that being saved had nothing at all to do with any actions or decisions by us, that it was all God's doing. That seemed to turn us into puppets rather than agents, with no way of knowing why God would choose one person over another. I was told that we were, nevertheless, responsible for our wrongdoing, but then it didn't seem right that we could take no credit for our right-doing. I was also troubled by the idea that because we are by nature sinful, and will therefore inevitably express that as we grow up, God also sends children to hell, with no one spared except for the elect. All non-elect humans are condemned, even before birth, with the awful implication that children dying in the womb, or not surviving birth, go straight to hell, with their only conscious

---

[21] My own attempt at a summary.

experience being the torments of hell. That, for me, was an intolerable implication of this teaching.

I have discovered since that some argue that babies and young children don't go to hell. They are spared and will be accepted into heaven. This view softens things a little, but only to create additional problems. Why should God spare babies and children whose nature is exactly the same as those who live beyond childhood? Moreover, when is the cut-off age? And doesn't such an exception prove that what people do or don't do is important? It also suggests, bizarrely and disturbingly, that we ought to be hoping and praying that children of non-believers die in their mother's womb, or before reaching an age when they will be expected to pay the price for their sinfulness.

Implications such as these disturbed me whenever I tried to think through the implications of Calvin's teaching on predestination. In this, I had a ready ally in my father who was lifelong in his rejection of Calvinism. Dad's background was Methodism, which tended to align itself with an Arminian rather than a Calvinistic understanding of this doctrine. Jacob Arminius (1560-1609), a contemporary of John Calvin, reacted against the idea that human freedom played no role in the salvation of individuals. He accepted predestination as Scriptural, but argued that God predestined those he knew would one day freely choose to avail themselves of the undeserved redemption offered by Christ. This was how my dad understood predestination.

But my father's view also had difficulties. A free-will approach has its own nest of problems. As I thought about my own Christian life, it seemed obvious that my becoming and remaining a Christian had more to do with influences outside of my control than with choices I had made. I noted, and have noted since, that what people are taught as youngsters is what they normally believe and keep on believing throughout their lives. Freedom to choose rarely results in life-changing choices and changes, particularly in matters of religion or worldview. The communities of faith we are born into tend to be the communities of faith we die in. Freedom is an overrated gift perhaps. Muslims, Hindus, atheists, and Mormons are free to become Christian and vice versa, but the modest and variable rates at which such conversions happen suggest that freedom of choice is a minor determinant.

Deciding on which side of the Calvinist/Arminian fence to sit was not something I had time for in my final year of university. Rashly, I had decided to attempt a joint Philosophy/History honours year—with natural law being the broad topic. I managed to successfully complete the necessary course work, but had no idea of what was being demanded of me in completing a thesis, and as the year went by, I became increasingly bogged down and anxious, choosing too often to escape into what was the highlight of my year, a burgeoning romance with my female best friend, Judy. She was beside me—literally and metaphorically—for the hours and hours of finally fruitless research and writing.

In the August holidays of 1976, I drove north to visit Mum and Dad at our home in Maclean. I was planning to then travel to Judy's home, a dairy farm just out of Killabakh Creek in the beautiful foothills of the Great Dividing Range, not far from the mid-north coastal town of Taree where Judy was doing a stint of prac (or practice) teaching. Judy's father and her two older brothers had been making bets with each other about when I would ask Judy to marry me.

Not long after arriving on the farm, I had the perfect opportunity to ask Judy. We went for an afternoon walk down to a nearby creek and up onto a nearby hill where we could sit and look down over the farm. The sun was out. The sky was blue. The paddocks were green, the cows content, and I lost my nerve. So momentous a question had me internally shaking. Later that night, one of my legs started shaking when finally I got up the courage to ask Judy to spend the rest of her life with me. Early the next morning, buoyed by Judy's 'Yes', I followed her father, Ted, out to the chook pen to ask his permission. He said, 'No', followed by 'What took you so long?' It was a fair question and a relief to know he was joking.

Teaching at Seven Hills and Hay

The last few months at university were spent madly preparing for a wedding. We didn't give Judy's mum, Peg, much notice. We decided to get married in January, in time to begin our teaching careers as husband and wife. Neither Peg nor Ted, nor my mum and dad, complained (to us at least) about being given so little time to get ready. As we were to find out years later, there is a lot to do to organise a wedding. We did help out a little, including arranging for Michael Hill to travel up from Sydney to Killabakh Creek's tiny Anglican Church to conduct the wedding service.[22]

Our university years closed happily enough; the prospect of marriage, and of a short career in teaching, softened the blow of failing to complete my honours year. The ambition to be a pastor and preacher had strengthened during my time at university. I hadn't lost my faith. On the contrary, it had become stronger and more sophisticated. I had also made some very good friends. Some, including Michael Dasey, would follow a similar path to mine into ordained ministry.[23]

Getting married was wonderful. Our first home was a suburban bedsit in Sydney's western suburbs. We weren't there for long before moving to a larger and fully furnished unit in nearby Harris Park, not far from Macarthur Girls High where Judy began work as a Maths and Science teacher. I taught English and History at Seven Hills High. Both schools kept us up late at night preparing for the next day's lessons. Neither was an easy school for young and inexperienced teachers like us. We had our share of out-of-control, or just-barely-in-control, classes. We both looked forward to weekends when we could relax a little and attend Harris Park Anglican Church. We were now happily Anglican and beginning to think about how long it would be before I left teaching to become a minister.

By a quirk of organisational disorganisation, the Department of Education hadn't caught up with the fact that I was married. A telegram arrived at the end of my second of three terms at Seven Hills instructing me to make my way to Hay in south-western New South Wales. Assuming I was single, they reasoned I could easily and quickly relocate. Judy and I didn't mind.

---

[22] Michael, at that stage, was teaching philosophy at Moore Theological College.

[23] From what I can gather, as many as 11, and maybe more, were significantly influenced in their decisions to enter ordained ministry by the chaplaincy ministries that so benefitted me during my time at New England University. The following seven returned to the Anglican Diocese of Armidale for periods of ministry: Michael Dasey, David Wiedemann, John Jenner, Cliff Ainsworth, Steve Williams, Andrew Dircks, and I.

Judy had already left the department to take up the directorship of a local pre-school, a job much more to her liking, one that she was eminently suited to. We thought, mistakenly, that Hay was nestled somewhere in the rich flood plains of the Murrumbidgee Irrigation area, an area that had been brought to life by the irrigating waters of the Snowy Mountains Hydro Electric Scheme. We imagined orchards and rice fields and slightly rolling hill country. What we found, after a long and tiring nine or ten hour trip from Sydney, was a vast and barren red soil flatness. We turned up in Hay at the tail end of a severe drought that had transformed the landscape into the likeness of a Drysdale painting. Hay was hot and dusty. Hay and Booligal (a nearby town) are known to have something in common with hell—heat![24]

But we fell in love with the town. My two cousins, Ken and Geoff, had both spent time teaching at Hay, and they had contacts, including Alan and Beth White who generously invited us to spend our first few nights with them. They became lifelong friends. We soon found a deserted shearer's cottage at Mungadal, a large sheep station just west of Hay. The house was rundown and needed some work to get it up to scratch, but we couldn't have been happier. We were within a short walk to the Murrumbidgee River where we could cool off after school on a hot day. Judy was now jobless, and rather than looking for work, and beguiled by the young children of our new friends, we decided that we'd begin a family. Just a little over nine months later our first son Damien was born.[25]

We have had our share of exciting moments in our lives, but none compares with the joy Judy and I felt at the birth of our first son. The labour was long, but the joy it delivered was unsurpassed. I remember driving away from the hospital to ring parents, siblings, and friends, and saying to myself, over and over again, 'I have a son! I have a son!' So enthusiastic was I, so euphoric, that God must have got the impression I only wanted sons. Four would follow Damien, and now two grandsons.

There is nothing you can do to fully prepare yourself for having a child. There is no experience like it. The arrival of your very own son or daughter

---

[24] Hence an expression used by locals and others, 'Hay, hell and Booligal.'
[25] On 1 August 1978.

is amazing, bordering on the miraculous. Can this little individual, so small, so vulnerable, so unique, so unlike you even in its likenesses, really be here? Nine months previous, he wasn't even a twinkle in his father's eyes, but here he was, fully formed, fully him, fully Damien.

Judy and I were fortunate to have fantastic parental role models. Even so, we didn't have a clue. This was so new, so scary, so daunting. Within days we were exhausted. Within a week, Judy's mum, Peg, was in Hay to help. A day or two later, she quietly walked into our room in the middle of the night to ask if everything was OK. Damien had been crying his eyes out for some time. Mum felt she had to get up. We were sound asleep, too tired by the new labours of parenthood to waken even to our son's increasingly urgent entreaties. We thanked God for Nan that night, albeit with some embarrassment.

We had more than our parents to thank for not making too big of a hash of parenthood in those early days. Within twenty-one months, another son, Jonathan, arrived.[26] Within a few months of Jon's birth, child number three, Daniel, was on the way. We needed help, and got it in bucket loads from more experienced fellow parents including Alan and Beth.

We were in Hay for just over three years. We enjoyed country town life. We attended the local Uniting Church, a congregation not large enough to afford its own minister, and so there were opportunities to do some lay preaching. During the preaching of my very first sermon in Hay, a visiting family up the back became increasingly restless as the sermon dragged on, and before it was finished walked out. I was somewhat relieved later to find that they had accidentally left a roast in an oven back at their caravan park. They had hoped that I would finish quickly enough for them to get back to rescue it.

Being in Hay was a good experience from the point of view of our Christian faith. We enjoyed midweek meetings with people from a couple of other churches in town. There was an Anglican Church, but at that stage, we felt more comfortable mixing with people of Uniting, Presbyterian, or Baptist backgrounds; Christians of a low church or non-conformist variety. Quite

---

[26] On 6 May 1980, just hours away from my birthday.

some years would pass before I would be able to understand or appreciate middle or high church varieties of Anglicanism such as we encountered in Hay. I was still very much in the thrall of Moore College and of its graduates who had so thoroughly impressed me while at university.

In thinking about where I would train to become a minister, I had no doubt that Moore College was the place for me, the only place. During my time at Hay, I talked with one or two Uniting Church ministers about where I might train. From what I could tell or now remember, they were at the conservative end of the Uniting Church spectrum, but even they were less than enthusiastic about my preference for Moore, and thought I could do better. I asked about whether becoming a Uniting Church minister was incompatible with attending Moore for at least the beginning of my theological training. I even wrote to someone at Leigh College to ask about this possibility. They weren't too keen, citing what they considered to be Moore's narrowness of theological perspective. That didn't quite wash with me, and I began to think about joining the Anglican Church, a church I had by then become comfortably associated with.

Being at Hay did somewhat broaden my outlook, however. In partial preparation for going to Moore College, I enrolled in some courses with the Melbourne College of Divinity, including New Testament Background. I began to read works from across the theological spectrum. I was thereby introduced to critical biblical scholarship with its interesting range of questions and proposed solutions. I was also mixing with people at church more conservative than me, people who were persuaded by or drawn to the doubtful conclusions and methods of Creation Science. I was thus simultaneously being drawn in opposite directions, a tension that would continue into the years ahead. In seeking to come to my own mind on issues of faith, I had an able and engaged ally in Alan White. Alan was the Maths master at Hay War Memorial High where I also taught. He would later train in Melbourne for the Uniting Church ministry. He and I both enrolled in these courses, to our benefit.

The only thing that might have stopped me from becoming a minister was that I enjoyed teaching. After surviving my baptism of fire at Seven Hills High, I arrived in Hay with an overlarge arsenal of disciplinary techniques which I really didn't need to use. There was so much to love about teaching. I became a debating coach and achieved relative success, or rather the students did, in inter-school debates in the region and beyond. I directed a number of school plays, and even had a minor role as a Bow Street Runner in a town-based production of Oliver. Small towns are known for their obsession with sports of all kinds. I was able to sample Australian Rules Football (AFL), at which I was totally inept. I preferred touch rugby and did much better at that. I even played enough squash to become moderately proficient.

Life was good. I did seriously consider remaining a high school teacher, especially when news of Judy's third pregnancy surprised us. We faced the daunting prospect of three children under the age of three. Maybe this wasn't the best time to leave a promising career for the relative poverty of four years of theological training. We did seriously consider not going to Moore College, at least not then—but not for long. This was something we both believed God was calling us to. We applied to enter Moore College and were accepted. A new chapter of our lives was about to open.

Chapter 4

Realising a Dream

The prospect of spending four whole years studying theology was joyous. I couldn't think of a better way to spend my time. I had loved high school teaching, but at theological college, I would be learning to teach theology. And not just to teenagers, but to people of all ages.

Moore Theological College

Because we already had two sons, with one on the way, we were allocated a large, two-storey former-shop-front house on King Street, Newtown.[27] All that now remains is the original façade, behind which is a lecture complex completed in 1994. The house was old and in need of constant repair. Tacked to the ceiling of our bedroom was a thick plastic sheet for collecting drops of water that trickled through from no-one-knew-where when it rained heavily. An irritating ritual on rainy nights was to drain the deepening bulge to avoid a deluge from above. But we loved the house. It was big, with enough rooms for me to have an office out the back. There was a sandpit and smallish backyard for the boys. It was an easy stone's throw from the dining room and lecture theatres.

---

[27] Newtown is one of Sydney's oldest suburbs—not far from the CBD.

A treat in that first year was to have as one of our near neighbours Keith Birchley who two years earlier had won the ABC's[28] Concerto Competition.[29] Judy and I had witnessed his award winning performance from the lounge room of our Hay home. Keith was a pianist of prodigious talent. Through the walls of our college home, we could hear him practising for about two hours every day, down from his previous seven. Even his scales were beautiful to listen to. His practising was the best possible inspiration for the latest looming essay.

First year at Moore College was amazing and wonderful in almost every way. There were about sixty people in our class.[30] I think it might have been a record up to that time. 1981 was the last year that Cash Chapel[31] could accommodate the whole student body, then around 150. Part way through the year, I wrote to my friend Michael Dasey, who, at that stage, was teaching at Mt Hagan in the Papua New Guinea highlands. He was about to follow me towards ordination. I wrote to him enthusing that first year was 'like an all-year house party' (or church camp). What was especially impressive for me was the calibre of the lecturers we encountered in that first year.

Rev. Dr Bill Dumbrell was an early favourite. We had Bill for Old Testament. Bill is an enormously talented linguist and biblical scholar, and one of the funniest and most engaging of lecturers we ever had. He had an amazing alacrity with language. Though somewhat cumbersome in his writing style, he was beautifully descriptive in his teaching. During his academic life, Bill gained at least partial mastery of nine ancient and four modern languages.[32]

Bill reintroduced me to Biblical Theology. I had already had a taste of it in the preaching of Tony, Michael, and Kevin, but here was the originating

---

[28] Australian Broadcasting Corporation—Australia's publicly funded radio and television corporation.
[29] Later renamed the Young Performers of the Year Award.
[30] Including part-time students—some of whom were spouses of students in other years.
[31] The College church for years and years.
[32] Hebrew, Greek, Aramaic, Akkadian, Syriac, Arabic, Coptic, Ethiopic, and Ugaritic; French, German, Italian, and Spanish.

engine room for them and us. Biblical Theology, as it was then beginning to be taught at Moore College, was an effort to discover and articulate a theology of the whole Bible, picking up key themes throughout the length of its pages, then seeing how they develop and find fulfilment at the Bible's end, and also at its middle, in the life, death, and resurrection of Jesus.[33] Towards the end of Luke's Gospel is a passage where a then-unrecognized Jesus expounds a Biblical Theology of himself with two unnamed disciples. When he suddenly leaves them, they exclaim, 'Were not our hearts burning within us while he was talking with us on the road, while he was opening the Scriptures to us?' It felt a bit like that for us as Bill took us on an excursion through the Jewish and Christian Scriptures.

Another highlight in first year, for me certainly, was being introduced to Graham Cole. Graham was then only in his second year of lecturing, and the gossip was that he was better the second time round, as I am sure most lecturers are. Graham was also highly talented. In fact, he and Bill were the closest to being polymaths of any of our lecturers. Graham has a prodigious and photographic memory. He could also read fast, very fast. Legends exist of Graham taking up to seventeen books home on a weekend and bringing them back on Monday all read and remembered; perhaps an exaggeration, but possibly not too far shy of the truth. Graham was a brilliant systematiser, able to bring information and ideas from multiple sources and lay them out helpfully and memorably. This skill he put to good effect in teaching us philosophy, apologetics,[34] and theology.

Graham and Bill had more in common than their mastery of multiple subjects. They both had an endearing habit of suspending judgment and admitting ignorance on issues they hadn't yet made their minds up about. My memory is that when asked a question with two possibly right answers, or two variously doubtful answers, they'd say something like, 'On Monday to Thursday I think x; on Friday to Sunday I think y.' There was a winning

---

[33] For more detail: Gibson, R. J. (ed.) *Interpreting God's Plan: Biblical Theology and the Pastor, Explorations 11*, (Carlisle/Adelaide: Paternoster/Open Book, 1997).

[34] Apologetics, from the Greek word, apology, meaning defence, is a theoretical discipline devoted to exploring how best to commend and defend the Christian faith.

humility in their approaches to many issues. In later years, they would both conclude y rather than x in areas where some of their more influential colleagues had concluded x—and it got them into trouble. I continue to admire them for their courage and scholarship.

Another person we warmed to easily was Bill Lawton. Bill had been converted into evangelical Anglicanism when a student at Moore. He had come from a high Anglican background and became, for a time, a persuasive and colourful advocate for evangelical Anglicanism. Bill was (and is) a great story teller. We marvelled at the rawness and realness of the experiences he so vividly described. Of all the things I learnt at college, the most memorable and practical were Bill's stories. We sensed that in Bill there were struggles not all of which he shared with us.

Our first year also featured cameo appearances from Peter O'Brien and Barry Webb. Peter was a meticulous exegete with a warm pastoral approach. Barry reminded me of Tony Doran. He had a similar combination of prayerful piety and sharp intellect. Barry had been nurtured in the Brethren movement, as had Tony Doran and Graham Cole. Barry and Graham stood out at college, in part because they were refreshingly different. They so naturally brought a devotional edge to all that they did and said.

One last, but by no means least, reason why first year was so special was that it included my first encounter with Broughton Knox. Dr Knox was an enigmatic figure. He was coming towards the end of his tenure as principal and seemed a little tired and disengaged. He had been principal of Moore College since 1959. He had taught Doctrine 1 for most of those years, and appeared bored by his own lectures, that is, until he could manage to hook one of us into a debate. Dr Knox was a master of the Socratic method of teaching. He enjoyed interrogating any who took him on, with the obvious intention of unearthing unhappy implications from what was being said. You had to have your nerves about you to speak up in his class. Some found him rude. I wasn't one of those. I was too used to the joy of debating my dad to be at all concerned by the cut and thrust of this ancient teaching method. I only wished I had the courage and wit to more fully join the debates.

Dr Knox was adept at being a devil's advocate, taking on contrary positions in order to discover from the inside what were their deficiencies. He was also committed to scholarship. It was his vision and the achievement of Noel Pollard, Bruce Smith, Bill Dumbrell, and others that Moore College develop a first-class library. The appointment of Kim Robinson in 1975 further was crucial to the creation of a large and well-resourced research library with journals, books, and other resources from right across the range of biblical and theological scholarship.

Broughton Knox's impact on the character of Sydney evangelical Anglicanism is immense. Yet there are puzzles I am not sure I have answers for. Dr Knox was committed to scholarship, but he himself rarely pursued direct engagement with that scholarship. He was comfortable with quite literal readings of Genesis 1-11, and did not, at least publicly, distance himself from creationism. He also appeared less fearful or cautious than those who followed him into theological leadership of the Diocese of Sydney. I am not sure why that is. Perhaps it was a matter of personality. Another possible explanation is that Dr Knox, by his sharp wit and teaching style, instilled a fear within his students that they might, even unwittingly, fall into one of the many heresies he would often accuse us of, hence the more cautious approach of his successors.[35]

Meeting and engaging with the faculty, as well as with those who came from outside the college to teach,[36] was stimulating and enjoyable. I loved first year at Moore College. So did Judy. It promised to be a much harder year than it turned out to be. When we arrived in Sydney, Judy was heavily pregnant with Daniel.[37] The prospect of even more sleep-deprived nights caring for three young infants was daunting enough, but even before Daniel was born, Jon (then only eleven months) required surgery entailing heart-rendingly painful recovery.

Also, we had come from the freshness and relative relaxation of a small country town into a busy, smelly, and noisy city. Police, ambulance, and fire engine sirens wailed past our front door at all hours of the day and night. As for me, I was often busily engrossed in essays, lectures, and

---

[35] See further chapter 7.
[36] Including, in our first year, Dr Alan Craddock and Canon Alan Langdon.
[37] Born on 25 May; a few weeks after I had completed an essay on the Biblical Book of Daniel, providing inspiration for the naming of our third son.

language work. It should have been a terrible year, but it wasn't. Judy looks back as fondly as I do to a very special year. Our parents were often down helping out. We made some great new friends, and friends we already had prayed for and supported us, in some cases financially. We felt cared for and upheld.

Reminding us a little of the country town we had come from was the little church we attended for our first two years at college, Taren Point Anglican Church. It was the branch church of St Philip's of Caringbah, a southern suburb of Sydney. The congregation at Taren Point was warmly accepting and generously overlooked my youth and inexperience. Our little family felt instantly at home, although it did take us a little while to readjust to Anglican ways, including for me the wearing of a white surplice when leading services. This practice was so new to Damien that on one early Sunday, when I had dressed up and was coming into the church, he exclaimed, in rapt excitement, 'Jesus!' My then bearded face and white flowing garment was enough to momentarily fool Damien into thinking what he has never had the slightest reason to think ever since.

From his earliest days, we wondered whether Damien was hyperactive. He was always inquisitive, always on the go, would almost never settle for a cuddle, and, as a two-year-old, was insistently involved in any conversation happening in his vicinity—with one notable exception. Towards the end of our first year at Moore, Tony Doran came to visit while on furlough from Indonesia. Judy and I were amazed by what we witnessed. Tony arrived at our back door to be greeted by Damien. Without looking in our direction or saying a word to us, Tony squatted down, his attention totally absorbed by the little two-year-old in front of him. He talked quietly with Damien for what must have been five, maybe even ten, minutes. Tony then got up to greet Judy and me with the same warmth and full attention. He sat at our kitchen table for the next half-hour and Damien didn't once interrupt our conversation. Instead, he stood quietly beside Tony holding his hand, such was the impact of this man's calming peacefulness.

Better placed judges than me believe that had Tony not died so young, he would have become principal of Moore College, and perhaps even archbishop of Sydney. It is tempting to think what this might have meant. Those who knew him best knew him as one who eschewed politics and was disappointed by the behaviour of those who chose to use political means to achieve their objectives. It may be that he would have avoided advancement. One thing is sure. Tony's gentle and gracious ways would have made him an excellent choice for either of these positions of influence.

Years two to four of Moore College weren't quite as inspirational as year one, but we did begin to delve in greater depth across the healthily wide spectrum of subjects offered, including Church History, Philosophy, Ethics, Apologetics, Old and New Testament, Biblical Theology, Systematic Theology, and Pastoralia. Our still infantile grasp of Hebrew and Koine Greek improved enough for us to at least get a taste for reading and understanding the Bible in its original languages. That was fun.

One subject we didn't study, except incidentally and along the way, was hermeneutics, which is the science and art of interpreting texts.[38] This was a weakness later acknowledged and addressed to some degree within the college curriculum.[39] We tended to pick up hermeneutical principles either tacitly through observing how our teachers handled the Scriptures, or more explicitly in teaching we received on the nature and authority of the Bible. We were taught from day one that the Bible was the Word of God and that through the Bible God's nature, purposes, and requirements are infallibly communicated. The faculty of Moore College was united in believing the Bible to be infallible or non-misleading in matters of faith and morals. I am not so sure that all believed the Bible to be inerrant, that is, without errors of any kind.[40] Not all who were faculty then think that now. However, inerrancy, for those who hold it, is clearly a very important hermeneutical

---

[38] Hermeneutics as a discipline or field of study has expanded significantly over the last hundred years to include the interpretation or understanding of human interactions with the world in general, including written texts.

[39] A course on hermeneutics has been offered as an elective at fourth year level in the BD program for some years now, with Graeme Goldsworthy its usual teacher. Central to the course are principles spelt out in Graeme's book, *Gospel-Centred Hermeneutics: Biblical-theological foundations*, (Nottingham: Apollos, 2006).

[40] Those who believe the Bible to be inerrant normally add the important qualification that this inerrancy applies only to the now unrecoverable original manuscripts. Errors of transmission and translation are obvious and undeniable.

principle. The belief that there are no errors of any sort in the Bible has a profound influence on how the Bible is read and interpreted.

There were other principles proposed for our guidance in interpreting Scripture while at college. These included *sola Scriptura*, the analogy of Scripture, and the perspicuity of Scripture. Forged in the fires of the Protestant Reformation, these principles reflect a high view of Scripture as God's primary communication to humankind. While there are other legitimate authorities to guide the Christian in coming to a true knowledge of God, Scripture takes precedence (*sola Scriptura*). Because of God's trustworthiness, Scripture is internally consistent. Scripture can therefore be used to interpret Scripture and is not to be interpreted against Scripture. Scriptural passages that are plain in their meaning should be used to interpret obscure passages (the analogy of Scripture). Because God intends to communicate effectively with people of all ages and abilities, the meaning of Scripture will mostly be clear and unambiguous (the perspicuity of Scripture).[41]

In recent years, I have come to see that these principles can be misleading. They can obscure what is true as much as reveal it. Moreover, they work against, or at least are qualified by, two other principles that guided our reading of Scripture. The first was sensitivity to genre. From my time at the University of New England, I had been blessed by the benefits of taking full account of the multiple genres employed by biblical writers. Proverbs needed to be interpreted as proverbs, poetry as poetry, metaphor as metaphor. All sorts of possibilities began to emerge for consideration. For example, was the story of Jonah a true story or a parable? Were the early stories of Genesis factual, mythical, or legendary, or, if none of these, what were they? Being aware that biblical literature is ancient literature helps in answering these questions, as does an awareness of the relevant

---

[41] The Westminster Confession of Faith articulates the doctrine in these terms: 'All things in Scripture are not alike plain in themselves, nor alike clear unto all; yet those things which are necessary to be known, believed and observed, for salvation, are so clearly propounded and opened in some place of Scripture or other, that not only the learned, but the unlearned, in a due use of the ordinary means, may attain unto a sufficient understanding of them.' (WCF, 1/vii)

literary, historical, and theological conventions. We couldn't expect of the historical books the same exactitude as might be expected of modern histories. Ancient historians tended to include myth and legend in their histories. Might the biblical writers have done the same? These were questions we needed to ask and find good answers to.

Also guiding us in how we read the Bible was Biblical Theology. We learnt, and learnt well, to read the Scriptures canonically, that is, as a completed whole of biblical books roughly laid out in chronological order. We were taught to build a Biblical Theology on the back of a respectful understanding of what was unique and distinctive about each book, employing a grammatical-historical approach to do this.[42] Only after we had come to understand each book as the sort of literature it was, and as shaped and conditioned by the historical background out of which it had emerged, could we isolate and highlight threads of connection with the wider story. Sometimes these threads would be so emphasized that each book's distinctiveness was lost, but when done skilfully, a biblical-theology approach was enlightening and helpful. Clearly, almost all biblical writers used themes found in their already existing Scriptures, making a biblical-theological approach possible.

Over time, I have come to see some significant shortcomings and blind spots in the biblical-theological approach we were taught at college. However, at the time it was revolutionary. Not only did it enrich the process of reading the Scriptures, it also provided a framework for understanding the world. All the major themes of life are touched on in one way or another within the unfolding storyline of the Bible. Answers are given to many of the major questions, including: where do we come from, why are we here, why is there evil, what is the purpose of our lives, where are we headed?

While I was at college, I encountered, not for the first time, but in more detail, a way of doing apologetics which is called presuppositionalism. Well, known and originating exponents of the approach include Cornelius Van Til (1895-1987) and Francis Schaeffer (1912-1984). Both argued that the

---

[42] The grammatical-historical (or grammatico-historical) method is that approach to interpreting the texts that seeks to recover the author's original intended meaning, drawing on relevant literary and historical information.

big themes of the Bible provide a way of understanding life that makes best sense of it. Van Til went one step further to argue that unless we assume the truth of what the Bible teaches we can make no sense at all of life. We can have no true knowledge either. I was never completely comfortable with this approach, but it does explain something of the appeal of Biblical Theology with its highlighting of major themes of the Bible, which are also major themes of life.

Moore College did its best to create a similarly integrated approach to life. Worship was considered an all-of-life devotion to God. Learning was thought to be best done in community. When we first arrived at college, it was almost fully residential. Most people lived in and around its campus. There were, however, some notable exceptions. Not long into our first year, we learnt about a 2½-acre, tree-lined oasis in the suburbs called But Har Gra.[43] In its middle was a suitably grand old homestead once boasting a ballroom and servants' quarters. We'd come from the country, and although we'd loved our first year at Newtown, the prospect of country-style living at But Har Gra was too good a prospect not to pursue. We applied to be there from second year.

But Har Gra did not disappoint in any way. Damien, Jon, and Daniel loved the extra space, the trees to climb, the sandpits to play in, the guinea pigs to chase, the budgies to feed, the wide open spaces to run in, the bushes to disappear into. It was a boys' paradise. We shared it with Graham and Julie Cole and their family. We also shared it with two other student families. The house was divided into four units, later reduced to three. All were big enough for us to live in comfortably.

But Har Gra was special to me because it was special for us as a family, but also because of daily trips in and out from college, usually taking about half an hour. On these trips, we almost always talked theology and philosophy or were able to get Graham Cole's take on what we were studying or he was teaching at the time. My classmates thought it was worth at least 5 per cent in every exam I sat for at college to be so tutored by Graham. They were probably right.

---

[43] The name is an abbreviation of the names of some former occupants of the house, the Buttons and the Hargraves

Moore College passed quickly and happily. In third and fourth year, we changed churches. The usual practice was for students to become catechists or student ministers throughout their time at college. Normally, we would spend no more than two years at one church before having to seek another appointment. Towards the end of my second year, I contacted Rev. Allan Blanch who had just left St Barnabas Broadway[44] after nine distinguished years of ministry there. St Barnabas had a strong ministry to students at the nearby University of Sydney, not dissimilar to the University Chapel at Armidale. I felt fortunate to be invited by Allan to join him at St John's Beecroft. Allan was a seasoned and talented preacher, and a thoughtful theologian. Many were the Sunday nights we would unwind together after the last of the parishioners had left. Mostly, I would leave before midnight, or before thoughts of a young family or college the next day would prompt me to drive home.

On Sundays, we would all come out for morning church, with Judy taking the boys home by train in the afternoon. I have always known what a champion mother Judy is, but I do feel some guilt in remembering what pressures this sort of lifestyle placed on her. Sundays were, nevertheless, often good for her and the boys. Allan's daughter, Fiona, was willing and skilful in helping to look after them. Allan's wife, Pamela, always went out of her way to make us all feel welcome. Having But Har Gra to go back to was good, but Judy still had a lot to put up with, especially on those Saturdays when I had a sermon to prepare for the next day. Saturdays were our only day off together, and I ruined about twelve of them a year because of my then tendency to last minute preparation.

Those who know me now would probably think of me as a confident person, and I have certainly become more confident over time, but I lacked confidence at college. Two things surprised me towards the end of my time at college. One was being asked by Broughton Knox to be one of three Senior Students. The other was the achievement of First Class Honours in my Bachelor of Theology exams, the last of which were sat for at the end of third year. I was thrilled by the result and decided to enrol in a Master of Theology degree. At that stage, it was possible to do the necessary course work in fourth year, and to at least begin the 30,000-word dissertation while still at college.

---

44 One of Sydney's inner-city churches.

Fourth year was occupied with taking early first steps towards this higher degree. We also did a number of subjects to prepare us for life after college, the pick of them being a course on contemporary theologians taught by Bruce Smith, the father of my present pastor, Dave Smith. Bruce was a brilliant thinker and communicator. What I remember most about his lectures was his ability to think his way into the minds and spirit of those he taught us about. It wasn't good enough to recount their theology. Bruce believed that the way to understand a person's theology was to enter deeply into their intellectual and cultural milieu, to attempt to breathe the same air, to feel the pressures and challenges, and to enter empathetically into their journey of faith and doubt. Bruce was an exceptional wordsmith and poet, with the ability to mesmerize audiences, including us as we sat in his class.

Fourth year was also noted for being only the second time that our touch rugby team was beaten. We lost an early game in first year, not long after assembling our team. The star of the team, without the slightest doubt or competition, was a lanky red head from Queensland, Graham Lawrence. Graham, his wife Sandra, and two young children lived just down the road from us in our first year, before we went out to But Har Gra. We became good friends, and still are. Graham was/is an exceptional athlete. He had played first-grade rugby league, cricket, tennis, and squash. He was also a first-rate golfer and is presently part-time chaplain to the PGA tour ministering to golfers with whom he still plays competitive golf. Though Graham was the most talented person in our team, the rest of us had sufficient talent to collectively ensure a long winning run that sadly came to an end in our final game (a grand final) at college. We didn't quite become the stuff of legends, except in our own eyes, perhaps.

One of the benefits and responsibilities of being a Senior Student was that we had opportunities to speak at various events. It was my privilege, towards the end of fourth year, to speak on behalf of the student body in farewelling Dr Knox. 1984 was his last year as principal of Moore College. Peter Jensen was the heir apparent. I remember the mad scramble to find stories, including some designed to amuse. It was a big occasion and a fitting farewell. Dr Knox left Moore College to become the Founding Principal of George Whitefield College in South Africa.

We also were on the move. When I came into college, all the way from Hay, I knew I wanted to study at Moore. I knew I wanted to be a minister. I had decided I would be happy to be an Anglican minister, but didn't care much about where I would do my ministering. I had always liked Sydney, had felt the lure of its crowds and ability to host big events, including cricket, football, and a Billy Graham Crusade. I was happy enough to become a Sydney Anglican and was already a candidate for ministry in the diocese, but I had also spent most of my life up to that point in the country. I had been introduced to evangelical Anglicanism in Armidale, a big country town. Judy had grown up on an orchard, and then on a dairy farm 10 kilometres out of town. She had an understandable preference for the country, and so encouraged me to at least think about going back there.

I wasn't at first keen, having gotten used to the idea that we would stay in Sydney. Somewhat reluctantly, I wrote a letter to the then Bishop of Armidale, Peter Chiswell, basically saying that I was happily en route to becoming a Sydney Anglican, but did he have anything he could offer us. This was very much an eleventh-hour letter, but I am thrilled, looking back, that Peter Chiswell saw fit to offer us a place. Judy, Damien, Jon, Daniel, and I were soon driving out through the gates of But Har Gra on our way to Tamworth in north-western New South Wales.

Pastoral Ministry: the Dream Coming True

Theological colleges of all varieties inevitably create a stamp that distinguishes their graduates. Moore College is no exception. Its strengths are discernible in the strengths of its graduates, its weaknesses in their weaknesses. One of the criticisms I now often hear is that the preaching of Moore College graduates is formulaic; one keeps getting the same type of sermon, with the same pet topics, chief among them being evangelism or justification by faith or Biblical Theology. I am sure I was similarly stamped by Moore College when I arrived to become deacon and assistant minister for Rev. Ken Allen at St Peters, South Tamworth. The sermons I preached in those first couple of years majored on just those themes.

At the time, I thought I was different to the norm. I figured I was older and wiser, and had more life experience than your typical graduate. I am now older still, and quite certain that I too had all the recognizable signs of being just out of college. The congregations at St Peters were gently understanding, as was their vicar, Ken Allen. Ken graciously let me learn my own lessons, gave me enough rope to use or to be hanged by. Mercifully and hopefully, I didn't cause too much damage.

Judy and I enjoyed our time at South Tamworth. Just as had been the case at Beecroft, we were wonderfully supported as a family. Ken and Helen Allen were great role models. Ken's daughter, Jenny, took over the mantle from Fiona Blanch of being a skilful and caring friend to our growing boys. Many were the games of cricket played in the backyard of our home, which also boasted a small swimming pool. During our second year in Tamworth, our family grew again with the happy arrival of Jared Paul Mascord on 5 August 1986, necessitating the acquisition of a Mitsubishi Nimbus, a nicely designed, seven-seater people mover.

After two years in Tamworth, I was champing at the bit to take responsibility for my own parish. I had heard about a tiny cotton-growing town about three hours drive to the south-west. Cotton was a young industry, and the town's average age was lower than elsewhere in the Armidale Diocese. It seemed a happening sort of place. When news came through that it would be to Wee Waa that we would go, I was thrilled. Judy and I went there for a drive to inspect the new church and vicarage and to meet one of the church wardens, Jean Barton. I will never forget the euphoria I felt as we drove in over the town's levee bank. Wee Waa sits within the rich, black-soil flood plains of the Namoi River. Before levee banks were erected, Wee Waa had been subjected to frequent flooding. The sign at the outskirts of the town, which never changed during the five years we were there, announced a population of 1,900 people. For me, this was amply large enough to constitute ministerial paradise. I have seldom been happier than I was on that day. Everything I had wanted to be, everything I had trained to become was about to become reality.

A year or two before we arrived in Wee Waa, the then Vicar, Graham Farley, had supervised the building of a new church building. The old church was decrepit and unsafe. The new church was beautiful, and beautifully functional. Some of the decor of the old church was incorporated into the new building, including its stained glass windows. The carpeted floor and comfortably cushioned bench-seats gave the church a contemporary feel. There was plenty of natural lighting and nothing of the dinginess of older churches.

We felt fortunate to come to Wee Waa at such a time. Graham and Pat Farley had done a great job of re-engaging and re-involving the local community in the church-building project. Before the Farleys came, the church had been all but on its knees. The previous two vicars had embraced the charismatic movement, and in the process had alienated most of the congregation and much of the town. Graham rebuilt bridges into the community, and although the congregation was still small when we got there, a reinvigoration of the church community had begun. We were able to build on Graham's and Pat Farley's good work.

We did notice the difference between Tamworth and Wee Waa. The pace of life in Tamworth was noticeably slower than Sydney's, but in Wee Waa, it was slower still. Conversations were longer, phone calls could last for half an hour before the often straightforward purpose of the call was made known. Walking the few blocks to the main street to pick up some milk could take an hour, or more, depending on whom you met on the way. On one of our very first days in Wee Waa, I was waiting to buy a newspaper at the local newsagent, and though I wasn't consciously in a hurry, I must have given the impression of impatience by the rebuke I received from the admittedly gruff newsagent: 'You're in a bl***y hurry, aren't you?' I introduced myself as the new vicar.

I probably was in a hurry. There was so much to do. I had come to Wee Waa with a strong sense that the gospel I was entrusted with was for all of Wee Waa, that it had relevance for all aspects of the life of every person in Wee Waa. I wanted Wee Waa Anglican Church to be a centre of worship for as much of the community as would happily attend an Anglican Church. Between 50 per cent and 60 per cent of the town and district's population was at least nominally Anglican. That made me the vicar of the majority of the district's population. There were only three other churches in town: a Roman Catholic, a Presbyterian, and a small charismatic fellowship.

I had a keen sense of wanting to minister to all the people who came across my path, and in a town as small as Wee Waa that was most people. I got to know many of the cotton farmers, some of whom had become very rich. The earliest cotton farmers were mostly American. They had discovered how similar the flat flood plains of the north-west were to cotton growing areas in California, and how suitably hot the climate was for growing cotton. There were soon more millionaires per square kilometre around Wee Waa than around any other town I knew of. Wee Waa's banks did more business than towns far larger.

I enjoyed the hospitality of rich and growing-rich cotton farmers, but was equally at home, perhaps more so, with those who were not so well off. A highlight of our time in Wee Waa was becoming a friend of Wee Waa's then small Indigenous community. I especially loved playing touch rugby with people of Indigenous background, mainly because they were so amazingly skilful. Fairly early on in our time at Wee Waa, I learnt second-hand that I'd been criticized for playing touch rugby with some local Aboriginal boys known to have been involved in criminal activity. I was disappointed by the criticism, but kind of chuffed to be criticized for such a thing. Some weeks, perhaps months after I had joined their irregular and fast-paced games, I received what I thought was the ultimate compliment. I hadn't noticed, but the boys had inhibited their normal more colourful swearing. One day, a couple of their cousins from Walgett joined us, and part-way through the game, one of them swore normally, only to follow it with, 'S**t, I forgot there was a priest here!'

I would later put together a team of Indigenous and non-Indigenous players to enter a mixed gender touch rugby competition which happened once or twice a year in town. We did pretty well. Some of these friendships fed into a night service we had begun, with Indigenous people from all over the district beginning to attend, attracted in part by the style of music we began to use. We had been able to employ a youth worker, Tim Baxter. Tim had come straight from university and was not only a highly gifted youth worker, he could also play a mean game of touch (a selection prerequisite), as well as being a skilful guitarist. Joining Tim on guitar was Lloyd Dewson, a young Indigenous man. On drums was Cathy Sumpter, a Burren Junction local. The band's music was lively and loud.

Ministry was not just to all people, it was to people throughout all the stages of their lives. I baptized, married, and buried them, sometimes in close temporal proximity. I had the honour of conducting the wedding of the daughter of our next-door neighbour. Within twelve months, I buried her and her young husband. They had slammed into an unforgiving gum tree; their new Brock Commodore becoming airborne at 220 kilometres per hour on a road just outside of Narrabri, a nearby town, the car's capacity and limitations becoming brutally obvious in one deadly split-second. A minister's life can be an emotional roller coaster. On the day of a funeral, you can find yourself visiting a newborn child in hospital, or teaching Scripture to children of all ages.

We bussed students to our church from the local high school for Scripture seminars, something we did in cooperation with the Presbyterian Church. Our churches worked together beautifully, though with a tiny competitive edge. I also got to know the local Roman Catholic priest. Not long after we arrived in Wee Waa, his parish was participating in a national Renew program designed to encourage a renewal of faith within their communities. They had enrolled 150 parishioners to participate in a number of small discussion groups. I saw this as an opportunity to encourage our parishioners to do the same. After hearing of the numbers about to be involved at the Catholic Church, I challenged our congregation with words to this effect, 'If they can get 150 people to their discussion groups, surely we could get 50.' We did get fifty, or just under, for six weeks of study and reflection. It was an early turning point in our life together.

The Christian faith I believed in and wanted to commend to the population of Wee Waa was not only for all ages and stages of life, it was for all aspects of life. I had long held that a mark of authentic and healthy Christian faith was that it made better human beings of us; it enhanced rather than detracted from our humanity. We'd enjoy the world more fully, would express our talents more skilfully, would engage in intellectual pursuits more freely. I inherited from my dad and mum what I would describe as a healthy theology of creation, a love of games, an appreciation for literature, art, and music, and for the value and joy of a hard day's productive labour. My understanding of the Jewish Sabbath is that it was a time to gratefully reflect on all that is good in God's creation and to not make an idol of it. My big hope for the people of Wee Waa was that they would stop their work for long enough to attend church to appropriately give thanks for God's help and blessing. Some did.

I am an optimist by nature. Theologically, I had some justification in the notion of a sovereign God. I felt that I was on the winning side. I also believed, naively, that I could persuade almost anyone of the truth of the Christian gospel. When I was deciding what thesis to write to complete my Master of Theology degree, Graham Cole suggested I study the works of John Warwick Montgomery, a then reasonably high-profile apologist for the Christian faith. There are different theories about how one should best defend Christian faith, but one very prominent theory, dating back to the European Enlightenment, is evidentialism. Evidentialists typically judge beliefs acceptable or unacceptable, rational or irrational, depending on how well supported they are by evidence. John Locke (1632-1704) cautioned against holding beliefs with greater assurance than the proofs they were built upon would warrant. W. K. Clifford (1845-1879), the English mathematician and philosopher, asserted: 'It is wrong always, everywhere, and for anyone, to believe anything upon insufficient evidence.'[45]

Whether or not one agrees with these articulations, most of us acknowledge the need to provide evidence for at least some of our important beliefs. John Warwick Montgomery believed his Christian beliefs required the support of evidence. He was also convinced that such evidence exists in more than adequate amounts. In fact, so compelling did he believe the case for Christianity to be, that not believing it was irrational. In his words,

> The facts of God's existence and of His incarnate revelation in Jesus Christ . . . stand over against man, judging him by their sheer veracity and compelling force—and unless he volitionally refuses to believe, and goes against all sound reasoning in so doing, they will move him to a Spirit-produced conversion and living relationship with Jesus Christ.[46]

I am not sure I ever believed the case for Christianity to be that strong. However, I did conduct my ministry in Wee Waa with the belief that Christianity was not only true, but could be shown to be true.

Helping the cause of Christianity in Wee Waa was the fact that Christianity was the only religion on offer. There were no other faith communities. Moreover, the Christians in town spoke with a largely unified voice. The

---

[45] W. K. Clifford, 'The Ethics of Belief', in *Lectures and Essays*, Leslie Stephen and Frederick Pollock, (eds), 2nd ed. (London and New York: Macmillan, 1886), 342-46.

[46] John Warwick Montgomery, *Faith Founded on Fact*, (Nashville: Thomas Nelson Publishers, 1978), 150.

Catholic priest was as conservative in his beliefs as were the town's other clergy. The Presbyterian minister, Russell Stark, and before him David Cook, were Moore College-trained evangelicals, as was the Charismatic pastor.

Also helping the case for Christianity in Wee Waa was the calibre of those who came to minister there, including Tim Baxter, Roger and Sue Chilton, Jeremy and Virginia Rice. Bishop Peter Chiswell devised a wonderful (for me and others) scheme of partially paying the salaries of deacons in their first year so they could work in small country parishes like Wee Waa. In my last two years at Wee Waa, the bishop sent us Roger and Sue, then Jeremy and Virginia. Two more talented ministers I have not met. It was such a privilege to have them and their families join us in ministry to the people of Wee Waa and surrounds.

Wee Waa has two branch churches, each about 50 kilometres out of town; the first is at Burren Junction, renowned for its hot springs; the second at Pilliga in the famous Pilliga scrub. It was great to have Roger and then Jeremy help out in making these outlying congregations feel cared for. Roger was, and I think still is, a workaholic, or, more charitably, has enormous capacity for work and people. Like Tony Doran, he gives himself completely to every person he encounters, always giving sacrificially of his time and energies. He threw his immense talents and drive into organizing a mission to Wee Waa. The year was 1990. We organized to have Rev. Ian Powell come to preach. Ian is a superb preacher with a great ability to relate to Australians and to Australian men in particular. Joining Ian was Owen Shelley, a seasoned puppeteer and communicator to children and families. Joining them was up-and-coming musician Phil Davidson, skilful at relating to teenagers. Co-hosting the mission was the Presbyterian Church.

We were quite blown away by the success of the eight-day mission. Its highlight was an invitation dinner held in the High School auditorium. A total of 430 people attended, along with about 90 children who we needed to supervise and keep relatively quiet in the school library. More than a quarter of the town's population, an eighth of the district's, attended that night. During the week of mission, up to a quarter of the district's population came along to at least one mission event. It was a remarkable week.

Not long after the mission was over, Roger and Sue moved on to be replaced by Jeremy and Virginia. Jeremy is among the funniest people I have met, a worthy rival to Ken Fraser, my friend from school days. Jeremy is tall, English, and not unlike John Cleese in shape, mannerisms and ability to be funny even when not trying. He and Virginia were also wonderfully caring and compassionate, and their ministry in Wee Waa was hugely appreciated.

Judy and I had hoped to stay in Wee Waa for at least ten years. That was a figure we had in our minds, but in our fifth year, I got a phone call from Peter Jensen, then Principal of Moore College. He said he wasn't offering me anything, at least not yet. He was just sounding me out about coming back to Moore College to teach. He had in mind someone to relieve David Peterson from some of the pastoral ministry subjects, allowing him to do more in New Testament studies, his specialty. I was flabbergasted. At the day of my graduation from Moore College, my dad had embarrassed me greatly by suggesting to one of the faculty that I might one day come back to teach at Moore. I never once imagined it would happen.

It was a very, very unsettling phone call. It wasn't a job offer, just an indication of the possibility of a job offer, which did later come. I travelled back to Sydney to be interviewed by Peter and also by Peter O'Brien. The job offer, when it came, was slightly enlarged by the fact that Graham Cole had by then accepted the position of principal of Ridley (Anglican) College in Melbourne. There was suddenly a need for someone to teach philosophy and apologetics, subjects I was keen on, and at that time addressing in my Master of Theology degree. It was a tempting and daunting offer.

One of the reasons for accepting it was that Judy (especially) sensed the need for a new start. Ministry at Wee Waa had been wonderful, but it had got busier and busier, and Judy at one point had to say to me, 'If you don't slow down, Keith, you will become a stranger to your family'. She was right. I was becoming engrossed in ministry. It was addictive. You begin to believe the hype that others start putting about, about how good you are, about what a difference you have made. It wasn't healthy.

On 29 May 1991, Kieran Barry Mascord was born, becoming the fifth Mascord boy to face the prospect of missing out on his father's rightful attention had I stayed in Wee Waa and not mended my ways. It was good to go when we did. Our decision to leave coincided with a succession of tragic deaths which were beginning to take their toll. Over the five years we were in Wee Waa, I took the funerals of a number of stillborn children as well as of some who had died inexplicably of cot death syndrome. I buried an aging bullocky who justified his decision to shoot himself by appeal to his lifelong practice of putting his bullocks out of their misery when injury or old age overtook them. I buried the daughter of my neighbour, along with her husband, but two further tragic deaths rocked me and our community to the core.

The wife of a Jewish cotton farmer started coming to church at a time of family crisis. Turning up at church was a tentative first step to rediscovering the faith of an earlier time in her life. Her children were facing challenges she needed help with. Not long after she started coming to church, I did a short sermon series on the problem of evil and suffering. I remember well her and her daughter laughing along with some attempted humour of mine as I sought to show the occasional benefits of pain, citing as an example the sometimes painful removal of infected teeth. On the Friday after that sermon, this lady realized she needed some bread for her husband's dinner. In the gathering dusk of evening, she jumped into the family utility, intending to drive three blocks to the nearest store. On crossing the first intersection, she didn't see a fully laden cotton truck bearing down on her. The driver, who had recently become a Christian, couldn't stop or turn his truck before it ploughed into and over her car, bringing her life to a sudden end.

I have no idea what God's purpose was in allowing this awful tragedy. It simply added to that family's woes, and, from what I could gather at the time, confirmed the atheism of this woman's husband. Just as perplexing was the death of a young boy whose family I had begun to get to know on a small farm the other side of Pilliga. I had visited the family maybe two or three times. They were struggling to earn a living, but were making a go of it. One day, not long after I visited the family, I heard news that a young boy had been run over by his father and was in intensive care at Wee Waa Hospital. I soon discovered it was Eric, the beautiful little boy I'd begun to get to know. Eric had seen his father drive past the family home on the way to a nearby shed, and had madly ridden his three-wheeler in pursuit. Not aware of his son's presence, the father had reversed, crushing his son under the wheels of his truck.

Eric's was as hard a funeral as I have ever taken. Just one funeral surpassed it, the funeral eleven months later of his elder sister, who, in another freakish accident, was thrown from the car she was travelling in to her death. She hadn't been wearing a seat belt. Her reason for not wearing a seat belt was that had she been wearing a seat belt in an earlier car accident, she would have been killed.

Events like this were deeply unsettling. They unsettled my faith. They made me wonder whether the beliefs I had about God and death and faith were adequate. The doubts were mostly momentary and soon dismissed, but they did linger at times. What did linger was the cumulative impact of tragic funerals like these. It got to the stage that I would jump—internally if not literally—every time the phone rang. I was fearful of hearing of someone else's death. Even after only five years at Wee Waa, I had so got to know and love its people that I hated the prospect of having to bury them.

We left Wee Waa resigned to the need and opportunity of moving on. We headed back to Sydney, not quite back to But Har Gra, but to a house that backed onto But Har Gra. The boys were staggered by the size of Sydney. On its outskirts, they began to ask, 'Are we there yet?' Half an hour later, we arrived at our destination, at the But Har Gra the older boys remembered—just. As the truck arrived with our furniture, another van arrived bearing flowers to welcome us into our new home. It had been sent by Eric's parents and surviving sister as a way of saying thank you for the hard road we had walked together. It wished us their best for the next stage in our journey.

CHAPTER 5

Cracks Appearing

The text for the morning's chapel service on my first day back at Moore College was Genesis 6, the first few verses of the Noah story. I can't remember much of what was doubtless an excellent sermon by Old Testament lecturer, Barry Webb, but I do remember thinking how appropriate it was for him to be preaching about the Nephilim, who in the early text of Genesis 6 are described as 'heroes of old and warriors of renown.' They were believed to be giants.[47] My very first class appeared giantlike to me when, a few minutes later, I delivered my first lecture in Pastoral Ministry One.

I should perhaps have been more frightened than I was. I was joining a talented faculty. I was taking over some of the lecturing load of Graham Cole, a person of prodigious gifts. I had come from the relative obscurity of being a small town vicar. I should have been intimidated, but strangely wasn't. I figured that I had more and more recent experience in pastoral ministry than most of my colleagues. I had stories to tell and experiences to share, as had Bill Lawton before me. The learning curve was steep, nevertheless, and I needed the generously given help of fellow faculty including new boss, Peter Jensen. Peter was and still is a very private person. You weren't ever too sure what he was thinking, but he was a good leader with an occasionally crazy sense of humour. We all thought he could easily have got a job as a stand-up comic, a talent he would mostly keep under wraps until bringing it out for all to see at light-hearted end-of-the-year celebrations.

---

[47] Numbers 13: 33

There was no censoring of what I taught. Peter was willing to trust those he had appointed. There was ample freedom and encouragement to pursue my own scholarly interests. David Peterson, then head of the Ministry Department and my immediate boss, hoped that I would pursue studies in pastoral ministry, but my interests and passions were in philosophy and apologetics. In my first year back at college, I completed my Master of Theology degree and then followed a suggestion by Graham Cole to study the works of American philosopher Alvin Plantinga, an excellent suggestion as it turned out.

An early challenge was to find a church to attend and throw our lot in with. In the first few months of 1992, we attended St Barnabas Broadway, then pastored by Robert Forsyth, future Bishop of South Sydney. We enjoyed the anonymity of being in so large a church and not feeling we needed to contribute other than by attending. We were still feeling the grief of leaving Wee Waa. We had so fallen in love with this town, with its people, its lifestyle, with the productive connection that existed there between church and community. City churches were very different. Because we had to travel across suburbs to attend St Barnabas, we never quite felt at home. It wasn't local. It was also very middle class, with nothing like the social variety or intimacy of a small country church. We started looking for something closer to home.

Someone suggested St James, Croydon, just up the road from But Har Gra. We are so glad they did. Not only was this our local Anglican Church, but its rector, Barry Dudding, had spearheaded an active and energetic ministry to children and youth. When we arrived there in late 1992, there was a youth group for each of our boys—except for Kieran. He was still being minded in crèche. We instantly warmed to Barry and his wife Jo. Barry is an inspirational preacher, one of Sydney's best. He inspires not simply by his ability to expound and apply the Scriptures, but is himself an inspiration for being so tirelessly passionate and prayerful.[48]

Becoming a teacher at Moore College allowed me to again take a slight step back from the coalface of Christian ministry, and, as I had done before at

---

[48] Barry retired as rector of St James, Croydon, in January 2012. He and Jo will not ever retire from ministry, which remains their passion.

university, to hold up my inherited Christian faith to critical scrutiny. It was, in fact, what I was being employed to do. I was being asked to teach apologetics. The word apologetics is used to describe the theory and practice of defending and/or commending the faith, in my case the Christian faith. I was being paid to ask 'Is my faith justified? Does it pass the sort of intellectual tests that healthily justified beliefs should be able to pass?' I felt up for the challenge. As was the case at university, I was also happy to become involved in ministry, to do my bit for the church we had joined.

At St James, there was a lot to do, lots to be involved in. I soon assumed the title of honorary curate (unpaid assistant). I was asked to preach from time to time. I helped out at one of the youth groups and got involved in ministry to men. Judy and I opened up our home for a study group and for pastoral care meetings. I co-started a Sunday-afternoon touch rugby game with Warren Darwall, then chef at a nearby Bible College.[49]

These were very special years—special for our boys, and special for us as a family. But they also had their challenges, including the tragic death of a member of our church. On the morning of a Sunday school picnic that still went ahead on the spacious grounds of But Har Gra, the newly married wife of now-good-friend Brian Tucker had just come into church for the morning service. She complained of feeling nauseous and moments later collapsed from the hidden effects of a rupturing blood vessel. She was rushed to hospital, but never regained consciousness. Bronwyn and Brian, who had wedded relatively late in life, thereby had the joy of their married life cruelly snatched from them after just four months.

Another not so challenging, but still unsettling experience was the slow discovery that there were a number of beliefs around the edges of the Reformed orthodoxy Moore College stood for that were fast becoming sacred cows, beliefs used to measure one's acceptability within the tribe that is Sydney Anglicanism, or, at least, within a growingly influential inner tribe. Acceptability had previously been measured by how solid or sound one was on the key subjects of Calvinism and Biblical authority. I expected that. I also wasn't surprised by the vehemence of opposition to Pentecostalism or to the ordination of women to the priesthood. I was happily in those camps

---

[49] Sydney and Missionary Bible College (SMBC).

myself, but wasn't as prepared to find that one's view of who was expected to do evangelism would create such heated disagreement.

Not long after arriving at Moore, I was asked to prepare a paper on the subject of mission in the New Testament and to bring to it my own experience of country ministry. We had certainly been involved in mission in Wee Waa. I wasn't sure where to start, and so did a comprehensive search of relevant passages in the New Testament. I soon discovered what many had discovered before me—that there are no explicit or straightforward exhortations directed to Christians in general to do evangelism. That intrigued me and sent me on a quest to develop a more holistic and community-based understanding of evangelism, taking into account the wide range, within any congregation, of gifts that can collectively determine its life and witness.

It all began to make sense to me, but when I finally delivered the paper,[50] I had the strangest experience of feeling I was sprouting heresy. I discovered then and later that what I was saying was not the position of a number of the more influential members of faculty, nor was it the position of Phillip Jensen, Peter's brother, then reaching the height of his powers as the controversial and free-spirited rector of St Matthias, Centennial Park. Phillip taught that it was the duty, even the primary duty, of every Christian to do evangelism. He was building a ministry among students at the University of New South Wales on this very premise.

I would later use a version of this paper in Pastoral Ministry One, and once again was surprised by the vehemence of reaction to what I was arguing. It was hardly an outlandish position. The then Archbishop of Sydney, Donald Robinson, had argued a very similar line in a paper written a few years earlier. He was good enough to critique a draft of my paper.[51] Significantly,

---

[50] Later published as a chapter entitled 'Equipping the Local Church for Mission', in B. G. Webb (ed.), *Exploring the Missionary Church,* Explorations 7, (Homebush West: Lancer Books, 1983), 125-150.

[51] In more recent years, Dr John Dickson, a graduate of Moore College, completed doctoral studies on the subject, concluding along similar lines to Archbishop Robinson. His book, *Promoting the Gospel: a practical guide to the biblical art of sharing your faith,* (Blue Bottle Books: Sydney, 2005), spells out some of the practical and contemporary implications.

those who reacted most strongly to what I was saying were those who had come to college from St Matthias and its associated ministries.

What I have come to see since is that here is another example of ubiquitous tribalism. As humans, we like to live in tribal groupings. We feel we need to find boundary markers to determine who is in and who is out of our tribe. Sydney Anglicans, not surprisingly, are very tribal, with various groups and even families ebbing and flowing in their relative influence. As lecturers, we became quickly aware of some of these tribes. We could quite easily pick those who had come from St Barnabas Broadway and its various Sydney University ministries. It was easier still to pick those who had come from St Matthias. One reason for this was that Phillip Jensen was, and remains, a seasoned boundary marker.

As for me, I was mostly oblivious to any angst I might have been creating by taking a different line to Phillip. I was simply saying what I thought and was very happy to engage in dialogue and debate with those who differed. I had a slightly different view on guidance; was much more willing to countenance extra-biblical sources of guidance than were those from the St Matthias tribe. Those of us who discussed such things on faculty believed it was good for those coming out of St Matthias to be exposed to different points of view. And some did moderate their dogmatism. Some did begin to see that there were greys and not just blacks or whites when it came to what we think or believe.

I lectured full-time at Moore College for ten years, between 1992 and 2001, and then a further five years part-time, teaching a one-semester course in philosophy. I enjoyed my time at Moore very much. I enjoyed teaching and developed a habit of sitting cross-legged on a desk up the front when we got into discussion, mostly in philosophy classes. The posture matched the style of discussion I enjoyed most. I wasn't so happy just to talk or read out lecture notes, and, as has become the practice at Moore, encouraged students to do most of their reading out of class. I enjoyed getting to know students, and, perhaps strangely, developed some of my best friendships with students who had come out of St Matthias. I appreciated the earnestness of their desire to know and defend the truth as they understood it.

I enjoyed the touch rugby (and sometimes gridiron, soccer, or cricket) we played at college. Most weeks I'd play in at least three games and sometimes more when the annual touch rugby competition was happening. I think I ended up playing in five grand finals, winning two, losing three, and that on top of four grand finals as an undergraduate. Perhaps the highlight of all this touch rugby was a win by But Har Gra in my final year of full-time lecturing. On that day, we had a number of genuine speedsters including my son Jon. As I got older and slower, the best I could do was to put these guys through gaps on their way to scoring tries.[52] It was good to finally go out a winner, unlike what happened at the end of my undergraduate career.

Returning to North America

Another highlight of my time at college was having the opportunity to begin and complete doctoral studies. Alvin Plantinga, whose work I studied, was Director of the Center for Philosophy of Religion at the University of Notre Dame in South Bend, Indiana.[53] One of the wonderful privileges of teaching at Moore is the institution of study leave, six months of it, every 3½ years—effectively a sabbatical. In the second half of 1995, Judy, the boys, and I, along with Judy's mum, Peg, flew out of Sydney for Los Angeles, on route to South Bend. This would be the trip of a lifetime for all of us. For me, it meant returning to Canada, the country of my birth and growing-up years. I hadn't been back since I was eleven, thirty-one years earlier. That in itself was special, but to have my family with me to enjoy and sometimes roll their eyes in amusement at the nostalgia was extra special.

We left Sydney on 4 July, arriving the same day in Los Angeles. After checking in at our hotel, we walked across to Disneyland, along with hoards of other Independence Day visitors. We waited in long queues for most of the rides and exhibits, but it was worth it, just to see the excitement on everyone's faces. Kieran was just four, but these constitute some of his earliest memories. We loved our two days in Disneyland. Back in Australia, I had just taken Jared to see the movie *Lion King*, one of the all-time great children's movies. Disney had organized a magnificent *Lion King* parade

---

[52] The equivalent of a touchdown in gridiron or a goal in soccer. The ball has to be put down over the try or goal line.

[53] Plantinga has only recently (2010) retired from this position.

with dancers in animal costumes and the music of the movie booming over loud speakers along the route. We couldn't have asked for a better introduction to the United States.

After Los Angeles, we flew to Portland, Oregon, to spend some days with my brother Alan and his wife Donna before buying a Chevy Suburban, a giant (to us) nine-seater people mover, and driving north for Vancouver and across to Victoria, British Columbia, my birthplace, and from there over the Rockies to Calgary where my sister Dorothy and husband John lived. For me, the highlight of the whole trip was a return to Three Hills, and being bold enough to ask permission of the new owners of both homes I had lived in to let us look around inside. I was uncontrollably euphoric, as I was when showing the family around the campus of PBI, including the massive auditorium, as I was when later driving out to Pine Lake, the site of the most wonderful childhood holidays.

From Calgary, we travelled to Claresholm, my mother's home town, then to Yellowstone National Park, from there across the top of the United States to Chicago, and from Chicago to South Bend. It took us five weeks from the time we arrived in the United States till we arrived, travel weary, at a house that had been organized for us, just up the road from the university campus. We would live there for the next five months.

This too was a special time for our family. The older boys went to school. Damien enjoyed making new friends at school and church. Jon trained for his school's gridiron team for a month before school went back; then scored a touchdown in his final game of the season. Daniel was alone in middle school and had a miserable first few weeks, with classmates struggling to understand his Australian accent. Happily, he went on to make many good friends. Jared enjoyed third class just up the road from where we lived. Kieran learnt gymnastics with some friends from church. Two sporting highlights of the trip enjoyed by the older boys were the chance to watch the Notre Dame College Football team in what was an always-packed 60,000-seat stadium, and the even bigger treat of travelling to Chicago to watch Michael Jordan score 44 of his side's 108 at the Chicago Bull's home stadium.

For me, one of the most special things about this time in South Bend was getting to know and going to church with Alvin Plantinga whose work

I would be studying. His church, which became ours, was South Bend Christian Reformed Church. A highlight, apart from the high calibre of preaching, was attending all-age Sunday school. Judy and I enjoyed presentations from ancient historians, biologists, and specialists of all sorts. Plantinga himself would sometimes take a class. What we encountered here was a church that was openly and honestly wrestling with issues of faith and life, without censoring alternative points of view. Plantinga was somewhat unusual in calling into question aspects of evolutionary theory, taking on Daniel Dennett, for example, more than once. I chatted at church with a biologist who was bemused by Plantinga's point of view, but also respectful of Plantinga as a philosopher and fellow Christian. I could easily have become a long-term member of this church. We were astounded by how welcoming the church was of us, how often we were invited out for meals, even with so many boys to feed.

Alvin Plantinga is a highly impressive human being. It was a privilege to study his work, and also to meet and be encouraged by him. When Plantinga began his career as a philosopher in the late fifties, he was aware of there being very few philosophers willing to identify themselves as Christian, certainly within Anglo-American circles.[54] Positivism was in the ascendency, and Christianity was on the back foot.[55] That situation has significantly changed, in part because of the influence and stature of philosophers like Plantinga. Plantinga was instrumental in the creation of the Society of Christian Philosophers, which boasts a membership of over 1,000, representing about 10 per cent of professional philosophers in the United States.

While at Notre Dame University, I managed to track down and plough my way through most of Plantinga's published as well as some of his unpublished work. I was initially intrigued, but became increasingly disturbed by what I was reading. When Plantinga first began teaching philosophy, he assumed, as I had always assumed, that the rationality of Christian beliefs could only be established by way of arguments and evidence. He also encountered the

---

[54] With the obvious and not only exception of philosophers teaching in Roman Catholic universities such as Notre Dame.
[55] A. Plantinga, 'Plantinga: A Christian Life Partly Lived', in J. C. Kelly, (ed), *Philosophers Who Believe*, (Downers Grove: InterVarsity Press, 1993), 81.

evidentialist objection to Christian beliefs, which was that these beliefs lack sufficiently strong arguments and evidence to be considered rational. This objection he encountered often in his early career.

The problem of not enough evidence

What was disturbing for me was that Plantinga came quickly to agree that his Christian beliefs are not rational if based upon the sorts of arguments and evidence that have traditionally been used to support them. Plantinga spent many years analysing arguments both for and against the existence of God. He himself devised and revised versions of these arguments. It is not that Plantinga thought these arguments were useless or without merit.[56] Individually and cumulatively they did contribute to the case for God. However, even when added together, they were not conclusive. They are certainly not strong enough to compel belief, or to render unbelief irrational. When strong arguments against the existence of God are taken into account, including arguments from evil and suffering, Plantinga concluded that the best one can say is that God's existence is slightly more probable than not. A reasonable thing to do in the light of this uncertain conclusion is to suspend belief and be agnostic.

This conclusion of Plantinga's is not overly controversial. In fact, some would argue that Plantinga is unjustifiably optimistic about the outcome of arguments in favour of God's existence. He himself comes from a Reformed or Calvinistic tradition which has been largely antagonistic to the enterprise of natural theology, which is the enterprise of developing arguments in favour of God's existence.

What was more disturbing for me was that Plantinga was even more pessimistic about arguments in favour of distinctively Christian beliefs, such as belief in the truth of the gospel. These also, according to him, fail

---

[56] Plantinga speaks positively of there being 'a whole host of good theistic arguments, all patiently waiting to be developed in penetrating and profound detail'. In this context, he mentions over 30 examples of such arguments. A. Plantinga, 'Christian Philosophy at the end of the 20th Century', in Sander Griffioen and Bert Balks (eds), *Christian Philosophy at the Close of the 20th Century*, (Kampen: Uitgeverij Kok, 1995), 40, 41.

to meet the evidentialist objection. Central to gospel belief is belief in the resurrection of Jesus. Evidence for this event has often been relied upon by apologists, me included, as the linchpin of their case for the gospel's truth. But Plantinga was different. He believed, and still believes, that the historical case for the resurrection of Jesus is weak—too weak to rest one's belief on. In *Warranted Christian Belief*, he makes the assertion that even if one had a fine command of the vast literature on the historicity of the resurrection, one would 'presumably think it pretty speculative and chancy, its probability being either low or inscrutable.'[57]

With respect to the Christian gospel as a whole, Plantinga thinks that if we simply try to assess its truth making use of our ordinary belief-forming mechanisms, such as induction, deduction and memory, or historical method fairly applied, the rational thing to do would be to *not believe*.[58] I found that disturbing, not just because I was an evidentialist, and was therefore convinced of the importance of evidence, but also because I began to think Plantinga might be right. Without going into details, he points out that a probabilistic case for the truth of the Christian gospel is likely to involve a number of related and mutually supportive truth claims (such as that God exists). When these are brought together to mount a case for the truth of the gospel, the probability of the conclusion of any such case cannot rise higher, and is almost certainly going to be lower, than any one of the constituent truth claims. So, for example, if you think that the probability of God's existing is slightly more probable than not, then the overall case for the truth of the gospel cannot rise higher than that; and is almost certainly going to be less; and so the rational thing to do is to not believe.

Now, it may be possible to argue a case for the truth of the Christian gospel in other ways than Plantinga has suggested, for example by arguing that the gospel explanation of the Jesus event is the best possible explanation of all the relevant facts; and that, in the absence of a better explanation, one is warranted in embracing that message as true. Maybe an alternative approach like this is possible. I hoped so. It unsettled me to think there

---

[57] A. Plantinga, *Warranted Christian Belief*, (Oxford: Oxford University Press, 2000), 276.

[58] *Warranted Christian Belief*, 133.

mightn't be. Having been an evidentialist for all of my adult life, I was entering new territory in even countenancing the possibility that evidence for my beliefs wasn't strong, or strong enough, to justify them.

Plantinga's Proposal

Plantinga was able to keep his faith intact, despite its claimed lack of evidentialist support, by developing an approach to justifying theistic and Christian beliefs very different to what I was used to. Rather than trying to meet the evidentialist objection by looking for more and better evidence to support the belief that God exists and that Christianity is true, Plantinga argued that there is a better and more direct way to justify these beliefs, a way that does not involve the use of evidence or arguments. In order to argue his case, Plantinga points out that there are other types of belief that we typically and justifiably hold without the need for evidence or arguments, like perceptual beliefs for example, such as that I am having the experience of seeing a computer in front of me. I could argue that my eyes normally work well, that I have had my eyes tested recently, and that my vision was judged to be pretty good for someone of my age. That would certainly provide me with some reasons for thinking that my experience of seeing a computer in front of me isn't misleading me. But far more persuasive than any argument I might construct is the experience itself. In seeing my computer, I form the belief that I am seeing a computer. I don't need an argument to come to this belief. In fact, arguments can have the undesirable consequence of making me less certain about what I formerly believed with great certainty. Maybe my eyes *don't* work so well. Maybe I have a rare and imperceptible tendency to delusions. Perhaps I am no more than a brain in a vat. All sorts of possibilities can present themselves when we start constructing arguments. They are not always the best way to justify our beliefs.

Plantinga suggests that belief in God and belief in the truth of the Christian gospel are like perceptual beliefs in that they arise much more directly and without the need of arguments to justify them. He calls them basic beliefs, because of this characteristic of not needing the support of still further beliefs. Memory beliefs and mathematical beliefs also fall into the category of basic, according to Plantinga. When I say that I had Weet-Bix for breakfast or that $1 + 1 = 2$, I don't typically need an argument to be convinced of the truth of what I remember or intuit.

Basic beliefs have varying degrees of warrant, which is Plantinga's preferred word for rational justification.[59] They have high degrees of warrant if formed according to belief-forming faculties that are working properly in the right sort of environment, and in a way that is likely to produce true beliefs. Plantinga argues that belief in God is normally, or often, and with the most warrant, a basic belief. He draws upon his Reformed heritage to argue that human beings have been created with a *sensus divinitatis*, a sin-damaged, but nevertheless still operational awareness of God that is typically formed in contexts where the beauty and splendour of nature is evident. In Plantinga's own words,

> Calvin holds that God 'reveals and daily discloses himself in the whole workmanship of the universe,' and the divine art 'reveals itself in the innumerable and yet distinct and well ordered variety of the heavenly host.' God has so created us that we have a tendency or disposition to see his hand in the world around us. More precisely, there is in us a disposition to believe propositions of the sort *this flower was created by God* or *this vast and intricate universe was created by God* when we contemplate the flower or behold the starry heavens or think about the vast reaches of the universe.[60]

Plantinga argues for the existence of a different, but similar belief-forming mechanism that is operational when someone comes to believe that the Christian gospel is true. He thinks that it also typically arises non-inferentially. What gives warrant to Christian belief is that it is produced in us by the workings of the Holy Spirit. Because God is God (and can be expected to produce true beliefs about himself), the beliefs formed as a result of the Holy Spirit's work are reliable and true. Plantinga describes the phenomenology of Christian belief formation in these terms:

> We read Scripture, or something presenting Scriptural teaching, or hear the gospel preached, or are told of it by parents, or encounter a Scriptural teaching as the conclusion of an argument

---

[59] For Plantinga's account of warranted belief, see *Warranted Christian Belief*, 46.
[60] A Plantinga, 'Rationality and Religious Belief', in S. Cahn and D. Shatz, (eds), *Contemporary Philosophy of Religion* (New York: Oxford University Press, 1982), 272.

> (or conceivably even as an object of ridicule), or in some other way encounter a proclamation of the Word. What is said simply seems right; it seems compelling; one finds oneself saying, 'Yes, that's right, that's the truth of the matter; this is indeed the word of the Lord.' I read 'God was in Christ, reconciling the world to himself,' I come to think: 'Right; that's true; God really was in Christ, reconciling the world to himself!' And I may also think something a bit different, something *about* that proposition: that it is indeed a divine teaching or revelation, that, in Calvin's words, it is 'from God'. What one hears or reads seems clearly and obviously true, and (at any rate in paradigm cases) seems also to be something the Lord is intending to teach . . . The process can go on in a thousand ways; in each case there is a presentation or proposal of central Christian teaching, and by way of response, the phenomenon of being convinced, coming to see, forming a conviction. There is the reading or hearing, and then there is the belief or conviction that what one reads or hears is true and a teaching of the Lord.[61]

Plantinga's efforts to construct Christian belief in non-inferential terms are admirable and even plausible. I can certainly understand his reasons for opting for such an approach. The spectre of irrationality is one worth avoiding. Nevertheless, I wasn't initially persuaded by his approach. I needed time to process what I was reading. I had time, fortunately. I had only just embarked on what would turn out to be a seven-year, part-time effort to complete doctoral studies.

Back in Australia and Thinking Through the Implications

We spent five months in South Bend, Indiana, before needing to make plans to fly back to Australia. We received news that Judy's mum had been diagnosed with pancreatic cancer. Judy and Kieran flew back early, with the rest of us following not far behind. Judy's mum's illness and death in early 1997 was hard on all of us, particularly hard for Judy. Along with friends from St James, Croydon, who came up the coast for her funeral, were Peter and Christine Jensen. We were very touched and are ever grateful for this

---

[61] *Warranted Christian Belief*, 250, 251.

expression of love and concern. Judy had been very close to her mum. She is like her in many ways. Peg was a hard working, big hearted, and hospitable person. She was a strong woman, very much the matriarch of the family. She was amazing in her ability not to interfere in Judy's and my flawed efforts to bring up our boys, while loving and putting herself out for them, as had Judy's father. Ted had passed away five years earlier.

Judy's relationship with God was numbed for about a year after her mum's death. She was grieving. She experienced something of a crisis of faith as she found herself wondering whether she would ever see her mum again, whether there really was a life after death, or a God to guarantee this. I also was unsettled by a growing sense of unease about the faith it was my job and lifelong passion to defend. It seemed at times that the challenges to Christian belief were winning. In class, I would sometimes play devil's advocate and pretend to be an atheist. I am a long way shy of being the world's best actor, but I had no trouble assuming the persona of an atheist. It wasn't hard to be entirely unconvinced by Plantinga's efforts to defend Christian belief, or to say I didn't believe in the *sensus divinitatis*, or to claim that belief in God was nothing more than a comforting projection of our desire for an enduring father figure. I was able to congratulate Plantinga for acknowledging how paltry was Christianity's evidential base. I was pleased (as an atheist) to have the wherewithal to silence budding apologists by reminding them of Plantinga's concession that it would be irrational for me to believe the Christian gospel without there being a work of the Holy Spirit in my life—and I didn't feel any such work. Along with Bertrand Russell on his death bed, I could say, 'Not enough evidence!' How can a person be condemned for doing what reason requires, reason that God himself has gifted them with, if indeed God exists?

It wasn't hard to play the part of an atheist. Perhaps it was too easy. The truth is that I was unsettled by Plantinga's torpedoing of the argumentative case for Christianity. Against Plantinga, I retained the conviction that Christian beliefs, and especially belief in the resurrection of Jesus, required evidence of sufficient strength to warrant reasonable belief. In my Th.D. thesis, I suggested a possible way forward by developing what I called a warranted-trust model of Christian belief formation. It was exploratory and very underdeveloped, but it highlighted the importance of trust and suggested that people were not unjustified in accepting the testimony of the New Testament, not in every detail necessarily, nor uncritically, but as a product of what could reasonably be seen as an authentic encounter with the risen Christ. It was not unreasonable to believe. That was the best I could do.

That the evidence for the resurrection is not conclusive or demanding of belief is widely accepted among apologists for the Christian faith, and especially among those with some background and sophistication in historical studies. Rev. Dr John Dickson, for example, whose doctoral studies were on early Christian history, is at pains in his books to say that the resurrection, even if factual, isn't able to be demonstrated by means of historical enquiry.[62] He quotes, with approval, Professor Graham Stanton of Cambridge University:

> The early Christian claim was that God raised the crucified, dead, and buried Jesus 'on the third day' to a new form of existence, the precise nature of which Paul and the four evangelists describe in rather different ways. That claim can be neither confirmed nor denied with the use of historical lines of enquiry. Whether it may be accepted as plausible depends both on careful assessment of the resurrection traditions and on convictions about God.[63]

This acknowledgement that the evidence for the resurrection does not compel belief or render unbelief irrational (by implication) is a long way shy of claims by John Warwick Montgomery that 'the facts of God's existence and of His incarnate revelation in Jesus Christ . . . stand over against man, judging him by their sheer veracity and compelling force.'[64] It does seem that people can withhold belief in the gospel, including its

---

[62] See, for example, John Dickson, *The Spectator's Guide to Jesus; An Introduction to the Man from Nazareth*, (Sydney: Blue Bottle Books, 2005), 121-123. Also helpful is James D. G. Dunn's magisterial *Jesus Remembered*, (Grand Rapids: William B Eerdmans, 2003). His discussion of the resurrection traditions is particularly illuminating, both because it acknowledges the limitations imposed by historical method, and also because of its fair treatment of the empty tomb and appearance stories, 765-879.

[63] Graham Stanton, *The Gospels and Jesus*, (Oxford: Oxford University Press, 2003), 291, quoted in *Spectators Guide*, 123.

[64] *Faith Founded on Fact*, 150.

claims about the resurrection, without being unreasonable in doing so, and especially if they are of a mind to ask, 'Is there sufficiently strong evidence for these beliefs?'

Further Examples of Inadequate Evidence

Lack of compelling evidence is an even bigger problem for other biblically derived beliefs, including belief in the Exodus from Egypt. The book of Exodus and subsequent books of the Pentateuch describe the enslavement of Abraham's offspring in Egypt and their subsequent miraculous rescue and return to their God-given land of promise. Much is made of this gifting by God in contemporary Israeli politics. However, there is no evidence that this event ever occurred, apart from the testimony of the Scriptures. A problem for archaeologists and ancient historians is that an event of this magnitude could reasonably be expected to have left historical traces. Exodus 12: 37 describes a fleeing population of 600,000 men on foot. Numbers 1: 46 is more precise in its count of 603,550 warriors 'from twenty years old and upward, every one able to go to war in Israel'. That is a very large army. Add women, children, and others and the number grows to around two to three million fleeing slaves, an extraordinary and amazing event, which is how the biblical writers describe it. Taken literally, the logistical implications are enormous.

I once received an email designed to encourage faith among Christians. Its argument was that if God could bring about an Exodus, he could certainly take care of the much smaller challenges we are likely to face. The scale of God's actions during the Exodus was spelled out in the following terms:

> Moses and the people were in the desert, but what was he going to do with them? They had to be fed, and feeding 2 or 3 million people requires a lot of food. According to the Quartermaster General in the Army, it is reported that Moses would have to have had 1,500 tons of food each day. Do you know that to bring that much food each day, two freight trains, each at least a mile long, would be required! Besides, you must remember, they were out in the desert, so they would have to have firewood to use in cooking the food. This would take 4,000 tons of wood and a few more freight trains each a mile long, just for one day. And just think, they were forty years in transit. And Oh yes!

They would have to have water. If they only had enough to drink and wash a few dishes, it would take 11,000,000 gallons each day and a freight train with tank cars, 1,800 miles long, just to bring the water! And then another thing! They had to get across the Red Sea at night. Now, if they went on a narrow path, double file, the line would be 800 miles long and would require thirty-five days and nights to get through. So there had to be a space in the Red Sea, three miles wide so they could walk 5,000 abreast to get over in one night. But then there is another problem . . . each time they camped at the end of the day, a camp ground two-thirds the size of the State of Rhode Island was required, or a total of 750 square miles long . . . think of it! This much space for camping. Do you figure Moses figured all this out before he left Egypt? I think not! You see, Moses believed in God. God took care of these things for him.

If that many people did leave Egypt, it would for sure have precipitated a demographic and economic catastrophe. One would also expect to find historical and archaeological evidence of so large a migration. Even if the number was many times less, say 60,000 or even 20,000, the impact of their forty years of wandering in the Sinai desert is likely to have left traces.[65] The fact is, it hasn't, not that we have yet discovered, and not for want of trying.

---

[65] Once it is conceded that the numbers involved in the exodus from Egypt may have been much less than the numbers used in the Biblical narratives, it does become more likely that an exodus of some sort may have happened, but we just don't have the evidence for it yet. Counting in favour of the conclusion that the numbers of Israelites leaving Egypt couldn't have been as many as described in Exodus and Numbers is the fact that Egypt's army at the time is thought to have been around 20,000. 600,000 Israeli warriors would have stood a good chance of overwhelming 20,000 Egyptians. However, if the numbers are greatly inflated, other legitimate questions are raised about the historicity of other aspects of the Exodus story. It is worth noting that many, even most conservative Biblical scholars are willing to concede that the numbers quoted in the Biblical texts cannot be accurate. This also raises questions about how to understand the presence of fictional elements within the text of the Bible. For a useful discussion, see V. Philips Long, *The Art of*

Lack of evidence doesn't, in itself, imply that the Exodus stories are factually erroneous. However, biblical archaeologists and historians working in the area appear to be less and less inclined to take the stories as factual. The accumulating evidence appears to be moving away from the conservative beliefs I had grown up with. In beginning to think and read about these issues, I had a book recommended to me by a colleague on Moore College faculty, a book by William G. Dever who is widely regarded as the doyen of biblical archaeology. He was recommended because of his tendency to resist the scholarship of more radical archaeologists such as Israel Finkelstein, known as 'revisionists'. Dever argues that the Exodus stories are broadly reflective of historical conditions existing at the time the Exodus was said to have happened. However, even he concludes:

> If we look at biblical texts describing the origins of Israel, we see at once that the traditional accounts contained in Genesis through Joshua simply cannot be reconciled with the picture derived from archaeological investigation. The whole 'Exodus—Conquest' cycle of stories must now be set aside as largely mythical, but in the proper sense of the term 'myth'; perhaps historical fiction, but tales told primarily to validate religious beliefs. In my view these stories are still 'true' in that they convey forcefully later Israel's self-awareness as a 'liberated' people.[66]

Dever points out that even conservative archaeologists from conservative religious backgrounds have had to submit to overwhelming evidence that Israelite occupation of Palestine was gradual and from within rather than by conquest or invasion.[67] At the very least, evidence of invasion is puzzlingly missing.[68]

Biblical History (Grand Rapids: Zondervan, 1994). Long notes the distinction between 'historical fiction' and 'fictionalized history.' He employs the second of these to describe Biblical history.

[66] William G. Dever, *What Did the Biblical Writers Known and When Did they Know it?* (Grand Rapids: Eerdmans, 2001), 121.
[67] *What did the Biblical Writers Know?*, 119.
[68] Lack of evidence for the Biblical portrayal of early Israelite history is readily admitted by the best of conservative scholarship. Iain Provan, V. Philips Long, and Tremper Longman III are three such scholars. In their co-authored

Evidence Moving in the Other Direction

Lack of supporting evidence is even more of a problem for those who continue to take the early chapters of Genesis literally. In this case, the evidence is not simply missing, it has moved entirely in the opposite direction. There is less and less reason to believe that the earth is no more than six or, at a stretch, twelve thousand years old. To hold out for a young earth in the face of mounting and overwhelming evidence is irrational and also counterproductive for those wanting to convert twenty-first century cultures to Christian faith. However, there are problems for Christian faith in abandoning a literalistic reading of these early chapters.[69]

Creation Scientists have a point when they insist that Christians are in danger of throwing out the baby (of the gospel) with the bath water (of these early creation accounts) if Genesis 1-11 is not taken literally, or, at least, as broadly factual. It was interesting that during my time at Moore a significant shift took place. As mentioned in chapter 4, Broughton Knox appeared happy enough to take the seemingly straightforward propositions of Genesis literally.[70] Peter Jensen, Broughton's successor, was more public in his non-literal or non-literalistic approach, and in his acceptance of mounting scientific evidence suggesting an old earth. He thereby quickly attracted the ire of creationists who now accuse Moore College of being liberal, with some warrant.

A Biblical History of Israel (Louisville: Westminster, 2003), they resist the efforts of those who argue that the Biblical narrative is of no or little historical value. However, even they concede that the 'Biblical narratives concerning the eras of Moses and Joshua are just as problematic with regard to external verification as those concerning the patriarchal era,' 26. In the associated footnote, they frankly admit that 'there is . . . no independent attestation of the Exodus,' 307, footnote 47.

[69] Some of these I will explore more fully in chapter 6.

[70] In researching for this book, I have not been able to determine Dr Knox's exact or final understanding of how to take the narrative of Genesis 1-11. Some who know him well believe he was not a literalist. One person remembers him saying that whether you take the early chapters of Genesis literally or not, you can still arrive at the same theology.

Peter Jensen was right to allow scientific evidence to modify his understanding of the early chapters of Genesis. However, there are some possibly uncomfortable implications of accepting not only an older earth, but the emerging story of the origins and spread of human civilizations. A number of scientific disciplines are cooperating to give us an increasingly detailed understanding of the development and spread of human life on this planet. These include geology, archaeology, biology, anthropology, and DNA studies. It seems that human life first emerged in Africa, contra Genesis that has it begin in Mesopotamia. Exactly when is still being debated, but evidence suggests that *Homo sapiens* came into existence as a species about 195,000 years ago, with examples of early tool-making going back 165,000 years, with the beginnings of language happening as far back as 100,000 years. Burial sites dated between 100,000 and 70,000 years ago suggest the emergence of religious consciousness, including belief in an afterlife. Seventy thousand years ago *Homo sapiens* first left Africa on journeys that would take them to Australia (between 60,000 and 50,000 years ago) and to the Americas (11,000 years ago). Along the way, they would settle in the Middle East, in Europe and Asia. Between 8,000 and 3,000 BC, an agricultural revolution occurred which would transform human culture, inform the development of religion, and allow for the development of cities and nation states, including Israel.

This broad story is still being written and refined. It is still in scientific draft form, but it does sit uncomfortably with even a broadly factual understanding of Genesis 1-11. For example, how should we understand Adam and Eve? What do we make of the threat of death following disobedience? Do we need to relocate Eden into Africa? If so, does that mean we are free to correct the biblical narrative? How do we understand 'the fall' of human kind? Did this happen at a point in time or is it better to understand the narrative as describing human experience at all times? These are questions of genre that require careful thought. My own conviction is that the only way to make sense of these narratives is to treat them as mythical, as theological myth, if you like, stories that are told to illustrate theological convictions. They should not be taken literally.

Rethinking Redemption

One of the advantages of taking these stories as myth is that they allow a more agnostic and open attitude to scientific studies. One can let the evidence speak for itself. One can even become involved in suggesting hypotheses to best explain the emerging evidence. But there are problems, and one in particular began to eat away at my thinking during my years at Moore. Becoming aware of how old and widely spread human civilization is raised questions about the theology of salvation I had inherited, a theology constructed on the traditional schema of creation, fall, punishment, redemption, and new creation. One version of it, an evangelistic tract entitled *Two Ways to Live*,[71] describes God as the loving ruler of the world that he has made.[72] It points out that God has given human beings responsibility to care for the world, 'but always under his own authority, honouring him and obeying his directions'. It goes on

> The sad truth is that, from the very beginning, men and women everywhere have rejected God by doing things their own way. We all do this. We don't like someone telling us what to do or how to live—least of all God—and so we rebel against him in lots of different ways. We ignore him and just get on with our own lives; or we disobey his instructions for living in his world; or we shake our puny fists in his face and tell him to get lost.[73]

A problem with this description is that it is not at all obvious how this description is true for most of human history. If the story of human origins and development emerging from scientific studies is anywhere near accurate, even with respect to how long humans have been around, then it is hard to argue that humans haven't been attempting to understand and worship deity from our earliest days. Moreover, there don't appear to have been any instructions given, other than what has been intuited from human experience, giving rise to the wide variety of religious expressions that have existed throughout history. Monotheism, the idea that there is only one God, seems to have been a relative latecomer on the religious scene. The Ten Commandments were delivered, biblically speaking, just a little over 3,000 years ago, which is about 47,000 to 57,000 years after

---

[71] Developed in the late 1980s by Phillip Jensen, currently published under the joint authorship of Tony Payne and Phillip Jensen, *Two Ways to Live: the choice we all face*, (Sydney: Matthias Media, 2003).
[72] *Two Ways to Live* (Pocket Edition), 2.
[73] *Two Ways to Live* (Pocket Edition), 5.

Indigenous Australians arrived on this continent. And so this description (above) raises more questions than it addresses.

There are similar problems with the story of God's rescue plan for humankind. The *Two Ways to Live* tract articulates the good news that despite humankind's hell-deserving rebellion against God, God sent his Son, Jesus, to suffer the punishment we deserve, to substitute himself for us so that we might be forgiven and welcomed into heaven at the end of our lives. That is certainly good news for those who accept it, but once again, what of those who haven't heard of it, or can't appropriate it? What of the multiple generations that existed before Christ or the vast majority of humankind who have lived after Jesus without any knowledge of this salvation? That is a question that I and many Christians have wrestled with for years. It is a question which was asked of Christians within years of the life, death, and resurrection of Jesus. It is an obvious question.

Celsus, the second-century opponent of Christianity, asked whether God could really be said to care about the human race when it had (apparently) taken him so long to express that care salvifically.

> 'Is it only now after such a long age that God has remembered to judge the life of men? Did he not care before?' (c. *Cels.* 4.7)

Two centuries later, Julian the Apostate had asked why God had sent prophets to the Jews,

> 'but to us no prophet, no oil of anointing, no teacher, no herald to announce his love for man which should one day, though late, reach unto us also? . . . Is he the God of all of us alike, and the creator of all, why did he neglect us?' (106d).

Porphyry (c. 232-c. 304), aware of Christian attempts to meet this objection by appealing to the antiquity of the Jewish tradition, wrote:

> 'let them not say that the human race was saved by the ancient Jewish law, since the Jewish law appeared and flourished in a small

part of Syria, a long time after [the ancient cults in Italy], and only later made its way into the Italian lands, after the reign of Gaius Caesar, or probably during his reign. What, then, became of the souls of Romans or Latins who were deprived of the grace of Christ which had not yet come until the time of the Caesars?' [Augustine, *Ep*, 102.8][74]

He could have asked, had he known, 'And what about Africa's first human inhabitants, or Australia's or North or South America's or China's or those from South-East Asia or the Pacific Islands? What way of salvation was open for them?'

While teaching apologetics at college, I would every year introduce students to presuppositionalism according to which people were encouraged to take on Christian or biblical assumptions as the key to making sense of life. Rather than argue to the truth of Christianity by mounting arguments and assembling evidence, people were encouraged to simply accept the Bible's teaching. They would then discover that their knowledge and experience was unified and justified. One problem with this position is that it runs the risk of creating an uncritical attitude to those parts of the Scripture, including Genesis 1-11, that can reasonably be interpreted in a number of different ways, which begs the question of which interpretation is likely to make best sense of our human experience. Another problem, not often recognized or acknowledged, is that some of these interpretations create more problems than they solve. This is certainly the case when it comes to the understanding of salvation I grew up with, certain versions of which create massive problems for faith.

---

[74] Quoted in Robert L. Wilken, *The Christians as the Romans Saw Them*, (New Haven: Yale University Press, 1984), 162. Note that the problem articulated in these quotations can be otherwise described as the scandal of particularity. A universal religion surely requires universal access. That God should reveal himself at a particular time and place disenfranchises all those who do not have access to such disclosure.

In chapter 1, I included the Doctrinal Statement of PBI, which spells out quite clearly what is a fairly standard fundamentalist and/or evangelical understanding of salvation. Three headings in particular spell out the basics of the doctrine:

> **Humanity and Sin**
>
> We believe humanity was created in the image of God. In Adam all humankind fell and incurred eternal separation from God. As a consequence, all humans are declared by God to be inherently depraved and in need of salvation.
>
> **Salvation**
>
> We believe the grace of God provides salvation from sin for all humanity only through personal repentance and faith in Jesus Christ and His atoning work.
>
> **Future State of the Dead**
>
> We believe in the bodily resurrection of both the saved and the lost, those who are saved unto the resurrection of eternal life and those who are lost unto the resurrection of eternal conscious punishment.

The teaching here is quite clear that humankind as a whole is sinful, lost, and depraved and that the only escape from eternal conscious punishment is personal repentance and faith in Jesus. Only Christians will be saved. That is the straightforward implication of these statements, although, even on a fundamentalist understanding, the borders of heaven are expanded enough to include at least some Jews and others who lived before Jesus, including Abraham. Everyone else will not be in heaven. They will be sent to hell. The problem with this position is that it appears to undercut belief in the expansive love of God for all people.

A Problem of Apparently Excessive Suffering

To sharpen the problem a little, there appears to be some obvious tension between the following two propositions:

(1) God is all-loving, all-powerful, and all-knowing, and

(2) Only those who have been the recipients of the biblical gospel[75] and have responded to it in faith and obedience will be saved. Every other person will suffer the eternal torment of hell.

Trying to reconcile these two propositions can be seen as a sharpened or targeted version of the problem of evil and suffering. Problems of evil and suffering normally draw attention to evil and suffering in this life and throughout human history, but introducing hell creates new challenges. The idea that there is a hell to pay for misdeeds committed in this life is not, in itself, a problem for Christian theism. In fact, the idea that justice will ultimately be done is attractive. It gives voice to a universal yearning of the human spirit. It may have been the impetus for Judaism appropriating the idea of hell.[76] We like to think that there will be justice done—if not in this life, then in the life to come. However, there are real problems with the above account of who is saved and who is not, and what that means.

For one, the idea of eternal conscious torment seems out of all proportion. This is punishment beyond anything we might devise. I now work with Corrective Services, NSW, and people I work with are regularly given sentences, sometimes for long periods of imprisonment, occasionally for life. But the idea of being punished forever is hard to comprehend or justify. In many of the cases I supervise, I agree with sentences that are handed down, especially where real damage has been done to the lives of others and where the person responsible isn't taking responsibility for his or her actions. Having to submit to appropriately apportioned punishment seems right and proper, but eternal conscious torment seems excessive, to say the least.

The *Two Ways to Live* tract describes hell as eternal separation from God. It goes on to describe hell as the absence of anything good, arguing that

---

[75] It is often pointed out, with some Biblical warrant (for example, Hebrews 10: 39-11: 40), that there was an Old Testament version of the gospel. Although not explicitly a gospel about Jesus, it is, nevertheless, ultimately about him.

[76] Historically, the idea of hell predates Judaism, which had no such notion for most of its pre-Christian history. Chances are it was appropriated from Zoroastrianism.

since God is the source of life and all good things, then being cut off from God involves the everlasting removal of all these good things. In hell, it states, 'we face the dreadful prospect of an eternity of separation from him, without life or love or relationship.'[77]

This is a horrific image of never-ending lonely torment, infinitely worse (literally) than any human torturer could devise. The worst human torture ends mercifully in death, but hell is a living death, with no relief. One can understand some Christian theologians proposing annihilation as an alternative, or as an appropriate climax to post-death punishment. It is hard to imagine God being justified in inflicting this much pain on any of his creatures—even the worst of them.

The trouble is that those who advocate eternal conscious torment as the best interpretation of the relevant biblical texts (with some warrant) mostly also believe that the vast majority of human beings throughout history will be suffering this form of punishment. It isn't just the Hitlers and Stalins of this world who will suffer in this way. Everyone will, except those who have come to believe and accept the biblical gospel. Every Indigenous population of the world will be there, with the exception of a small proportion of their number who were around when the Christian gospel arrived, and who accepted it. Every adherent of every religion other than Christianity will be there. And so the numbers will be huge, billions upon billions of people, with the numbers increasing every day, but if the *Two Ways to Live* account is correct, not one of these people will be in contact with any other—each will be alone and lonely in never-ending torment.

Now it may be that this is simply the way it is. We mightn't like it, but God has decreed it, and God knows best. That may be the case, but from almost every human point of view, it doesn't seem credible. Presentations of the gospel that I have heard over the years emphasize the amazing love of God in forgiving sin, even more amazing for its having impelled God to absorb the equivalent of hell for those who believe the gospel. That does seem amazing, and does evoke wonder and gratitude for many. However,

---

[77] *Two Ways to Live* (Pocket Edition), 13.

I wonder how upfront evangelists and apologists are about how few the beneficiaries of this love are. Hell for ever for most of God's human creatures doesn't immediately strike one as the action of a loving God, of a God whose love we are often told is deeper and greater than any human love. It also doesn't strike one as the action of a God who would have the wherewithal to win over any and every one of those creatures.

Some people point to human freedom as a possible reason that God cannot win over every creature. If that is the case, one might justifiably ask whether freedom is worth the cost of the suffering it occasions, especially if eternal conscious torment is its widespread result. If, as some argue, human freedom is compatible with a divine sovereignty which is able to effect any logically possible outcome, then one could reasonably ask why God hasn't actualized a world in which every human creature freely and lovingly chooses to love God and neighbour. This would be something God could do.

A further complication for those who believe in eternal conscious torment as the destiny for most of the world's population is that this belief is likely to have the effect of making the gospel appear incredible. Being told about God's love is attractive. Being told that this love entails or results in eternal conscious torment for most of the world's peoples creates a reason not to believe in a God so conceived. Plantinga argues that when people hear the Christian gospel, they simply believe it to be true, in a basic or non-inferential way. My hunch is that many would not find it so immediately credible if spelt out in terms of this doctrine of hell (as in the *Two Ways to Live* tract). I would think that they would have good reasons not to accept it.

A friend recently gave me a copy of a book written by John Wenham. John Wenham wrote the New Testament Greek text book that I used to my profit at theological college. Towards the end of his life, he wrote an autobiography entitled *Facing Hell: The Story of a Nobody*. It tells the story of Wenham's quite early rejection of the doctrine of hell as eternal conscious torment. He includes in his book a long passage from one of C. S. Lewis's early books, *The Pilgrim's Regress*. This book tells the story of C. S. Lewis's own spiritual pilgrimage written in the form of allegory.

Chapter one starts in Puritania, where he dreams of a boy frustrated by the prohibitions of his elders who is one day taken to see a Steward appointed by the Landlord to oversee obedience to the Landlord's rules:

> When John came into the room, there was an old man with a red, round face, who was very kind and full of jokes, so that John quite got over his fears, and they had a good talk about fishing tackle and bicycles. But just when the talk was at its best, the Steward got up and cleared his throat. He then took down a mask from the wall with a long white beard attached to it and suddenly clapped it on his face, so that his appearance was awful. And he said, 'Now I am going to talk to you about the Landlord. The Landlord owns all the country, and it is very, very kind of him to allow us to live on it at all—very, very kind.' He went on repeating 'very kind' in a queer sing-song voice so long that John would have laughed, but that now he was beginning to become frightened again. The Steward then took down from a peg a big card with small print all over it, and said, 'Here is a list of all the things the Landlord says you must not do. You'd better look at it.' So John took the card: but half the rules seemed to forbid things he had never heard of, and the other half forbade things he was doing every day and could not imagine not doing: and the number of rules was so enormous that he felt he could never remember them all. 'I hope,' said the Steward, 'that you have not already broken any of the rules?' John's heart began to thump, and his eyes bulged more and more, and he was at his wit's end when the Steward took off the mask and looked at John with his real face and said, 'Better tell a lie, old chap, better tell a lie. Easiest for all concerned,' and popped the mask on his face all in a flash. John gulped and said quickly, 'Oh, no, sir.' 'That is just as well,' said the Steward through the mask. 'Because, you know, if you did break any of them and the Landlord got to know of it, do you know what he'd do to you?' 'No, sir,' said John, and the Steward's eyes seemed to be twinkling dreadfully through the holes of the mask. 'He'd take you and shut you up for ever and ever in a black hole full of snakes and scorpions as large as lobsters—for ever and ever. And besides that, he is such a kind, good man, so very, very kind that you would never want to displease him.' No sir,' said John. 'But, please, sir . . .' 'Well,'

said the Steward. 'Please, sir, supposing I did break one, one little one, just by accident, you know. Could nothing stop the snakes and lobsters?' 'Ah! . . .' said the Steward; and then he sat down and talked for a long time, but John could not understand a single syllable. However, it all ended with a pointing out that the Landlord was quite extraordinarily kind and good to his tenants, and would certainly torture most of them to death the moment he had the slightest pretext. 'And you can't blame him,' said the Steward. 'For after all it is his land, and it is so very good of him to let us live here at all—people like us you know.' Then the Steward took off the mask and had a nice sensible chat with John again, and gave him a cake and brought him out to his father and his mother. But just as they were going he bent down and whispered in John's ear, 'I shouldn't bother about it all too much if I were you.' And at the same time he slipped the card of rules into John's hand and told him he could keep it for his own use.[78]

It is a remarkable passage, no doubt reflecting early experiences of being exposed to hell-fire and brimstone preaching, a commonplace in the Northern Ireland of C. S. Lewis's youth. A few things stand out from this passage. One is the obvious moral tension that exists between words about the great kindness of the Landlord and the completely unrealistic expectations and nightmarish consequences of disobedience. It is hard to imagine a young boy, or anyone, coming to love the Landlord of this story. What also stands out from the passage is the contrasting humanity of the Steward who when he takes off the mask of his required duty clearly doesn't believe what he is saying or trying to justify.

I have a sneaking suspicion that most Christians today no longer believe in the theology of hell that I and many of them grew up with. Many, I suspect, are like the Steward in this story in being profoundly conflicted as they attempt to retain apparently incompatible beliefs. For those who are not yet Christian, it represents a formidable barrier to belief, especially when added to other reasons not to believe that have been considered in this chapter.

---

[78] Included in John Wenham, *Facing Hell: The Story of a Nobody* (Carlisle: Paternoster Press, 1998), 252-54.

What has become clear to me is that the Christianity of my growing-up and early adult years faces a major and serious credibility problem. Its doctrine of hell runs counter to the moral intuitions of most people. Many other of its stories and doctrines either have no evidence to support them, or too little evidence, or are contradicted by evidence mounting in the opposite direction. The discovery of this created cracks in the formerly solid edifice of my faith, cracks that became fissures, and then chasms that I could no longer fill or paper over.

As I now look back on my time at Moore College, and immediately after, it is a wonder I did not give up on Christian faith altogether. I didn't. Nor was I seriously tempted to. Maybe it was my native optimism. Maybe it was because of the wonderfully warm nurturing I had received as I grew up into Christian faith. Maybe it was because there still were good reasons to believe in God, including, supremely for me, the man Jesus, who remained worthy of a following. Whatever the exact reason, I kept on believing, or at least hoping that there might be some way through the increasingly tangled thicket of challenges facing my Christian faith. I did know that I would need to find a different way forward, perhaps a very different way. I was aware that the fundamentalism of my early days was not a bridge I could any longer put weight on. It had too many weaknesses. The evangelicalism that I had more lately come to embrace had many of the same weaknesses. I had at first believed that Sydney evangelicalism had the intellectual rigor to keep me in the faith, and it certainly did that. But now even Sydney evangelicalism was beginning to creak under the weight I was attempting to apply to it.

Ten years was a long time to be teaching at Moore College. Peter Jensen had suggested to me towards the end of his tenure as principal that I should move on. Perhaps he had some inkling of the problems I was increasingly having with evangelical Anglicanism. I am not sure. Regardless of the reason, I wanted to leave, wanted to get away from the academic ivory tower of college. I had come to miss the grass-roots ministry I had so enjoyed in Wee Waa. It was time to go.

I also felt the need to rediscover or reconfigure my faith, to see whether within praxis and away from theory I could find the core or kernel of a legitimate faith. I thought seriously about having a break from ministry altogether. I paid a visit to Bill Lawton. Ten years earlier, when I was about to begin lecturing at Moore College, I had sought Bill out to get his take on what lecturing at Moore entailed, and how I could do it justice. It was time to visit him again, to learn from his own transition out of college. I floated the idea of taking a year or two off to think through my faith in the context of some secular occupation. I suggested working in a pub. Bill very quickly threw cold water on that suggestion and recommended that I go and have a chat with John McIntyre at the Parish of South Sydney in inner-city Sydney. John was known for his courageous support of women's ordination and Indigenous rights. This was appealing, as was the chance to again work with and alongside Aboriginal people as I had done in Wee Waa. It was appealing to work with someone who as an integral part of his ministry hung out in a local pub.

Meeting John was the clincher. I knew within minutes of sitting down to talk that I'd be able to work with him. I sensed that we would become friends, which we have done, as my family has with his. South Sydney Parish had three centres: St Saviours, Redfern (the main church), Crossroads Aboriginal Fellowship (also in Redfern), and St James, Beaconsfield. There were, at that stage, only four or five people attending St James. Not too much earlier, the congregation had been larger and more vibrant. The church building had been completely renovated in the wake of a very big and destructive hail storm. When John took Judy and me through its doors, we were instantly impressed and enthused by what would be the setting of a new stage in our lives and faith journeys.

I still had faith, a faith that was being buffeted and redefined that's for sure, but faith nevertheless. I believed, or sensed, that God was big enough and patient enough to accommodate my struggles and to guide me towards a more sustainable faith.

Chapter 6

Hermeneutical Humps

Leaving But Har Gra was challenging. Judy and I had spent thirteen years there all up. Our boys had spent most of their lives there. As a family, we had no experience of inner-city living. Not all of the boys came with us. Damien had already moved out. Daniel took the opportunity of our move to launch himself into independent living.

Moving to Rosebery[79] and then to Beaconsfield was not entirely unlike the move to Wee Waa, however. Even though these were inner-city suburbs, they weren't entirely un-country-like. Rosebery was a long-settled, predominantly Greek-speaking community. Beaconsfield is one of Sydney's tiniest suburbs, not unlike a country village. It still has a lingering small-town feel. One of the best things we did when we got there was to tap into this more cohesive past and to form a community action group through which we later organized two highly successful community fairs.

Almost from day one, we began to letterbox drop. I started door-knocking to let people know of our little church and of its connection with the community. It was great to be back at the grass roots, good to again be pastor of a small, and, we hoped, growing church. People were flooding back to the inner city from the suburbs as it became trendier and cheaper,

---

[79] Rosebery adjoins Beaconsfield, and, along with Zetland and Alexandria, make up the southern end of South Sydney Parish.

transport-wise, to live so close to the centre of town. We were living in a growth area,[80] touted to become a city centre itself.

But this wasn't Wee Waa. There wasn't anything like the same excitement. We weren't all together as a family. The boys were beginning to go their own ways spiritually. So had most of the people I encountered as I walked and talked and door-knocked around these suburbs. Most were three, four, or more steps away from any association with church. And they were still walking. The best I could do was to get some to pause, maybe for a moment or two, before resuming their walk. The only people attracted to church were people already used to church, people who had moved into the area and were looking for a church. Almost no one else was interested in beginning a practice that in Australia was fast becoming a dying art.

One challenge we faced was that we were small. Small churches tend to stay small. Large churches snowball, gobbling up nearby smaller churches, as was the case with Hillsong City Church, a short suburb away. Hillsong is a church with many strengths, including the ability to change and remain contemporary. But our little church, part-funded by the local Anglican Regional Council, was always going to struggle. In five years at Wee Waa, the weekly congregation grew from 40 to 160. At Beaconsfield, we did much better in percentage terms, growing from 4 to 40, but that was drawing from a population of about 10,000 in comparison to 4,000 within the Wee Waa district.

We did manage to attract some people. We were also blessed to have a succession of highly talented catechists, or student ministers, who, while studying at Moore College, needed the sort of church experience I had so benefitted from when I was a student.[81] We simply could not have achieved what we did without their help. But as important, and more lasting than any achievements, were the close friendships formed and nurtured within the congregation in those years. The attractively refurbished church at

---

[80] The Green Square Development Area.
[81] We were much blessed to have Paul and Angela Beeston, Neil and Emily Durrant, Charles and Jenny Hebblewhite, Martin and Wayowa Telfer, and Angela Cook join us for varying lengths of time.

Beaconsfield had a slow combustion heater to warm us in winter. The fellowship we enjoyed was warm all through the year.

These were special years. But they weren't easy. I came to Beaconsfield with the mentality of a church planter. I wanted to see the church grow, and felt I had the talents, energy, and necessary help to achieve this. But circumstances were different. I was different. The world we were ministering to had changed. I had come to Beaconsfield to grow a church, but I had also come to reconfigure a faith which had become unsustainable. It wasn't just the church that was a work in progress. I was. What had become clear to me was that I needed a new way to read and understand the Scriptures. I needed a new hermeneutic. The old one wasn't working.

Noah's Flood: a Hermeneutical Test Case

One of the early things I did when I arrived at Beaconsfield was to set up a hermeneutics discussion group. It was exploratory in intent, set up for those especially interested in hermeneutics.[82] Included within the group were Bishop of South Sydney, Rob Forsyth, a number of the faculty of Moore College, and a number of other clergy and lay friends. The group kicked off with a paper I had written on Noah's flood. For all of my life that story had fascinated and disturbed me, but I had also come to see it as having significant hermeneutical implications, so significant that the story became a watershed (appropriately) in my thinking. As with the Exodus of Israel from Egypt, Noah's flood is the sort of event that could reasonably be expected to leave ample evidence of its occurrence, if indeed it was factual. It should have been able to pass the evidential test.

---

[82] Hermeneutics is a vast and complicated field of study, more so in recent years under the influence of a succession of modern and postmodern philosophers including Schleiermacher, Dilthey, Heidegger, Gadamer, Derrida, and Ricoeur. Hermeneutics as the study of interpretation, or, more broadly, of human understanding, has a long history, stretching back to the beginnings of Greek philosophy. In the Middle Ages and into the Renaissance, hermeneutics became a crucial branch of Biblical studies. My own interest in hermeneutics, and the interest of those attending the hermeneutics discussion group, was largely restricted to an interest in how best to interpret the Bible. Broader concerns were, nevertheless, relevant.

It is worth pausing to consider what is said about this flood in the narrative of Genesis. At the beginning of Genesis 6, God decides to wipe out every living creature (6: 6-8), including the entire human race, 'for all the people on earth had corrupted their ways,' (6: 12). Noah and his family alone are spared by being given instructions to build an ark into which they were to bring seven of every kind of clean animal, two of every unclean animal, and seven of every kind of bird (7: 2-3). In Noah's six hundredth year, the springs of the great deep burst forth, the floodgates of the heavens are opened, and a forty-day and forty-night deluge is unleashed. With no let up, the floodwaters rise and rise until 'all the high mountains under the entire heavens' are covered to a depth of at least seven metres, (7: 12, 20). 'Every living thing on the face of the earth' is thereby wiped out (7: 23), except for Noah and those with him on the ark.

This was no localized flood as some commentators have tried to assert. To even suggest that it was localized entirely misses the point of the narrative, which is that God 'regretted having created human beings on the earth' (6: 6), and would have entirely obliterated all life had it not been for his gracious sparing of Noah, had it not been for his decision to make a fresh start (6: 6-8).

What makes this story so interesting and important is that it is so unambiguous. As a Sunday school child, I got the point—easily, quickly, and frighteningly. Moreover, whenever the story is referred to elsewhere in the Bible, it appears that the writers are taking the story as straightforwardly factual. Luke includes Noah in the genealogy of Jesus,[83] suggesting that Luke believed Noah to be an actual person. The writer of Hebrews includes Noah in his list of heroes of faith, along with other characters mentioned in Genesis 1-11. That he accepted the story as straightforwardly factual is suggested by his description of Noah:

> 'By faith Noah, warned by God about events as yet unseen, respected the warning and built an ark to save his household; by this he condemned the world and became an heir to the righteousness that is in accordance with faith.' (Heb. 11: 7, NRSV)

---

[83] Luke 3: 36

Jesus himself appears to have accepted the story of Noah as factual, as indicated by these words from the Olivet Discourse:

> 'As it was in the days of Noah, so it will be at the coming of the Son of Man. For in the days before the flood, people were eating and drinking, marrying and giving in marriage, up to the day Noah entered the ark; and they knew nothing about what would happen until the flood came and took them all away. That is how it will be at the coming of the Son of Man.' (Matt. 24: 37-38 NRSV; parallel passage Luke 17: 26-27.)

That Jesus accepted or appears to have accepted the Noah story as factual is good reason for his followers to take it that way as well, as is the fact that the Bible as a whole appears to take it that way. From a Christian point of view, it seems a no-brainer that we should accept the Noah story as factual. For most of my Christian life I did accept it that way. The hermeneutic I inherited from Moore College gave me all sorts of good reasons to continue accepting it that way. The principle of *Sola Scriptura* encouraged me to give much greater weight to what I read in the Scriptures than to other sources of knowledge, including the natural sciences. The principle of the analogy of Scripture encouraged me to be guided by what Scripture says about Scripture, to interpret the doubtful bits by the plain bits. With respect to the Noah story, Scripture appears to be uniformly unambiguous. Add in the doctrine of the perspicuity of Scripture and there doesn't appear to be much room to move beyond the plain and obvious meaning of the text.

Moreover, Jewish and Christian interpreters have mostly taken the story as straightforwardly factual. Norman Cohn, in *Noah's Flood: The Genesis Story in Western Thought*, chronicles the history of theological reflection on the flood story from Old Testament times to the present, and notes the near universal acceptance of the Noah story as factual, along with the chronology of Genesis implying a young earth.[84] Not only was the story

---

[84] Norman Cohn, *Noah's Flood: The Genesis Story in Western Thought*, Yale University Press, 1996. See also David A. Young, *The Biblical Flood: A Case Study of the Church's Response to Extrabiblical Evidence*, (Grand Rapids: Eerdmans, 1995).

accepted as factual, it was used apologetically,[85] and made an assumption to guide geological and archaeological research.[86] Many of the first geologists were men of Christian faith. Some were trained clergymen. As they did their geology, they had their Bibles in one hand and their pick or shovel in the other. They were doing exactly what presuppositionalists say we should do. They were assuming the truth of what the Bible quite plainly was saying as their way of making sense of the world.

The trouble is, it didn't. The genealogies of Genesis 1-11, if taken literally, date Noah's flood at around 2,300 BC, or about 1,700 years after the creation of the world.[87] According to this dating, the flood happened not that long ago. One would expect there to be some pretty significant evidence of its occurrence. There is none. While there is evidence of floods, even large floods, happening at around that time, and earlier,[88] there is no evidence whatsoever of a universal or worldwide flood happening then, or at any time in the world's history.

---

[85] The Apologists Justin Martyr and Theophilus of Antioch, for example, argued for the trustworthiness of the Biblical account by contrasting it to Greek myth and invention: H.S. Benjamins, 'Noah, the Ark, and the Flood in Early Christian Theology: the Ship of the Church in the Making', in Florentino Garcia Martinez and Gerard P. Luttikhuizen, *Interpretations of the Flood*, (Leiden: Brill, 1999), 138. See also Young, *The Biblical Flood*, 15-18.

[86] Amply illustrated in both Young and Cohn.

[87] Bishop James Ussher (1581-1656), on the basis of the Biblical genealogies and their correlation with various Middle Eastern and Mediterranean histories, calculated that the earth was created on Sunday 23 October 4004 BC and that Noah's flood happened in 2349 BC. Gordon J. Wenham, in *Word Biblical Commentary, Genesis 1-11*, (Waco: Word Books, 1987), implicitly accepts the reasonableness of this dating in his discussion of the genealogies, 133.

[88] There is evidence of a very large flood that occurred in 5,600 BC, when waters from the melting snow of the last ice age flooded the Black Sea. Memories of this flood may have found their way into the many flood stories of the wider region. So argue William Ryan and Walter Pitman in their fascinating book, *Noah's Flood: the New Scientific Discoveries about the Event that Changed History*, (New York: Simon and Schuster, 1998).

This lack of evidence is a concern. It is certainly a concern if you are inclined to take the story literally. What was interesting to me as I thought about this is that this story would have seemed entirely credible in the ancient world. It would have been accepted as reasonable up until the last few hundred years. Those who first told and then wrote down Noah's story are likely to have believed in a flat earth, above which was a firmament, above which were store houses of water able to be released in the form of rain. They would also have believed that the earth rested on water and was surrounded by water.[89]

This understanding makes highly credible the possibility of a universal flood. That the waters above and below and around the earth could flood the earth to a depth greater than the earth's highest mountains would have seemed very possible. That the earth's entire population of humans and animals could be wiped out by such a flood, that an ark could be built to house the world's animals, and that these animals were within walking distance of the ark would have been plausible. The story is credible given ancient assumptions. However, we no longer share those assumptions. As a result, the Noah story, as it stands, faces formidable challenges to be accepted as credible today, challenges that can be expressed in the form of questions such as the following:[90]

- Where did all the water come from? 4.4 billion cubic kilometres of water would have had to be added to the oceans for Mt. Everest and other large mountain ranges to be covered.
- Where did all the water go after the flood, and in so short a time?

---

[89] See, for example, Nahum Sarna's *Understanding Genesis: The Heritage of Biblical Israel*, (New York: Schocken Books, 1966), 5, for a diagrammatic representation of Biblical cosmology. See also P. Seely, 'The Geographical Meaning of 'Earth' and 'Seas' in Genesis 1: 10', *Westminster Theological Journal*, 59 (1997): 231-55.

[90] For these questions, I am indebted to the expert analysis of Ian Plimer in his tellingly critical book, *Telling Lies for God*, (Sydney: Random House, 1994). I was also expertly assisted by geologist Dr David Cohen, Associate Professor and Head, School of Biological, Earth and Environmental Sciences, University of New South Wales, Sydney. David is also Chair of the Academic Board of Moore Theological College, appointed in June 2011.

- How did the world's plants survive being submerged for between five months and a year?
- How did the world's freshwater fish survive their marine environment being swamped by salt water—or vice versa if the water was fresh?
- How did Noah and his tiny family keep the animals alive—many with highly specialized dietary requirements? How, for example, were the carnivores fed and kept apart?
- How did Noah manage to keep so many species alive? We now know that there are between 50,000 and 75,000 species of birds and animals and about 30 million modern and extinct species of organisms, which raises the problem of how they would all fit on the ark. Even if we assume that there were only two of each animal, rather than 2 plus 7 of some, it has been estimated that each of these animals would have needed to squash into the volume of a milk carton just to fit into the ark.[91]
- How did the animals manage to return to their specialized environments—many across un-crossable seas (e.g. Tasmania's tiger; animals from North and South America)? How did the sloth, who doesn't walk on land, manage to get all the way back to South America?
- Where is the evidence of this massive destruction in places like Australia?

Questions such as these made it impossible, for me at least, to accept the Noah story as factual, even as largely factual. This non-acceptance wasn't in itself a problem. It did, however, run counter to the hermeneutic I had inherited from Moore College, and, further back, from my fundamentalist roots. I remember talking with my mum at around the time I was writing the paper on Noah's flood and telling her that I didn't believe that we should take this story literally. She laughed. Not derisively, not dismissively. It just seemed comical to her that I should think such a thing. She may have thought I had lost my theological marbles. Over the years, her husband (my dad) had come out with some peculiar opinions. She was maybe thinking I was taking after him.

---

[91] *Telling Lies for God*, 110.

But it wasn't just my mum who seemed disturbed or puzzled by my take on Noah's flood. Others in my family had similar reactions. Some friends and former colleagues expressed alarm and probably did think I was losing my theological judgement. I now think a reason for this is that they (like me in earlier days) had no good reason to doubt the story of Noah. They hadn't looked at the scientific evidence. They also had every good reason to accept the story, guided as they were by the principles of *Sola Scriptura*, the analogy, perspicuity, and inerrancy (or infallibility) of Scripture.

One of the things that began to surprise me was how few people, in my circles at least, had thought about these things. The evidence has been in for generations. It was Christian geologists who had come to the conclusion that the story of Noah cannot be taken literally, not even as the hyperbolic account of a localized flood.[92] Scientific evidence about this continues to accumulate. Whole fields of science are involved, including geology, biology, physics, chemistry, cosmology, archaeology, and history. And yet in spite of this, it was amazing for me to find that so few of my Christian friends and former colleagues had even begun the work of bringing this information into relationship with their theology and, as importantly, with their hermeneutic.

One possible additional reason for this lack of engagement with emerging scientific evidence is that Moore College is so strong, admirably strong, in its biblical-theological approach. It does a great job in bringing Scriptural texts into illuminating relationship with each other. The grammatical part of the grammatical-historical approach[93] they do very well, but this has happened to the neglect of historical and scientific considerations. The unfortunate result of this is that students keep coming out of Moore College to preach about Adam and Eve and Noah with no reference whatsoever

---

[92] Note that geologists have found evidence in various Mesopotamian cities such as Ur, Uruk, Nineveh, and Kish of flood deposits dating back to the fourth and early third millenniums BC. However, and significantly, other cities of the region show no such evidence, suggesting that there was no flood large enough to cover Mesopotamia, let alone its surrounding mountains.

[93] The grammatical-historical (or grammatico-historical) method is that approach to interpreting the Biblical text that seeks to recover the author's original intended meaning. This typically involves making full use of linguistic, literary, historical, archaeological, and other data bearing on the author's environment.

to how what they are saying lines up with contemporary understandings, leaving scientifically informed audiences scratching their heads.

Complicating things for Moore College graduates like me is that it is not altogether clear what genre or genres are involved in Genesis 1-11. A long debate has raged over how to classify the genre or genres of Genesis 1-11. Most critical scholars agree that the early stories of Genesis are a mixture of myth and legend (*Sage*),[94] with the Noah story likely to be a mixture of myth and legend. Flood stories were common in the ancient near east, and it is now widely believed that the Noah story is a variation and adaptation of earlier Mesopotamian flood stories such as the *Epic of Gilgamesh* and the *Atrahasis Epic*, both documents dated to around the turn of the second millennium BC.

What scholars have been less clear about is how to classify Genesis 1-11 as a whole. Genesis 1-11 is part of a larger history of the world, and of Israel in particular, that begins in Genesis and concludes at the end of the second book of Kings. It appears to be designed to be a history. But if that is so, what are we to make of the (apparent) inclusion of myth and legend? This question has puzzled scholars. It has puzzled me. The best answer to the question I have come across is that of John Van Seters.

Van Seters argues that the book of Genesis, including Genesis 1-11, is a work of ancient history, an *archaeologia*, designed to serve as a 'prologue' to the national history of Israel. It has a number of significant similarities with other ancient histories, including the works of Herodotus, Dionysius, Livy, and Pausanias, each of whom included myth and legend within their histories, particularly the earlier (prehistorical) parts.

---

[94] John Van Seters defines a myth as 'a traditional story about events in which the god or gods are the primary actors, and the action takes place outside of historical time. In addition, myth contains some structure of meaning that is concerned with the deep problems of life and offers explanations for the way things are'. He defines legends as stories about heroes and eponymic forefathers, which, because they are usually about godlike figures and set in a time that is essentially ahistorical or prehistorical, are more similar to myth than history, *Prologue to History: The Yahwist as Historian in Genesis*, (Westminster: John Knox Press, 1992), 25.

Van Seters notes two possible processes at work in the formation of Genesis 1-11; firstly, the historicization of myth, and, secondly, the mythologization of history. The historicization of myth he describes as 'a process of rationalization of myths or mythical elements by the use of historical categories of arrangement or explanation, such as the imposition of genealogical or chronological succession on myths and legends.'[95] The mythologization of history is 'the imposition of mythical motifs and elements onto historical materials and traditions.'[96] Given the essentially prehistorical nature of Genesis 1-11, one would be inclined to see historicization of myth as predominating.

If Van Seters is right that the content of Genesis 1-11 is largely mythical—myth[97] in the service of national self-understanding—then we misread these chapters if we take them to be factual. We misread and misuse them if we appeal to them to work out the age or shape of the earth, or to guide us in our geological or archaeological digs, or if they send us on a search for the Garden of Eden or Noah's ark, or the remains of the Tower of Babel.[98] To use the texts in those ways is to misunderstand them—it is to misunderstand their genre.

In my struggle to understand Genesis 1-11 and to develop a new hermeneutic, I was helped by a number of other discoveries. One of those was that the problems I had been struggling with are by no means new. It has long been recognised by Jewish and Christian theologians that the

---

[95] *Prologue to History*, 25.

[96] *Prologue to History*, 25.

[97] Or, perhaps, anti-myth, which, in my opinion, amounts to the same thing. It has long been recognized that the writers of Genesis were skilfully engaged in critiquing Ancient Near Eastern myths. They would employ the storylines and the language of such myths, while stripping them of unacceptable elements, all in the service of theological correction. But the upshot of such critique was the production of alternative myths, albeit theologically corrected alternative myths.

[98] On this way of seeing things, the stories of Genesis 1-11, although deliberately set within, or at the beginnings of history, tell us more about historical existence than they do about historical or prehistorical events, such as the fall, a flood, or the confusion of languages.

early chapters of Genesis, and other parts of the Scripture as well, had fallen out of synch with post-biblical and extra-biblical understandings. One way of acknowledging and accounting for this, while retaining a high view of Scripture's authority and divine inspiration, was to suggest that God had accommodated himself to the limited and understandably erroneous understandings of the biblical writers. Augustine was an early Christian theologian who suggested a doctrine of divine accommodation. Calvin concurred. He employed accommodation to account for the then-no-longer accepted belief in a firmament, referred to in Genesis 1.[99]

Another helpful discovery or, better, rediscovery was a similarly long-held belief among theologians that biblical revelation must be understood as progressive. Even those with the most conservative of instincts can't help but notice that Scriptural beliefs change over time. Earlier beliefs are superseded, sometimes contradicted, by later beliefs. For example, resurrection belief emerges quite late in biblical literature contradicting earlier belief in the shadowy near-death, afterlife experience of Sheol.

What isn't often acknowledged by those who happily accept doctrines of accommodation and progressive revelation is that both of these doctrines relativise teachings found in the Bible. What is implied by them is that biblical statements can be and often are inaccurate. An inevitable implication of both doctrines is that the Bible does contain erroneous beliefs and assumptions, with some of these already discarded within the lifespan of its composition.

New Interpretive Possibilities

Realising this was liberating for me. It suggested the need for a more dynamic model of inspiration and revelation. One could argue, and many have,

---

[99] For a discussion of Calvin's use of the accommodation principle, see Kent Sparks, 'The Sun Also Rises: Accommodation in Inscripturation and Interpretation', in V. Bacote, L. C. Miguelez and D. L. Okholm, *Evangelicals and Scripture: Tradition, Authority and Hermeneutics*, (Downers Grove: InterVarsity Press, 2004), 114-118. See also, Stephen D. Benin, *The Footprints of God: Divine Accommodation in Jewish and Christian Thought*, (NY: State University of New York Press, 1993).

that revelation ends with Jesus and the New Testament. However, the New Testament itself doesn't make such a claim. Moreover, the need for divine accommodation can hardly be said to cease in the first century. A host of cosmological, anthropological, geographical, biological, and geological understandings have changed since New Testament times suggesting once again the need for a dynamic model of inspiration and interpretation.

In working my way through to a new hermeneutic, I revisited topics that suddenly had new interpretative possibilities. In earlier days, I had been persuaded by the arguments of those who argued that women should not lead men. Although the horse had well and truly bolted within the secular world, with women routinely and skilfully leading men in business, in politics, in the academe, and in almost every sphere, those whom I had been rubbing shoulders with theologically were still holding out against this tide of social change, arguing that women shouldn't lead men in church or in the home. Here at least were domains that could be closeted off from secular practice, despite the fact that the arguments employed implied that women shouldn't lead men anywhere. Male headship, so the arguments went, was built into the very fabric of our created natures as men and women. Some also argued that male/female role-distinctions mimic eternal relationships within the Trinitarian Godhead.

I became less and less persuaded by these arguments, though I had been an ardent advocate in my country ministry days. The exegesis seemed forced. Possible inferences were piled upon other possible inferences to conclusions that not only flew in the face of sensible contemporary experience, they were hard to sustain in practice. What I have noticed is that advocates of this position tend to go in one of two directions; they either so heavily qualify male headship as to make it practically meaningless, or, to make it meaningful, they go looking for ways to exclude women from leader-like involvement in congregations, with results that would be comical if they weren't so demeaning and disrespectful, not to mention archaic.

I therefore began to toy with the idea that there might be another way to approach this subject. Might it be possible that just as the biblical writers had cosmological assumptions that we no longer accept as true, they were also assuming a patriarchal understanding of male-female relationships no longer appropriate to twenty-first century life. Supporting this was the observation that within the Bible itself there is significant development.

Starting at the beginning of the Bible, it is possible to plot a gradual, but real and sometimes radical dismantling of patriarchal assumptions as the biblical story unfolds. It is likely that patriarchal assumptions do underlie the account of the creation of Adam and Eve and their subsequent fall. Those assumptions were ubiquitous within the Jewish culture that spawned that account. They are evident, and in some cases disturbingly evident, in the law codes of the Old Testament. Jewish law gave to men exclusive right to divorce their wives (Deut. 24: 1-4); a wife was considered the property of her husband, with few or no property rights herself (Exod. 20: 17, Deut. 21: 16-17, Num. 27: 5-8); virginity and fidelity requirements were more deliberately and ruthlessly applied to women than to men (Num. 5: 11-31).

Patriarchy comes under significant attack in the ministry of Jesus, or at least earlier expressions of it do. Women are given the right to divorce their husbands (Mark 10: 12). Jesus treats women with great respect, and readily accepts them as his disciples. He significantly elevates their status and role. Jesus' example is followed by his apostles, including Paul. Paul may not have gone all the way towards dismantling patriarchy. However, one could argue that the trajectory established by Jesus and honoured by Paul was of such a nature that patriarchy, like slavery, can reasonably be set aside, especially in a world where women have come to show themselves capable of holding their own at all levels of human endeavour.

On the Way to a More Biblical Hermeneutic

A third very useful discovery that became influential in the development of a new hermeneutic was the discovery that the way I had been reading the Scriptures was un-biblical. The grammatical-historical hermeneutic,[100] with all of its Reformation and post-Reformation components, simply wasn't biblical. Not one of the biblical writers employed it, nor did Jesus whose opinions on everything else have been considered normative.

What is so surprising about this discovery is that it took so long for me to make it. I had spent four years in intensive, postgraduate theological studies at a college touted by some in Sydney to be the best theological

---

[100] On the grammatical-historical method, see footnote 93, this chapter.

college in the world. Leaving aside the unfortunate and unjustified hubris involved in such overstatement, Moore Theological College is committed to high standards of academic excellence. It is hard to comprehend how I could have gone through its training, and even become a teacher there without even once thinking through the implications of the fact that the hermeneutic we were learning and having illustrated on a daily basis was not found anywhere in the Bible, especially baffling in a college priding itself in being so thoroughly biblical.

I am sure we did do some work on a Reformed hermeneutic, but I, for one, didn't pick the disjunction between the way the biblical writers read their Bibles and the way I was being encouraged to read it. There was certainly no exploration of the implications of this disjunction. As so often happens in every academic discipline, the assumptions guiding that discipline are seldom examined.

It was therefore instructive to look more closely at how the biblical authors read and understood their Bibles. What I noticed was that biblical writers often drew on material we would consider to be doubtfully reliable and even mythical. The New Testament letter of 1 Peter contains the following puzzling description of a post-resurrection descent by Jesus into the world of the dead:

> [Jesus] was put to death in the flesh, but made alive in the spirit, in which also he went and made a proclamation to the spirits in prison, who in former times did not obey, when God waited patiently in the days of Noah, during the building of the ark, in which a few, that is, eight persons, were saved through water. And baptism, which this prefigured, now saves you. (1 Pet. 3: 18-21, NRSV)

2 Peter has a similar account with some extra details added:

> For if God did not spare angels when they sinned, but sent them to hell, putting them into gloomy dungeons to be held for judgement, if he did not spare the ancient world when he brought the flood on its ungodly people, but protected Noah, a preacher of righteousness, and seven others . . . (2 Pet. 2: 4-5, NRSV)

Taken together and at face value, these texts report an expedition to hell by the resurrected Jesus to make some sort of proclamation to a group of angelic beings, who in Genesis 6: 1-4 are described as having sex with human beings, these unions resulting in gigantic offspring. In all sorts of ways, this is a problematic account. As we have already seen, there are strong reasons for believing that the story of Noah's flood is non-factual, as would also be the story of angels having sex with humans and creating giants. This account of Jesus preaching to imprisoned spirits closely resembles the mythical account of Enoch, Noah's great-grandfather, who in a book named after him (1 Enoch)[101] descends to the underworld to inform the imprisoned angels that they should not expect mercy from God who had already condemned them to eternal punishment. It seems likely that the authors of 1 and 2 Peter were drawing on this story, while modifying it by substituting Jesus for Enoch.

Over the years of my Christian life, I have often been puzzled by these two passages. They breathe a spirit and imply a hermeneutic that is very different to mine. But these are by no means isolated passages. There are many other passages that appear to deviate from sound Reformed and/or evangelical principles of interpretation.

I had been taught to be suspicious of myths and legends because they weren't true to fact. This discomfort is apparently not shared by biblical writers who happily include mythical and/or legendary elements in their writings,[102] which is perhaps an indication that we moderns shouldn't be so hung up about the distinction between factual and fictional narratives.

I had been taught to seek out the most reliable or accurate text or translation to be as close as I could to the original text. This doesn't seem to have been a priority for biblical writers who not uncommonly choose one text or translation over another if it suited their purposes better. The author of Matthew's Gospel, for example, appears to have done just that in choosing

---

[101] An Apocalyptic text written between the third and first centuries BC, 1 Enoch is not currently regarded as belonging to the canon of Scripture, apart from the Beta Israel canon (for Jews) and the Ethiopian Orthodox Church (for Christians).

[102] For two other examples, see Jude 9: 14-15.

to rely on the Greek translation of the Hebrew Scriptures (the LXX) in his story of the virgin birth of Jesus. Isaiah had prophesied that a 'young woman' (Hebrew *almah*) would conceive and bear a son called Immanu-El; the LXX has 'virgin' (*parthenos*).

I had been taught not to read meaning into texts (eisegesis), and to at least attempt to discover a biblical author's original intended meaning. Biblical writers appear to have been more concerned to find new, fresh, or hidden meanings in the original texts. For them, it was more a case of what the texts now meant. Jesus illustrates this approach in his use of Exodus 3: 6 to prove the general resurrection. In Luke 20: 34 and following, Jesus impresses his Sadducean audience by claiming that 'even Moses showed that the dead rise, for he calls the Lord the God of Abraham and the God of Isaac and the God of Jacob. For he is not the God of the dead, but of the living, for to him all are alive.' No sensible reconstruction of the original meaning of this passage from Exodus would conclude that this meaning was intended by the original author or authors.

Quite clearly, Jesus, along with the authors of the New Testament, was marching to a very different hermeneutical drum to the one I had been marching to. The unsurprising reason for this is that they were employing techniques and strategies current at that time—that time being the Second Temple period of Jewish history, the period between the completion of Jerusalem's Second Temple in 516 BC and its destruction by the Romans in 70 CE. These techniques and strategies included typology and pesher midrash,[103] which was an exegetical practice used at Qumran. By this method, Old Testament texts were given an interpretive shaping so that contemporary events could be presented as their eschatological fulfilment. The meaning of older texts was not self-evident. One had to go searching. One also had to wait for events that would fulfil those ancient texts.

---

[103] *Pesher*, meaning solution or deciphering, *midrash* meaning exegesis or interpretation. For more information, see Richard B. Hays and Joel B. Green, 'The Use of the Old Testament by New Testament Writers', in Joel B. Green, *Hearing the New Testament: Strategies of Interpretation*, (Grand Rapids: Eerdmans, 1995), 222-238, as well as E. Earle Ellis's excellent monograph, *The Old Testament in Early Christianity*, (Tubingen: J.C.B. Mohr, 1991).

Like the Qumran community, Christians developed their own *pesher* exegesis, scouring the Torah and the Prophets for prophetic references to Jesus. They used a variety of interpretive methods, sometimes taking a more literal and straightforward approach to the text, at other times reading their own experience into the text, at yet other times taking a more spiritual or metaphorical approach. There was no one approach that ruled out others, but rather an interweaving and blending of interpretive approaches, unified by a Christological reading of the Old Testament texts.[104]

What is clear is that Jesus and the New Testament authors did not use a grammatical-historical approach. That approach emerged many years after the writing of the New Testament; many years after a number of other approaches to reading the Scriptures had developed.[105] Those who use the grammatical-historical approach are departing from biblical practice.

Does that mean that they are to be criticised for doing this? I don't think so. In fact, one could argue that in adopting new methods, like the grammatical-historical method, we are being entirely biblical. We are doing just what the biblical writers did as we bring our own contemporary methods to bear on our reading and appropriation of our inherited faith. We are following their lead. Moreover, we cannot go back to adopting New Testament methods. We are on the other side of 2,000 years of post-apostolic interpretive practice. Our understandings have been irreversibly altered by the Dark and Middle Ages, by the Renaissance, the Reformation, the Enlightenment, and by Post-Enlightenment critiques of what has gone before. We simply cannot go back. Moreover, critical studies of the Bible have been hugely helpful in expanding our knowledge of the Bible and its background. We have at our disposal a much larger

---

[104] R. Longenecker, *Biblical Exegesis in the Apostolic Period*, (Grand Rapids: Eerdmans, 1975), 103.

[105] Origen (185-254) developed a three-fold hermeneutic involving attention to the literal, moral, and allegorical senses of Biblical texts. John Cassian (360-435) added a fourth, the analogical or mystical sense, which is their eschatological significance.

range of interpretive tools and approaches, including historical criticism,[106] which seek to unearth and understand the historical factors that gave rise to biblical religion and to the biblical text. With such tools as these, we too must re-appropriate the traditions which have given rise to our faith. We too must constantly rethink what it means to be a twenty-first-century follower of Jesus. That, at least, is how I have come to see it.

In the process of my own rethinking, I was greatly helped by an encounter with the writings of French philosopher Paul Ricoeur (1913-2005). As seems to have happened often in my life, it was both chancy and timely. I happened to notice the title of a book written about Ricoeur. Though I cannot now remember the title or the author, I was enthralled enough to read it from cover to cover. The writer was appropriating a Ricoeurian approach to a hermeneutical issue he was attempting to work through. In an essay written in 1967,[107] Ricoeur articulated a three-part hermeneutic involving movement from a 'first naïveté' through critical engagement to a 'second naïveté'. In the first naïveté, we simply encounter the symbolic and mythical representations of our culture at face value, without critique. In my case, this meant accepting the beliefs of my parents and of the religious culture in which I grew up. I had entered a world already well furnished with ideas and beliefs which soon came to define my approach to life. I wasn't at all critical of this heritage to begin with, but over time, and as I grew up, I did begin to subject my inherited beliefs to critical scrutiny. I entered, and came in and out of the second phase of Ricoeur's hermeneutic; the phase of critical engagement.

In lots of ways, I am still there. I have been within this phase of critical engagement for most of my life. Ricoeur observed that Western culture

---

[106] Associated with the historical-critical method are textual criticism, literary criticism, genre criticism, redaction criticism, historical criticism, rhetorical criticism, narrative criticism. There are also canonical, sociological, psychological, anthropological, liberationist, and feminist approaches to Scripture.

[107] Paul Ricoeur, *The Symbolism of Evil*, (Boston: Beacon Press, 1967).

has followed a similar path away from earlier non-critical and mythical cultures. From at least the time of the Enlightenment, Western thinkers have embraced a hermeneutic of suspicion,[108] with the Judaeo-Christian faith often squarely in its sights. Ricoeur's recommendation is that we re-engage and re-appropriate earlier symbolic representations, including those of Christianity. As we do this, we enter a second naïveté from which we can benefit.

Moving out of full-time teaching and into ministry at Green Square allowed me time and space to attempt to do just that. A small, but significant and now permanent step in that direction was to engage devotionally in this process of re-appropriation. With our boys now almost grown up, Judy and I began a practice of beginning each day with a coffee, a short reading from the Scriptures, followed by prayer. Guided by Ricoeur, we would start by noting our initial reactions to the text we were reading, taking the text at face value, not worrying if we were reading into it the results of our upbringing or theological education. But then we would draw on whatever critical resources we had at our disposal, not by grabbing commentaries, but by asking critical questions of the text, thinking about it with a bit more rigour. Then we would come back to it to let it speak to us again. Rather than getting stuck at a critical or cognitive stage, we allowed the text, and also God, to speak to us, hopefully in fresh ways. That, at least, is the theory, and, in broad terms, that is what we have done right through to the present.

I also began to use Ricoeur's approach in preaching. One of my early sermon series at Green Square Community Church[109] was a series on Genesis 1-11. What I endeavoured to do in this series was to move beyond a literalistic reading of these chapters and to draw out, as best I could, the meaning

---

[108] Ricoeur took issue with hermeneutical approaches, such as those represented by Freud, Marx, and Nietzsche, for being both suspicious and reductionistic in their approach to mythical or symbolic consciousness. See, for example, in Paul Ricoeur, *Freud and Philosophy: An Essay on Interpretation*, (New Haven and London: Yale University Press, 1970), 32-36, and Paul Ricoeur, 'The Critique of Religion,' in *The Philosophy of Paul Ricoeur: An Anthology of his Work*, (Boston: Beacon Press, 1978), 213-222.

[109] The additional name that we gave to St James, Beaconsfield.

of these texts for contemporary life. For me, it was a landmark series. It marked the beginning of a new approach, although not new in every respect. The preaching that resulted from this approach wasn't radically different to how I had always preached. A lifetime of respectful engagement with the text of the Bible had bequeathed an ongoingly respectful attitude to whatever text I was encountering. I had been taught to allow texts to interrogate me as much as I would interrogate them. I was aware of the pitfalls of allowing contemporary assumptions and beliefs to have the only say, or even the most say. I knew the importance of being self-critical, and not just text critical. I had been taught that Scripture, reason, and tradition all play a part in the interpretive process. This continued, but with some difference. I was now allowing myself to ask questions of biblical texts that I had previously never felt I could ask. There was a new freedom to discover and to take issue with assumptions and beliefs embedded within the text which can no longer be reasonably accepted.

This new model was more dynamic than the one I had inherited. It was also more respectful of the text, in the sense of being more willing to see what was there, less willing to excuse and to smooth and to harmonize, more sensitive to differences and developments within the text. It meant a less tortuous and more honest approach to what one finds in the Scriptures. For me, it was an approach that allowed me to follow the truth wherever it might lead, without being afraid or in denial about what I might find.[110]

An Early Test Case

One subject I felt I needed to rethink was homosexuality. Not only would this be another important step on the way to developing an intellectually satisfying hermeneutic, it was also an issue which was beginning to encounter me as I door-knocked my way around Beaconsfield and adjoining suburbs. South Sydney Municipal Council houses a higher than average

---

[110] As I began to employ Ricoueur's broad method of reading Biblical texts, I found to my delight that others were already well-advanced practitioners. Included among these was one of the world's leading Biblical scholars, Walter Brueggemann. Brueggemann draws on insights gleaned from Ricoueur in his work. See, for example, *Redescribing Reality: What do we do when we read the Bible,* (London: SCM Press, 2009).

percentage of gay, lesbian, bisexual and transgender (GBLT) residents. I was meeting, getting to know, and becoming friends with people whose sexual orientation was different to mine. What surprised me was how ordinary these people were, how normal in almost every aspect of their lives. They were just like me. I really shouldn't have been surprised, but I had had something of a sheltered background. However, I also found GLBT people to be extraordinary, to be quite special in their way of being, in part because of some heightened sensitivities and talents that appear to cluster around those whose sexualities are different, in part because of the often tortured and challenging lives many of them have lived, very often because of prejudices I once shared.

I wanted to have my prejudices challenged and, if necessary, overturned. I was heartened by changes I had noted within Sydney Anglican circles. There had been, in the past, an almost universal tendency to claim that homosexuality itself was sinful, regardless of behaviour. To be homosexual was to be sinful. That stance had already begun to be challenged when I first went to Moore College as an undergraduate. It has certainly been challenged since then, with many now recognising that homosexual orientation is simply that, an orientation, a possibly hard-wired tendency to be erotically aroused by people of the same gender. This understanding did not result from a careful reading or rereading of the relevant biblical texts. It came about under pressure from advancing scientific understanding. It also came about because of a new willingness by many to listen to homosexual people who were now bolder in telling their stories.

A year or two into my time at South Sydney Parish, I initiated, with the help of John McIntyre and good friend, Vic Branson, a pub discussion group called Quest.[111] It was a little like the hermeneutics discussion group in raising topics like homosexuality for discussion. We ran it at the Parkview Hotel in Alexandria, a nearby suburb. One of the people we asked to speak at Quest was Rev. Dr Canon Stuart Barton Babbage. He had recently written his memoirs, *Memoirs of a Loose Canon*.[112] In a long and distinguished

---

[111] The name Quest was chosen as a way of encapsulating an Augustinian approach to faith, an approach he described as 'faith seeking understanding.'

[112] Stuart Barton Babbage, *Memoirs of a Loose Canon*, (Brunswick East: Acorn Press, 2004).

career, Canon Barton Babbage had been principal of Ridley College (in Melbourne), dean of St Andrews Cathedral (Sydney), dean of St Paul's Cathedral (Melbourne), and dean of the Australian College of Theology. What stuck longest in my memory from that night was Dr Babbage sharing with us the impact on him and his thinking of discovering that his son was gay. I can't remember his exact words, but they were something along these lines: 'This experience forced me to rethink my theology and to reassess the adequacy of earlier understandings.'

Running Quest, mostly as a monthly, Sunday night event, was one of the most enjoyable and enlightening experiences of my time at Green Square. We had some great speakers, including such high-profile politicians as Peter Garrett, Tanya Plibersek, and Bruce Baird. We had a geologist, a boxer and kick-boxing Anglican priest (now my pastor), a Muslim, a sexologist, an ethicist, even an Archbishop in Peter Jensen. Peter spoke about his then recently published book, *The Future of Jesus*.[113] What especially interested me from what Peter said was his answer to a question asked of him after his talk. He was asked if he himself was still 'questing' for better understandings in some area of his thinking. His answer was that he was rethinking Genesis 1-11. There are certainly very good reasons to want to do this.

That was the rethink I had been engaged in for the previous few years. It was to make a huge difference for me in all sorts of ways. In my last couple of years teaching Philosophy 3 at Moore College,[114] I began to include some hermeneutical issues. They were relevant to a number of issues we were exploring in that course; one of them being apologetics, which is the study of how people might defend or commend their faith to others. One question that needs to be considered in this is: what exactly is being defended? Is it the Bible's cosmology or geology or chronology? Given that biblical writers had various assumptions we no longer share, what exactly is it that the Christian is commending or defending? I raised that question in class, against the backdrop of some discussion about divine accommodation. One very perceptive student asked, 'If accommodation is a fact, and we are at liberty to disagree with at least some of the assumptions

---

[113] Peter Jensen, *The Future of Jesus: Does He Have a Place in Our World*, (Sydney: ABC Books, 2005).

[114] The only course I was teaching there up until 2006.

and beliefs found throughout the Bible, what is to stop one from arguing that the Bible's teaching on homosexuality can be set aside because it is based on inadequate or pre-scientific understandings of this condition?' This possible implication was clearly alarming to him. It was, perhaps, a warning light against going too far down this path.

To even countenance the possibility that anything other than the Bible's apparent condemnation of homosexual practice was possible was to walk onto very dangerous ground. I realized that I had begun to walk on that ground. A very common view of many in Sydney Anglican circles is that homosexual practice is so abhorrent, so obviously contrary to God's will, that nothing should be conceded that might even open the door to a reconsideration of this issue. Any appeal to cultural relativities is resisted because of the fear that this might put one on an inevitably slippery slope towards accepting homosexual practice. There is some justification for this fear, and I was certainly now on that slippery slope.

Chapter 7

Fearful Fundamentalism

Sydney Anglicanism does not have a good reputation in Sydney or around the world. To be frank, it has a terrible reputation. In five years of walking the streets of Sydney's inner suburbs, I can't remember a good thing ever being said about the Sydney Anglican Church. I did hear a lot of criticisms from people who were sometimes surprisingly informed. It was strange, because I hadn't encountered this sort of negativity earlier in my life. Maybe it was because I myself had become a Sydney Anglican and was spending most of my time in the company of Sydney Anglicans. Certainly that was the case when I was a full-time teacher at Moore College.

But even in those years, I was aware of things about Sydney Anglicanism that disturbed me. At first, they were more like a niggle or slight disquiet, but they did grow over time into full-blown concern. I had benefitted from Sydney Anglicanism, greatly. There is every chance I would have ditched my faith altogether had I not met a succession of highly talented and winningly humble exemplars of this form of evangelical piety and scholarship. These included Tony Doran, Bill Dumbrell, Graham Cole, and Barry Webb. That I only include men in this list is fair commentary on my long-nurtured male biases, but what also unifies this list is the essentially humble approach these persons exemplified. All were comfortable in expressing uncertainty. All appeared willing to think outside of conventional boxes. All were willing to be different, even if that meant becoming outsiders or fringe dwellers to the dominant Sydney ethos.

It was this humbler strain of Sydney's Anglicanism that won me over. But it wasn't its only or most dominant strain. Sydney Anglicans are not generally known for their humility, in fact the opposite. They are better known for being abrasive and opinionated. I have heard it suggested that Sydney Anglicans are like this not because of theology, but geography. Sydneysiders in general are known to be arrogant and abrasive. Perhaps, though this is a pretty harsh assessment.

Arrogance can be a function of youth. I am quite sure I was arrogant as a young man. I was certainly intolerant of other expressions of Christian faith. Arrogance can be a function of self-belief. One of my all-time favourite cricket players was the West Indian batsman, Vivian Richards. It was always a thrill to watch Richards stroll out to bat, normally chewing gum, with the nonchalant and menacing ease of an assassin—which he often was to the reputations of otherwise capable bowlers. He oozed confidence. I supported a rugby league team known for its arrogance, the Manly Sea Eagles. They too oozed an arrogant self-belief, with practised contempt for those who opposed them. I wouldn't be surprised if I came across as arrogant when I first left Moore College to begin ordained ministry in the country. I was certainly proud to have come from Moore College. It is easy to be arrogant or to be perceived as arrogant.

But arrogance, even on the sporting field, is seldom justified, if ever.[115] It is never justified when it comes to matters of theology or faith. When I arrived back from the country to teach at Moore College, I began to be aware, only vaguely at first, of attitudes that bordered on being arrogant. Students and even some faculty seemed unsettled, even alarmed by expressions of difference on matters that were hardly central to evangelical faith. A growing undercurrent of theological correctness was beginning to run on topics such as evangelism or on whether a woman could preach to men. I began to hear of students telling other students to 'repent' for holding contrary views and of whispered conversations about people who were 'not to be trusted' because of their heterodox, but hardly heretical beliefs.

---

[115] One could argue that arrogance, or at least the appearance of arrogance, is justified on the sporting field as a form of gamesmanship designed to unsettle opponents, or as a ploy to mask nervousness and uncertainty which can afflict even the most talented of sportspeople.

It didn't take long to realize that a potent cause of this emerging theological correctness was the highly successful ministry of Phillip Jensen, Anglican Chaplain to the University of New South Wales and Rector of St Matthias, Centennial Park. Phillip's influence in those years (the 1990s) was immense. Increasing numbers of people, mostly young men, but also women, were coming into college from burgeoning student and post-student ministries. I was aware that some of the attitudes I didn't especially like were being expressed by students coming from these ministries. I didn't have much to do with Phillip. I had heard he was quite shy, belying his confident and typically combative upfront style. He seemed a somewhat shadowy figure when he'd occasionally come to college; was inclined to look out for people he knew, and appeared to be uncomfortable among those he didn't.

Every year at college, faculty and students would scatter to the four corners of Sydney and beyond for a week of mission, starting on one Sunday and finishing the next. They were often the highlight of the year. I enjoyed the opportunity of getting to know students better, and of putting into practice some of the things we were learning. One year, it was decided that there would be a mission to St Matthias, Centennial Park. I volunteered to lead a team there. I was keen to put to rest, if I could, some prejudices I'd begun to form against the ministries happening there. I wanted to be proved wrong. Damien, my eldest son, had benefitted from St Matthias ministries when he attended UNSW.[116] Consequently, I threw myself into preparation for this week with as much keenness and generosity of spirit as I could muster.

The week was interesting and positive in lots of ways, but it didn't at all disabuse me of my prejudices. Instead, it confirmed them. I was left with two abiding impressions. The first was the lack of warmth I felt among many of the people I met. With some notable and welcome exceptions, the leadership appeared cool, aloof, and watchfully suspicious. It rocked me at the time. I didn't expect so cautious a reception for a team from Moore College. I learnt later that St Matthias students were warned not even to trust people who attended Moore.

---

[116] Though not without forming his own reservations, some of which echo concerns expressed in this chapter.

A second abiding impression was more serious. Phillip Jensen wasn't around for most of the Mission week. He had been overseas. The only brief encounter I had with him was at a weekly meeting of students taking part in a Ministry Training Scheme (MTS) set up by St Matthias. There was a large group of students, most of them young and keen to learn. Phillip led the session, and we were invited to observe. For the best part of two hours, Phillip dialogued with the students. It was clearly a coaching session, but I couldn't help notice how guru-like Phillip appeared. He exuded confidence. The group was in his thrall.

Observing this for so long a time was simultaneously fascinating and disturbing. It was fascinating to observe someone who could talk for so long with such authority. It was disturbing to think about the impact of so authoritative an approach on people who were so young and impressionable. Those two hours niggled away at me as I thought about them. As the week of mission was coming to an end, I was driving home one evening and a thought came into my mind that I couldn't subsequently shake. It was that what I had been observing was a cult, or, at least, was cult-like. What I had been sitting in on was a nursery for the inflexible attitudes and beliefs I had observed prior to coming to St Matthias, but was now observing up close, at their source.

I did not say anything to anyone at first, except to one or two close friends. I was unsettled by this thought of mine. It would have been quite a damning assessment to make public. Over the years since that week, I have often wondered how warranted it was. Was I being too critical? Was it an example of my tendency to demonize those I don't approve of? Maybe it was all of those things. The very word 'cult' is emotive and always negative when used of others. I had read and seen documentaries about cults, many of them in the United States, a country that so values freedom of thought and religion that it has become a breeding ground for some of the world's most outlandish new religious movements, as cults are now often referred to. There is lively scholarly debate about cults, with some of it concentrating on characteristics of groups or movements that might start out healthily, but can become unhealthy, even dangerous. Included among these characteristics are the following:[117]

(1) Led by a strong leader who can claim divine authority for his/her deeds and directions;
(2) The leader not being accountable or feeling accountable to others;
(3) Deceptive recruitment; not telling the full story of what involvement will entail;
(4) Use of covert or disguised hypnotic techniques;
(5) Isolation in new surroundings apart from old friends or reference points;
(6) Having a philosophy, ideology or theology that seems logical and appears to answer all or the most important questions in life;
(7) Older or alternative ways of thinking criticized;
(8) Pressure applied to avoid engagement with competing or contrary ideas;
(9) Questioning, doubt or dissent discouraged, even punished;
(10) Sharp distinctions made between 'us' and 'them';
(11) A 'we are right and others are wrong' mentality;
(12) Committed to and focused on achieving a certain goal;
(13) Calling on adherents to sacrifice their time and money for the common cause;

---

[117] These characteristics have been drawn from a number of authors who have sought to isolate characteristics of groups that either are or run the risk of becoming cultish. These include Shirley Harrison, *Cults: the battle for God*, (London: Christopher Helm, 1990), Steve Eichel, 'Building Resistance: Tactics for building resistance to manipulation and unethical hypnosis in totalistic groups,' *Suggestion: The Journal of Professional & Ethical Hypnosis*, *1*, (Summer 1985), pp. 34-44; Eileen Barker, 'Watching for Violence: A Comparative Analysis of the Roles of Five Types of Cult-atching Groups,' in D. G. Bromley and J. G Melton (eds), *Cults, Religion and Violence*, (Cambridge: Cambridge University Press, 2003), 123-148.

(14) Highly structured activities giving little time for privacy or independent action;
(15) Threats of exclusion from the group used to keep people in the group.

The list is instructive, because it highlights the importance of coercion and control. Cults result when otherwise normal tribal boundaries are hardened to keep some people in and others out. What feeds them is the desire to exercise control over others, sometimes with the best of motives to begin with. Dissent and independence of thought, because they inevitably undermine group cohesion and purpose; because they also represent a challenge to the authority of the leader, must be resisted. Cults become especially sinister when the control of people and their thinking is justified by an appeal to God or Scripture. This tends to mask what is going on underneath, which is power being used and abused for the benefit of those wielding it. All sorts of unconscious and unacknowledged needs are fed by processes that end up being cultish.

It may be that my assessment of St Matthias ministries as cultish was too strong, but even if it was, it ought to be of some concern that many (though not all) of the above-mentioned characteristics were observable during the week of mission, and in observations before and after that week. Some were obviously the case. Others were more subtly present. There can be no doubt that Phillip Jensen was and is a strong leader. To his credit, he has consistently sought to decentre ministry so as to avoid being put on a pedestal. From what limited conversations I have had with him, and from what others have told me, Phillip is aware of the dangers of being constructed as a guru. However, the truth remains that he is deeply revered by those who are and have been his disciples. Even the effort of distancing himself from the centre of control has only served to accentuate his stature as elder statesman and founding father of the St Matthias ministries.

He has also tended to be a law unto himself. When it has suited him, he has ignored the directives of archbishops; has absented himself from Synod, has innovated changes to the way he has done and described church, justifying his actions by direct appeals to Scripture. He has been quite the maverick and renegade, and that was a big part of his appeal.

Phillip also benefitted from the fact that every year at university he had a new batch of mostly eighteen-year-olds, inclined like him to be rebellious, inclined like him to be idealistic. Phillip gave them a cause to believe in: evangelical Christianity of the Reformed and reforming variety. He gave them a mission to preoccupy their time, even to the detriment of their studies—the mission of converting as many of their fellow students as they could. And they were given all the on-the-job training they would need. There was nothing necessarily unhealthy about any of this from an evangelical point of view, although we did notice, while on mission, how highly structured the ministry had become, with trainees expected to work hard for little remuneration, females being paid even less.

Little of what I have mentioned so far would have made me think that what I was observing was cultish. My own university experience was similar. I too was young, idealistic, and ready to part company with the religion of my parents. I too was isolated by distance from my family home, and was taken in, positively, by a succession of highly able and inspirational leaders. None of this was cultish, but what I encountered at St Matthias seemed different. It felt different. It felt colder and more patterned. It also appeared simplistic.

Phillip was deliberately provocative in his preaching with an acknowledged preference for hyperbole, believing this was how Jesus preached. He preached in black and white. Though he may privately have seen some greys, he wasn't at all interested in preaching them. And that was attractive to those who became his disciples. Every issue was simple, because Phillip made it sound simple.

The trouble is that most things in life are not simple. There are greys, and lots of them. Eighteen-year-olds might not be so aware of them, but most of their parents are, and many became understandably alarmed by the new dogmata being espoused by their children. The wiser among them would have been patient enough to wait for their children to grow up and discover that life isn't as simple as they were claiming. But parents did have good reason to be concerned, because along with the dogmatism and black-and-white thinking was an even more alarming tendency to vilify and marginalize those who thought differently.

On the issue of whether women can preach to men or lead them, Phillip was fervent in his denunciation of those who thought otherwise, for no good reason. For years, there was a book on my dad's bookshelf by the long-time principal of PBI, L. E. Maxwell. The book was compiled and published after his death, and is entitled *Women in Ministry: A Historical and Biblical look at the Role of Women in Christian Leadership*.[118] What is so interesting about this book is that it was written back in the 1980s by a self-styled fundamentalist who was as conservative, and more, than Phillip Jensen, with essentially the same hermeneutic. But he comes to entirely different conclusions. The principal who followed Maxwell at PBI[119] would tease Maxwell that the ordination of women to positions of leadership followed logically from his arguments, though Maxwell wasn't quite prepared to take that final step. The fact is that many evangelicals think differently on this matter, and with good warrant, both exegetically and hermeneutically.

What was of even more concern was that disciples of Phillip and of those he mentored were actively discouraged from sympathetic engagement with alternative points of view. They were warned off attending events run by those not trusted by St Matthias and were told who could be trusted and who couldn't. They were even told that those they needed to be most suspicious of were those closest to them in Christian belief, on the assumption that these were the ones most likely to entice them onto slippery slopes to theological error. It is at this point that St Matthias ministries were most cult-like. Not only was the approach highly paternalistic, it also evidenced a lack of confidence in the black and white certainties being espoused. As with all movements that become cultish, it is fear that people will think for themselves which drives efforts to control. Behind the bravado is fear and uncertainty.

What has also disturbed me over the years is the almost total lack of self-criticism which seems to have accompanied this approach. By self-criticism I mean putting the spotlight on one's own ideas and beliefs. It seems to me that if we are going to criticise others, we need to be open to criticisms of our own way of thinking.

---

[118] L. E. Maxwell, *Women in Ministry: A Historical and Biblical Look at the Role of Women in Christian Leadership*, (Wheaton: Victor Books, 1987).
[119] Ted S. Rendall

Some years after the week of mission and after I had left Moore College to minister at Green Square, I was talking to a friend who had spent some years at St Matthias. He is one of a number of friends and acquaintances who were once active in student ministries at the University of New South Wales. He had been an insider, but told me that he now has a ministry to people needing to disconnect from what had been a powerful influence in their lives. What struck us both in conversation was how similar these experiences were to teenagers needing to cut themselves adrift from their parents. Phillip has been a powerful father-figure to many people. As with any father, his children are likely to share both his strengths and weaknesses. His insecurities and fears are likely to be theirs as well.

Reflections on My Own Father

The example of my own father has left an indelible mark on me, for good and ill. My dad passed away on 18 November 2005 at the age of eighty-eight. He had been deteriorating in physical and mental health for two years and more and had become a shadow of his former self. A sad thing happened as he grew weaker. He gradually lost the art of arguing, the joy and frustration of engaging in theological debates. A day came when I knew I could no longer argue with him, and that it would be cruel to even try. There was a song being played on the radio at around that time, Josh Groban singing, 'You raise me up'. Included among its soaring lyrics are the words,

> You raise me up so I can stand on mountains;
> You raise me up to walk on stormy seas;
> I am strong when I am on your shoulders
> You raise me up to more than I can be.

They reminded me of times my dad had lifted me onto his shoulders, or, more excitingly still, up onto his hands as he lay on his back. Once I was stable and standing, he would gently lift me, helping me to keep balanced, before dropping me back onto his knees. It was a practice I borrowed for each of my sons, and now grandsons. For months before Dad died, I would completely dissolve into tears when I heard that song; would sometimes even have to stop the car to let the impact pass. My dad was no longer strong enough, even metaphorically, to lift me up, other than through memories of his former strength and stature.

Being a leader of any sort brings awesome responsibilities to be the sort of leader whose example is worth following. It was my privilege to speak at my father's funeral. These were some of the words I spoke:

> Dad had an active mind. He also had a questioning mind. He taught us not to just accept a point of view simply because we had been told it. He taught us to question, to probe, to think.
>
> Dad was happy for us to argue with him. I've come to understand that that is rare. If we could argue a good case; if we could persuade him that our case was stronger than his, he'd accept it. He was less interested in winning an argument than in discovering the truth (about whatever). That is remarkable.
>
> He didn't always agree with us, of course—often didn't—especially if it was theology we were debating. A good friend of mine, Michael Dasey, remembers the animated, often heated, theological discussions we would have, and Dad saying, 'Ah, Keith; ah, Keith.' In other words, 'You don't believe *that* do you!'
>
> I am forever indebted to my father for the way he allowed us to question, to think, and to come to our own conclusions. He let us decide for ourselves which career path to follow, which church to join.

It is clear that I would always struggle with authoritarian approaches to faith and life. My inherited mindset was very different from the one I increasingly encountered in Sydney. It has been interesting to think about Phillip Jensen as a father-figure, and about how different he was to my dad. The truth is they are not that dissimilar. When I sat observing Phillip coaching his group of disciples those years ago, he most certainly was encouraging them to think, to debate, to establish the truth of their conclusions from Scripture. Those who came to college from St Matthias were terrier-like in trying to discover what the Scriptures were saying. They hadn't been indoctrinated with conclusions so much as by a method. That is hard to criticize. It also separated St Matthias from groups that are cultish. Perhaps the difference was that Phillip appeared inflexible in his opinions. Combine that with the powerful influence of being a father-figure, and you end up with disciples frightened to arrive at different conclusions. They had not been encouraged to do that.

I was more comfortable with my dad's approach than I was with Phillip's. I was more comfortable with the approach of John McIntyre, who I had gone to work with after leaving full-time teaching at Moore. John was one of Sydney's most capable clergy. Not only was he academically able and widely read, he was wonderfully approachable and winningly laid-back in his approach to ministry. John had a patience I lacked. For me, he was the perfect boss, allowing me freedom to do my thing, but always in concert with him, the parish's Indigenous Pastor, Ray Minniecon, and Ray's close associate in Aboriginal ministry, Pastor Bill Simon.[120]

Early Expressions of Concern

John was a determined advocate for the rights of Indigenous Australians. He was also a long-time and vocal supporter of the Movement for the Ordination of Women, putting him on the outer among more conservative members of the diocese, including the Jensen brothers. Peter chose to appoint Phillip as dean of Sydney in 2003, two years after he had become archbishop of Sydney. John was, at the time, a member of the Standing Committee of the diocese and often found himself isolated within that increasingly powerful and sometimes dangerously independent body.

In early 2004, I wrote a letter to Peter Jensen expressing my concerns about the direction in which the diocese appeared to be moving. I also expressed some regret that I hadn't said anything earlier. I had tended to stay out of diocesan politics, but felt I now needed to speak up. The sorts of things which had disturbed me throughout the years of my teaching at Moore seemed to be increasingly in evidence. In the letter, I drew attention to what appeared to be a serious lack of epistemic humility; people making overconfident claims about issues which were, at best, debatable. I

---

[120] Bill Simon tells the captivating story of his life and faith in *Back on the Block: Bill Simon's Story*, co-written with Des Montgomerie and Jo Tuscano, (Canberra: Aboriginal Studies Press, 2009). The book is dedicated to deceased members of the Stolen Generations. Bill himself is a member, having spent many of his growing up years in Kinchella Boys Home near Kempsey, NSW.

mentioned the marginalizing of people and spoke about what appeared to be an emerging ethos of preachiness; people being preached at, or preached against, rather than being engaged with respect and a willingness to learn. I didn't think it likely that the people of Sydney would be attracted to such an approach.

Peter wrote back to me and suggested we meet to discuss the letter, which I was very pleased to do. We met for an hour and more from memory. It was good to meet and talk. We ranged across a number of topics, but for me what was most memorable was Peter's insight into why the diocese had the ethos it did. He quite generously, and not entirely accurately, observed that I might be confident and assured in my beliefs, but many weren't. He went on to mention a succession of challenges that have been faced by evangelical Christianity, including critical biblical scholarship, Anglo-Catholicism, the feminist movement, Pentecostalism, secularism, and the gay rights movement. These he described as being like one wave of attack after another on traditional Christianity, with the church now reeling and churchgoing numbers plummeting under their cumulative impact. He didn't mention the New Atheists, who weren't then around under that name, though they could easily be added.

In essence, what Peter was saying was that Sydney's ethos, whether emerging or not, is defensive. It is understandably defensive in the face of powerful and sustained challenges. That perspective made sense to me. As I thought further on this, it dawned on me that Sydney Anglicanism was displaying all of the hallmarks of classical fundamentalism. The term 'fundamentalism' had its origin in a series of twelve booklets published between 1910 and 1915 entitled *The Fundamentals: A Testimony to the Truth*. These were distributed free of charge to Christian workers right across the USA. They were written to galvanize Christian belief in the face of the threatening advance of theological liberalism. Five beliefs in particular were chosen as fundamental and, therefore, non-negotiable Christian beliefs. These were: (i) the verbal inerrancy of Scripture, (ii) the deity of Christ (including his virgin birth), (iii) the penal substitutionary atonement, (iv) the bodily resurrection of Jesus, and (v) Christ's second coming.

Although it is not always helpful to generalize about what 'Sydney Anglicans' believe, one can safely say that many, perhaps the majority of Sydney Anglican clergy, if not laity, hold to each of these five doctrines.

Those currently with most influence within the diocese certainly do, with the possible exception of inerrancy. Peter Jensen has argued the case for inerrancy, though others are happy with infallibility.[121]

Christian fundamentalism, as I understand its origins and history, is evangelicalism on the defensive. The fundamentalist movement began as a loose coalition of Calvinists and Arminians, dispensationalists and anti-evolutionists who united in opposition to theological liberalism. The coalition worked well for a time, with liberalism being resisted in the denominations and Darwinism in the schools. However, disunity soon emerged as more militant fundamentalists moved to separate from their denominations[122] and from those seen to compromise or cooperate with people not considered biblically sound. Billy Graham, as previously mentioned, was considered suspect by more ardent fundamentalists for cooperating with liberals and Roman Catholics in his evangelistic Crusades.

Edward J. Carnell characterized fundamentalism as orthodoxy gone cultic, because it chose to go beyond the historic creeds in specifying additional doctrines one needed to hold to be considered Christian. Fundamentalism began by specifying five non-negotiable doctrines. It was perhaps inevitable that a movement born of anxiety would produce off-spring keen to outdo each other in deciding who were truly Christian and/or biblical and who not. Fear begets fear. Anxiety begets anxiety, and when you are feeling under threat, you can't be too careful about who to trust.

---

[121] Peter spells out his understanding of inerrancy in his book, *The Revelation of God*, (Nottingham: Inter-Varsity Press, 2002), 'Those wishing to assert inerrancy [as I do] use the word "inerrant" to signify "the quality of being free from all falsehood and mistake", and hence assert that "Holy Scripture is entirely free from all falsehood in all its assertions",' 199, 200. This includes all matters historical and scientific in its scope. Peter prefers inerrancy to infallibility. Infallibility makes the lesser claim that the Bible is trustworthy in matters of salvation or faith, though not necessarily in matters of science or history. As I understand Peter, his reason for preferring inerrancy is that any lesser doctrine could lead one away from historic Christian beliefs. See further *The Revelation of God*, 197-204.

[122] For further detail, see Harriet A. Harris, *Fundamentalism and Evangelicals*, (Oxford: Clarenden Press, 1998), 29-39.

Carnell believed that fundamentalism was more of a mentality than a movement.[123] I think he was right. There is a feel about fundamentalism, a spirit, a vibe, which, in essence, is defensiveness.[124] I felt it at St Matthias. I was beginning to feel it within the wider diocese. In late 2004, I attended a School of Theology at Moore College, and the topic was 'The Word of God'. About all I remember of it now was an exchange at the end of a lecture given by Peter Jensen.[125] Peter's son, Michael, asked his father whether it was time to give up on the doctrine of inerrancy. Peter's reply was that we mustn't give it up because of what it safeguards. If I have understood Peter right, inerrancy is like a dam wall. It might not be the best of walls. It may even be a leaky wall, but without it there is no guarantee that what is being held back by the wall won't crash through and flood away.

It is a remarkable admission of uncertainty and epistemic fragility. Perhaps it goes some way to explaining the culture of anxiety and control that has become so evident within the Sydney Anglican Church. When your own faith is fragile, you are more likely to be overprotective of those you have responsibility for. When your own doubts cannot be silenced, you will feel more urgently the need to warn people off listening to those expressing alternative points of view, or who examine too closely the state of the dam wall.

If it is true that fundamentalism is more of a mentality than a movement, then it is something people can choose to shed, even while holding on to

---

[123] Referred to by R. V. Pierard, in Walter A. Elwell (ed), *Evangelical Dictionary of Theology*, (Grand Rapids: Baker Book House, 1984), 381.

[124] Other words have been used to characterize fundamentalism including angry and militant. George M. Marsden, who has written extensively on North American fundamentalism, described it this way in *Fundamentalism and American Culture: The Shaping of Twentieth-Century Evangelicalism 1870-1925*, (New York: Oxford University Press, 1980), 4: 'Briefly [fundamentalism] was militantly anti-modernist Protestant evangelicalism . . . Fundamentalism was a loose, diverse, and changing federation of co-belligerents united by their fierce opposition to modernist attempts to bring Christianity into line with modern thought.' Underlying this militancy was an understandable defensiveness in the face of perceived challenges to the faith.

[125] Peter's lecture was entitled, 'The humanity of the Word of God.'

some or all of the things they believe. If a hallmark of fundamentalism is fear coupled with efforts to control and conserve, then it is possible to choose a different way. It is possible to choose trust over fear, permission over control; freedom, inquisitiveness, and a willingness to learn over coercion, conformity, and closed-mindedness. It is possible to choose love, joy, peace, and patience over suspicion, inhibition, and rancour. There are different ways of being a Christian, some manifestly better than others, some more attractive than others.

Fundamentalism wasn't good for evangelicalism. Under its influence, evangelicalism tended towards sectarianism and, at its extreme edges, into cultism. It also retreated into an anti-intellectual obscurantism as the only way of retaining a literalistic reading of the Bible. But evangelicalism didn't stay there. From the mid-1950s, evangelicalism and fundamentalism began to diverge as evangelicalism began to re-engage the always evolving world of contemporary scholarship. It sought to benefit from the best of that scholarship, thereby becoming more sophisticated. I was one of the beneficiaries of that re-engagement.

Contemporary evangelicalism exists somewhere on a continuum between fundamentalism and theological liberalism. Liberalism, as I understand it, is that broad approach to the interpretation and appropriation of Christian faith that is, in principle, open to contemporary scholarship, and to making whatever adjustments to Christian belief that are believed to follow from the variously assured results of that scholarship. Liberalism is typically proactive in its engagement with contemporary knowledge and belief. It may not always be astute or careful in accepting what can turn out to be unfounded fashion. It is not always sufficiently wary of its own guiding assumptions, but it is, nevertheless, willing to follow the evidence wherever it might lead, regardless of the consequences. It is, in that sense, courageous.

Fundamentalism is the mirror opposite of liberalism. It is, to varying degrees,[126] closed off to contemporary scholarship, and especially to

---

[126] It is important to note that Christian fundamentalism is by no means monochrome. It too is on a continuum with some versions more willing to engage with contemporary scholarship than others. Complicating things

scholarship that contradicts its understandably treasured beliefs. It is reactive rather than proactive. It is defensive rather than inquisitive. Its most characteristic affirmation is: 'If the Bible says x, then God says x'. If so-called experts or intellectuals say otherwise, they are wrong. Fundamentalists, despite their admirable passion for God, are often critically unaware of the philosophical and cultural influences that have shaped their distinctively modern (as opposed to premodern or postmodern) approach to Christian faith.

Evangelicalism is an essentially unstable position simultaneously pulled in the direction of fundamentalisms to its right and liberalisms to its left. It is unstable because it retains a fundamentalist hermeneutic while being variously committed to scholarly excellence and to accepting adequately supported scholarly conclusions. One interesting result of this is Sydney Anglicanism's lack of support for Creation Science, its jettisoning of a literalistic reading of Genesis 1-3. Sydney Anglicanism is a liberal-fundamentalist hybrid. It doesn't quite know what it is. It may be that this internal tension has contributed to efforts to define itself over against liberalism, helping to create an unhealthily defensive culture.

Working at Green Square and in the Parish of South Sydney had me one or two steps removed from this emerging culture, although I was aware of its impact. Back in 2001 when Peter Jensen became Sydney's latest archbishop, I was still at Moore College and was there to welcome and congratulate the winner of what had been an acrimonious electing Synod. Peter came into the auditorium of the college with the faculty and students standing to cheer him in. It was an historic moment, and I, like everyone there, was thrilled for Peter and impressed by his humble and statesman-like demeanour. He was the winner, but he avoided any expression of hubris and was quick to say that this was not something he had sought and to ask for our prayers.

---

further is the fact that most fundamentalists would also describe themselves as evangelical, but not all evangelicals would describe themselves as fundamentalist. Peter Jensen, for example, is not willing to accept the label of fundamentalist, in part because of negative associations that have attracted to that term, in part because Peter is more open to critical scholarship than are many fundamentalists.

It felt like a new era was beginning, and it was. Peter very quickly set a vision for his archbishopric; the conversion within ten years of 10 per cent of Sydney into Bible-believing churches.[127] There was, even in this, an implied critique of liberal Christianity, as well as a not-too-subtle hint of a fundamentalist-like exclusion of those not deemed to be acceptably biblical.[128] Nevertheless, there was an undeniable sense of excitement and new purpose. Peter began his episcopate by organizing a Billy Graham-like rally at a stadium recently built for the Sydney Olympics. People who didn't attend the event had the chance to watch a packaged version of the presentation at churches throughout the diocese on an adjoining Sunday.

I, like many others, wanted to believe that Peter would be a great archbishop; that he would grow in the job, as, no doubt he has; that he would become more accommodating of differences and would benefit from inevitably greater contact with leaders of different theological and faith traditions. That probably has happened as well. However, in the early years of his episcopate, Peter oversaw a gradual, but real tightening of theological and ecclesiological boundaries. It became harder for clergy from outside of the diocese to secure positions within the diocese. It became a requirement for all but a few exceptional cases that clergy be trained, or at least do some of their training, at Moore Theological College. Ordination candidates appeared to be more carefully scrutinized with new efforts to tighten doctrinal boundaries.[129] Phillip Jensen was handed responsibility for the

---

[127] It was an extraordinary vision entailing the conversion of 300,000 Sydneysiders into 'Bible-believing' churches.

[128] Excluded from the list of Bible-believing churches were Orthodox and Roman Catholic churches, as well as many or most Uniting churches.

[129] For example, a questionnaire was devised in 2005 or 2006 for third-year ordination candidates, which asked twenty-four questions covering subjects that went well beyond the five fundamentals identified by early fundamentalists. More than half of them were about subjects not included in the historic creeds of the Christian faith, and even those that were, asked for a level of belief specification that was not included in those creeds. There were questions on hell, on the nature of justification, on predestination, on the gifts of the Spirit, on divorce and remarriage, on the ordination of women, and on homosexuality. Prefacing the questionnaire was the observation that 'within our Diocese there is a degree of acceptable diversity in regard to various

training and development of ministers in 2003, becoming the Director of Ministry Training and Development.

I was kept reasonably up-to-date with what was happening in the diocese by John McIntyre, with him being a member of the Standing Committee. Moves were then under way to develop semi-formal links with evangelical church-plants on the New South Wales central coast and elsewhere around the State. Student ministries were being set up around the country patterned on the ministry pioneered at UNSW. From my then slightly removed vantage point, it felt as though the ethos I had encountered at St Matthias was spreading throughout the diocese and beyond. It worried me, but there was nothing much I could do to prevent it.

But that was about to change. 2005 and 2006 were to become pivotal years for me. 2005 was a simultaneously sad and happy year. It was sad because it was the year of Dad's slow decline and death. It was happy because my eldest son had fallen in love with a beautiful and talented Singaporean. It was my great pleasure to conduct their wedding back in Sydney, at St James, Croydon, his and our old church. The wedding occurred within days of Dad's funeral. Almost all of my family was able to attend both the funeral and the wedding. The most poignant moment for me was glancing across to my mum at one point in the wedding to get just a glimpse of her inner turmoil of grief and joy.

Disturbing Developments

2005 was also John and Jan McIntyre's last year in the Parish of South Sydney. After fifteen highly productive years as rector, John received a call from the Parish Nominators of St Johns, Darlinghurst. It is the job of Parish Nominators to go looking for a replacement minister if their rector

---

issues.' Immediately following is the statement: 'Other issues, by their very nature, will require greater unanimity and clarity of conviction.' There was no explicit indication of what those issues were. However, students would have been well aware of the views of those administering the instrument, giving them little room to move in without being justifiably nervous that their candidature might be jeopardized by too many alternative (to the party line) answers.

dies or retires or goes elsewhere, and Darlinghurst had become vacant. Darlinghurst parish adjoins South Sydney and is not dissimilar in its ethos. In all sorts of ways, it was (and is) a strategic parish, including within its boundaries the well-known inner-city suburb of Kings Cross. It was a high-profile and colourful parish with an obvious ministry to tourists, and a long-established ministry to prostitutes, junkies, and street kids. Bill Lawton had been rector there between 1989 and 1999.

John would have been great for Darlinghurst. He was eminently suited, overqualified even, with so much to give. He was evangelical by conviction and actions. His advocacy and concern for people on the margins was classically evangelical and classically Christian, but he had one major blemish. He supported the ordination of women to all levels of leadership in the church. Even in this, he was within the mainstream of evangelical scholarship worldwide, but it wasn't the view of those currently in power in the diocese. Almost certainly because of this, he was knocked back by the three diocesan representatives on the Presentation Board, all members of the powerful Anglican Church League.[130]

The reason given for John being knocked back was that he had 'no proven track record in growing a church.' Not only was this not true, it demonstrated a complete misunderstanding of the realities of inner-city life. It was also alarmingly revealing of a new obsession with 'bums on seats' to the detriment of other more balanced, and, for Redfern, appropriate models of church life and growth. By this criterion, the majority of ministers in Sydney wouldn't get a job or be able to move from one parish to the next.[131]

Fortunately for John, the Victorian Diocese of Gippsland was, at this time, looking to find and appoint a new bishop. Someone suggested John. He was at first considered to have an outside chance of being selected, but in interview went from being a rank outsider to the one chosen to be their next bishop, so impressive was he in interview, so impressive is he.

---

[130] More on the Anglican Church League in the pages that follow.
[131] Those chosen to follow John at South Sydney, or instead of John at Darlinghurst, have failed to grow their parishes numerically, and the diocese has lost one of its most talented ministers in John.

It was a thrill to see him honoured at his installation at St Paul's Anglican Cathedral in Melbourne in early February, 2006. It was a very special few days in Melbourne; special to join a large contingent from Redfern; special catching up with family and friends, some of whom I hadn't seen for years, including Maurice Betteridge, my first university chaplain.

Losing John and Jan was hard. We felt orphaned, but not dispirited. The pub discussion group, *Quest*, went from strength to strength. The congregations of the parish continued to grow at snail's pace.[132] Crossroads Aboriginal Fellowship continued to be pastored by the impressive and statesman-like Ray Minniecon. Ray is enormously talented. He is a gifted musician, an eloquent speaker, an uncompromising advocate, and an insightful thinker. He has a degree in theology from Murdoch University in Western Australia. He was (and still is) chairperson of the diocese's Indigenous Peoples Ministry Committee. John McIntyre had made enquiries about having Ray deaconed or priested. Ray himself had made enquiries. It was a pity that this wasn't followed through; that 200 plus years of paternalism wasn't set aside. It was an opportunity lost.

For Judy and me, 2006 was a year for waiting and for thinking what we might do next. I had been happy to work alongside John and Ray in the work of engaging our respective communities. But with John leaving, the big questions became what next and who next? Complicating matters was the fact that the parish had lost its right of nomination. It had fallen just under the required parish income level. This was not surprising given that many in the parish were on low incomes—a testament to the parish's ability to attract a mixture of people in what had been a working class and variously disadvantaged area. Finances had been steadily improving, however, so much so that the projection was that we would meet our income target by the end of 2006. We weren't quite there yet, however, and so, technically, the archbishop had the right to make an appointment himself—without consulting the parish at all. No doubt there could be circumstances where such an action should be taken, where parishes have become dysfunctional, for example. South Sydney was anything but.

---

[132] The Redfern congregation benefitted from the skilful and pastorally sensitive interim ministry of Rev. John Cashman, who, with his wife Robyn, fitted beautifully into the compassionate and inclusive ethos of the church.

Regional Bishop, Rob Forsyth, promised that the parish would be fully consulted in the process of selecting a replacement for John. This was appropriately respectful. I indicated that I was willing to be considered for the position; should this be what the parish wanted; should this be the archbishop's decision. I learnt at around this time that Peter was a notorious procrastinator. I hadn't realized this. Nor was I worried or impatient. There was enough to keep us busy.

Retrospect is a wonderful thing. There is much that we can see clearly from the vantage point of the present. I should have realized from the start that I had, at best, an outside chance of being appointed rector. I had for years been making unsettling noises. I had been forging unsettling friendships, with John McIntyre for example. I should have been more aware than I was of the politics that was so powerfully at work and had been for many years within the diocese. Right from its beginnings, Sydney Anglicanism has been theologically conservative. There have been times throughout its history when a more gentle and open evangelicalism has prevailed or, at least, has happily coexisted with more conservative or fundamentalist strains. When the Anglican Church League was formed, in 1909, it began as a party of comprehension. Although it was self-consciously evangelical, with an originating intent to preserve Sydney's evangelical heritage, it eschewed narrow or extreme expressions of evangelicalism, and had within its ranks those who were being gently pulled in a liberal direction, along with others of a more fundamentalist mindset.[133]

Throughout its early history, the Anglican Church League managed to accommodate differences, though with tension at times. These tensions came to a head in the early 1930s when more conservative elements succeeded in electing a similarly conservative missionary Bishop, Howard K. Mowll. An alternative and more liberal candidate had been proposed by the then Principal of Moore College, D. J. Davies, who was then president of the Anglican Church League. Supporting him was A. E. Talbot, dean of St Andrew's Cathedral and an ACL vice president. Sydney Diocese turned decisively in a conservative direction under the leadership of Howard Mowll, so much so that those in the diocese who were more open to contemporary scholarship felt sidelined.

---

[133] Stephen Judd & Ken Cable, *Sydney Anglicans,* (Sydney: AIO, 2000), 167.

In 1933, the Anglican Church League began a practice which continues to this day of putting out a 'how to vote' ticket after carefully selecting suitably committed evangelicals to stand for positions on diocesan committees. So successful did this practice become that the diocese came to be dominated by conservative elements. By 1936, less than 20 per cent of important decision-making positions in the diocese were held by non-conservatives, including a smattering of High and Broad Churchmen. Ten years earlier that figure had been over 40 per cent.[134]

Tension between liberal-leaning and conservative evangelicals led to the creation of a new party, the Anglican Fellowship.[135] Its aim was to encourage freedom of inquiry on the premise that new knowledge is a gift from God and doesn't need to be seen as a threat to his Word.[136] However, the creation of this Fellowship was considered threatening by conservatives who went on a recruitment drive to strengthen even further their dominance in Sydney. So successful were they that in 1938, a group of fifty clergy, or a quarter of all clergy within the diocese, wrote a long letter, 'The Memorial,' to Archbishop Mowll mildly protesting against the apparently relentless monochromisation of the diocese. The Memorialists asked to see Archbishop Mowll in person to discuss their concerns. He refused to see them, instead asking the newly appointed principal of Moore College, T. C. Hammond, to pen a letter in response. It was a brusque and uncompromising letter which effectively soured relations with these more liberal clergy, though hardly liberal by today's standards. In the years that followed, conservative or fundamentalist leaning clergy came to dominate the polity and theology of Sydney Diocese.

As I waited for Peter to decide the appointment, I knew nothing about the Memorialists. If I had known, it may have helped me understand the currents swirling around in the background to his delayed decision. Almost certainly, Peter saw himself as a custodian of the same conservative evangelicalism that had won out against more liberal versions back in the 1930s. He has been consistent in his anti-liberal rhetoric. He had certainly

---

[134] *Sydney Anglicans*, 237.
[135] In May 1933.
[136] *Sydney Anglicans*, 234.

been involved in all sorts of efforts to keep theological liberalism at bay, and about these I was aware.

Peter was a long-time member of the Anglican Church League, a body still committed to preserving the 'reformed, protestant and evangelical' character of Sydney Diocese. A friend of mine, who is something of a retrospective mole or fly-on-the-wall, has told me of ACL meetings punctuated by career assassinations effected ever so easily by a word or two from one or more of its esteemed members. People's progression within the diocese could be halted by even the suspicion of being Pentecostal, liberal, or feminist.

The Anglican Church League was not the only guardian of theological correctness. Back in the 1990s, a movement known as REPA,[137] sometimes dubbed 'the grim REPA,' burst onto the scene in response to the growing success of moves to ordain women as priests in Anglican dioceses across Australia.[138] REPA began as a call to 'revolution' by Phillip Jensen. After years of sitting on the sidelines of diocesan life, Phillip was stirred into action by what he regarded as flagrant disobedience to the plain teaching of the Scriptures. He enlisted a small band of trusted clergymen to join him in resisting liberalizing trends and in creating a new movement of evangelism and church growth. His co-combatants dubbed themselves 'colonels' in symbolic preparation for a battle to turn around the flagging fortunes of Anglican Churches around the nation. Their ambitious aim was to create a grass roots movement able to change the character and priorities of Australian Anglicanism.

REPA's vision was bold, even audacious. The appeal of joining a revolution must have been intoxicating, but, as with any revolution, there are inbuilt dangers and risks. Critical to the success of any revolution is that its participants have a clear idea of who they are and who their enemies are. There must be enemies, or, at least, rivals, and in the case of REPA that

---

[137] The Reformed Evangelical Protestant Association, formed in 1992.
[138] Anglicans from Sydney had previously attempted, unsuccessfully, to thwart efforts by other dioceses to ordain women as priests, even to the point of taking legal action. Those enlisted to join REPA began talk of secession from the national church.

was pretty much anyone who didn't share their particular understanding of the gospel and its implications. This necessary strength of REPA was also its great weakness. In so carefully defining itself against almost every other expression of Christian faith, it failed to recognise its own limitations and weaknesses, some of them created by the negativity of their opposition to rival versions of Christianity. Reactions easily become overreactions. In wanting to safeguard their faith from the excesses of Pentecostal enthusiasm, or from being distracted by the never-ending need for social justice, or from the uncertainties of those more liberal than themselves, they ended up with a truncated form of the faith. Though it claimed to be Reformed, Evangelical, and Protestant, REPA was only selectively so. In cherry-picking just those features of its heritage it was comfortable with, REPA could rightly be accused of being unhealthily individualistic,[139] rationalistic,[140] and other-worldly[141] in its understanding of Christianity. Theirs was by no means the only or best way to be Christian.

Another of REPA's weaknesses was its treatment of its enemies. One way to treat enemies is to seek to turn them into friends by way of respectful and loving engagement, in line with how Jesus said we should treat our enemies. It might not be the most efficient way. It does not always 'work',

---

[139] Missing, or seriously lacking, from this stream of Sydney Anglicanism was a corporate or communitarian dimension—illustrated by an individualistic approach to evangelism, with foot soldiers being endlessly trained to recruit more soldiers whose primary task would be to recruit more soldiers. Church and small group gatherings were little more than recruitment and training grounds. It was also illustrated in a fundamentalist-like fixation on issues of personal morality to the detriment of issues of social, global, or environmental responsibility.

[140] Converts to REPA style evangelicalism are typically encouraged to ever increase their knowledge of the Bible, through attending studies and listening to sermons, the most useful of which are long and filled with content. Also critical to this style is that people have the right beliefs. What one believes, on a whole range of subjects, is deemed more important than what one does.

[141] One of REPA's 'colonels' recently told me that his particular strain of Sydney Anglicanism was defined by its passion to save people from hell and for heaven. This was what their mission was all about. Anything that distracted from that central task was suspect.

and it wasn't the way that REPA chose. I wasn't aware at the time, but was informed years later, of REPA's strategy of cleansing the boards of non-diocesan organizations by stealth to make them more acceptable to the dominant Sydney ethos—and of the dubiously ethical 'success' of this strategy in the boards of New College (UNSW), Robert Menzies College (Macquarie University), and in organizations such as Scripture Union and the Australian Fellowship of Evangelical Students.

I was aware of other impacts of the REPA way, including the sidelining of people not considered safe or sufficiently similar. Included among those so sidelined were people once highly regarded in the diocese who, for a range of reasons, were not comfortable to sign up to the revolution. Some followed their consciences by admitting to variations of belief, often arrived at through scrupulous, even courageous scholarship, and have now vanished from sight. One of the most telling examples of this is the growing list of former Moore College lecturers no longer considered kosher. Included in this list are Mark Harding,[142] Graham Cole,[143] Bill Lawton,[144] and Bill Dumbrell.[145]

REPA didn't last long, only for a couple of years. Its final organisational act was to throw its weight behind the unsuccessful push to elect Phillip

---

[142] Mark is the current dean of the Australian College of Theology. After a brief stint of lecturing at Moore College, he spent four years completing doctoral studies at Princeton Theological Seminary in the United States before being told there was no position for him back on the faculty of Moore, the reason being that he had come to the opinion that the Pastoral Epistles might not have been written by St Paul.

[143] Despite Graham's scholarly stature and impeccable evangelical credentials, he has not once been invited back to Moore College to speak. There is little to no doubt about the reason for this: he has come to a different conclusion about women's ordination than have the diocese's powerbrokers.

[144] Bill Lawton has occasionally been asked to lecture at Moore College, but his well-known support for women's ordination and more radical causes have thoroughly marginalized him.

[145] Bill Dumbrell has similarly vanished from diocesan sight. He has come under suspicion for having views which resemble the views of one of the world's leading evangelical, N. T. Wright.

Jensen as archbishop (1992-93). Its ghost lived on in the sometimes nasty white-anting of Harry Goodhew's archbishopric (1993-2001), and in the relentless mainstreaming of what came to be described as 'hard' evangelicalism.[146]

In waiting for Peter to make up his mind, I received, in July of 2006, an unexpected phone call from Richard Grellman, then chairman of the Board of Mission Australia. He rang to sound me out about the possibility of becoming Bill Lawton's replacement as National Chaplain of that organization. Mission Australia is a large, not-for-profit, non-denominational Christian charity with staff of between 3,500 and 4,000 scattered across Australia. I didn't know too much about Mission Australia, but was intrigued by the offer to consider.[147] The thought of doing something new and different has always been attractive. The chance to work for an organisation committed to a practical and compassionate expression of Christian faith was appealing.

The more I thought about it, the more inclined I was to at least be interviewed for the job. I got in touch with Peter to let him know of my need to decide one way or the other. I needed to know what his intentions were. He said he would think and pray about it, but also mentioned that he still hadn't made up his mind whether to appoint me or not.

As the time came for me to make my decision, Judy and I were on our way by car to visit some good friends of ours. Peter rang me to say he wasn't able to make a decision by the time I required. I immediately burst into tears, unexpectedly. I surprised myself (and Judy) by the strength of my reaction. It wasn't something I would have anticipated or, even now, can fully understand.

---

[146] This was the self-designation of the movement itself, employed as a way of differentiating itself from 'softer' forms of evangelicalism, for example, evangelicalisms committed to social justice.

[147] I had been working as a chaplain with *WorkVentures*, a much smaller faith-based charity, for a number of years already, one day a week, and loved the work.

Not too long after this career-changing decision (or non-decision) by Peter, a friend of mine was told in hushed tones by Phillip Jensen that the reason I had not been offered South Sydney was that I was 'unsound'. This was disturbing to hear, because I had been told nothing of the sort. I was also perplexed, and a bit angry to hear this in so roundabout a way. I can remember being slightly amused. It was a new thought that I might be 'unsound.' I had, it is true, been exploring the possibility of a new hermeneutic, but this, in itself, could hardly be the sensible basis for a verdict of unsoundness, even if the implications of any such hermeneutic might be alarming or discomforting. My explorations were just that, explorations, carried out openly and in the company of others, including a bishop and three or four Moore College faculty. It seemed strange, even bizarre, to hear this description of me, especially coming the way it did, accidentally and without elaboration or explanation. At the time, I shrugged it off, though it did contribute to feelings of hurt I was already experiencing in the aftermath of Peter's phone call. Looking back, I am sure that all sorts of emotions deeply associated with my own recently deceased father had been aroused. I was upset more than I thought I would be. Peter must have been taken aback by the emotion of that call. He didn't seem uncaring.

Judy sometimes jokes with people that if I am down or depressed for more than a day, she considers calling a doctor. It doesn't happen very often. Our friends, to whose house we were travelling, were wonderfully supportive and understanding. They were a godsend that afternoon. But I did bounce back. In retrospect, I would not be at all surprised to find that Peter had wrestled long and hard in trying to make up his mind about South Sydney and about whether to offer me the job. Without a doubt there were factors pulling in both directions. A lifetime of trying to protect the diocese from any move whatsoever in a liberal direction would have certainly pulled him in the direction of being cautious, especially given the noises I had been making for as long as he had known me. Pulling in the other direction, I guess, was his knowledge of me and of the effort I had put in to grow a church at Beaconsfield. I respect the fact that he couldn't come to a decision in the time required.

I said yes to Richard Grellman of Mission Australia, yes to being considered for the job of National Chaplain. I did feel some relief at knowing that one door was closed and another was opening. I was called in for an interview with the Mission Australia Board, was offered the job, and began work part-time while wrapping up responsibilities at South Sydney.[148]

Needing to Speak Up

The transition to a new stage of life would have gone smoothly had it not been for some further disturbing developments within the parish I was soon to leave. Not too long after I made my decision to accept the Mission Australia offer, the parish was informed that Peter had someone in mind for the job, Rev. Paul Dew. I knew Paul and his wife Heather from our time as students. They had been at But Har Gra when we arrived there in 1982. Paul was, and still is, a straight-talking former agronomist. He was NSW State Secretary of the Bush Church Aid with pastoral experience in the Armidale and Grafton Dioceses. He also had experience working with Indigenous Australians.

Rob Forsyth and Paul organized a meeting with the Parish Nominators and a number of other representatives from the three congregations. It was a fairly last-minute arrangement, and Ray Minniecon wasn't able to attend. He was away in Switzerland at an Indigenous Peoples' Conference. No one else from Crossroads Aboriginal Fellowship could make it that night. At the time, this didn't appear to be a major problem. Full consultation had been promised. There would surely be time for more meetings and enquiries.

There wasn't. Within two days of this one and only meeting, Rob Forsyth phoned the President of the Nominators to inform him that a letter of invitation would be sent to Paul Dew inviting him to become rector of South Sydney. Neither Rob nor the archbishop asked for the opinions of those who had attended that night. No view was sought as to whether they believed Paul was suitable or not. These parish representatives had only just begun to ask that question.

Dismayed by this sudden decision, the nominators wrote to Peter asking to be given more time. They received no reply. I myself wrote to the archbishop asking for an extension of time. I also received no reply. Paul

---

[148] I began work with Mission Australia in July 2006, and was formally commissioned on 27 September.

was asked to delay acceptance, but decided he wouldn't. The parish as a whole was rocked by this development. It felt like a betrayal. In the swirl of emotions which followed, I learned of a further act of disrespect, this time involving Pastor Ray Minniecon. That Ray had not been consulted before Paul's appointment was disrespectful in the extreme. That he wasn't even asked his opinion was mystifying. But this wasn't the only time that one of Australia's most able Indigenous leaders wasn't consulted. Earlier in this same year, four new appointments were made to the diocese's Indigenous People's Ministry Committee. Ray was its chairperson. He wasn't consulted, merely informed of who they were; four new non-Indigenous members, appointed by Peter,[149] imposed without consultation.

It is hard to remember emotions from the past. I do know that I was angry on hearing of this high-handed action. At the time, I was still a member of the South Sydney Regional Council and was coming up to what would be my last meeting on that council. I felt I needed to speak, and did, in words charged with emotion as I remember. Members of the Regional Council were supportive and sympathetic. Archdeacon Deryck Howell described the treatment of Ray Minniecon as 'inexcusable.'

In the days that followed, nothing appeared to be resolved. There were no phone calls or meetings of explanation, no apologies, just that lingering feeling of being disrespected. We did hear from some well-connected sources that consultation was no longer valued by those now making decisions in the diocese, that consultation was viewed as counterproductive because it raised unrealistic expectations, that the best thing to do was just to act, and, over time, the protests would dissipate. I wondered if that was the policy being pursued here. Someone had even cynically suggested that it was easier to act and apologize later than to consult. What was galling, for all concerned, was the lack of respectful engagement.

An Open Letter

I can't exactly remember the process of my thinking or how I came up with the idea of writing an Open Letter, but I do remember deciding that I would need to write to the Standing Committee of the diocese. This was the least

---

[149] Deryck Howell, Ken Allen, Greg Anderson, and David Woodbridge.

I could do to fulfil my continuing pastoral responsibilities to the people of South Sydney, not just to its church people, but to the wider community who were similarly incensed by the way the parish had been treated. But I also realized that a letter to the Standing Committee was almost certain to be disregarded. It would probably just be noted and buried. What also was playing on my mind was that the culture of the diocese was continuing to run in entirely the wrong direction, and not just in my opinion. Scores of conversations that I had had with people at every level of influence within the diocese confirmed widespread disquiet and even alarm.

How does one change a culture? Not easily. Not by simply writing a letter. Somehow and somewhere along the line as I began to compose my letter to Standing Committee, I decided to make it an Open Letter. I would write on behalf of those many people who were concerned about the diocese and where it was headed. I also wanted to test the waters. Maybe I was talking to all the wrong people. Maybe my perspective was so biased by my own experiences and family background that I was an unreliable critic of what I was observing. I didn't think so, but this was a way to find out.

I was aware that within a few months I would not be able to pursue this course of action. By the beginning of 2007, I would be in the full-time employ of Mission Australia. I would no longer be acting rector of South Sydney. I had already ceased teaching at Moore College. I knew that if I was to speak up in this way, I would need to do it then. And so, with the invaluable help of a small group of trusted friends, I began to pen the letter (Appendix 1). It went through a dozen or more drafts. The letter, when it was finished, was a version of the letter I had sent to Peter Jensen three years earlier. It also included an account of what had happened at South Sydney. The details of this were never contested.

At the same time that the letter was sent for consideration by Standing Committee, it was also sent out as an Open Letter. I sent it to people on my own mailing list. It was deliberately not sent only to those likely to agree with me.[150] It was sent to people who had connections to the Sydney

---

[150] I encouraged people to distribute it not just to those who were likely to agree with me. Within a very short time, it travelled widely enough to give people of all persuasions a chance to read it.

Anglican Church, either because they still attended Anglican Churches in Sydney or had done. It was important to find out what Sydney Anglicans thought about their church. It would also be useful to find out the views of those looking on, people attending other churches or none. Making it an Open Letter meant that the city of Sydney could express its views on its Anglican Church. In chatting with Rob Forsyth just after the Open Letter was sent, he made the quite valid point that the wider Sydney community had every right to inspect what is an essentially public institution. A church seeking to commend itself to the wider community needs to be transparent and open to critique.

What I wasn't prepared for was the strength, breadth, and depth of the response. Within days of the letter going out, it had travelled around the world, literally. Responses began to pour in from Africa, the United States, and the UK, from within Sydney and around Australia. The letter went out on Thursday night, November 30. On Saturday, three people attending an ordination service in Bathurst had independently read the letter. That was the speed of internet connections. I was suddenly inundated with emails, all of which I attempted to answer; many of which began dialogues that continued well into the months ahead. I was amazed and humbled. It seemed I had hit a nerve.

December 2006 was an unusually busy time in the Mascord house, all because of me. We went on a pre-Christmas holiday to Nelson Bay. It was a great holiday to a great holiday location, but the family had to cope with a distracted father and husband, who was given increasingly strict rules about when and for how long he could access the continuing flood of emails. By the time the flood subsided to a trickle, and then petered out, I had received emails, letters, and phone calls from well over 300 people.[151] Over 100 of Sydney's Anglican clergy and over 150 of its lay people responded. Most, from within or outside of the diocese, were supportive of the letter's call for a more loving, humble, and open diocese.[152]

---

[151] I ended up having to put a cap on the process, alerting people to not send emails after 10 February 2007, except for the purpose of ongoing dialogue. Up until that date, I received 137,000 words of reply and comment.

[152] I kept a rough tally of emails, letters, and phone calls in response to the Open Letter until they petered out in mid-2007. Within Sydney, respondees

In the months and years following these frenetic few weeks, people often suggested that what I did was brave. They also suggested or assumed I must have been damaged or hurt as a result of the action I took. The truth is I never felt brave, or the need to be brave. At the time, it was just something I knew I had to and could do. Lots of people had protested before, in many cases only to be dismissed as uninformed outsiders or disgruntled insiders with some axe to grind. I wasn't so dismissed, certainly by those who knew me. I was still lecturing at Moore College within months of this action and had been for fifteen years.[153] I was as well-connected as most within diocesan inner circles. I could therefore speak with some authenticity and insider knowledge.

As to whether I was damaged or hurt as a result of speaking up, I don't believe I was. It did damage some relationships, my relationship with Peter Jensen, for example. I met with Peter not long after the letter had gone to Standing Committee. It wasn't the warmest or most cordial of meetings, but I could understand him feeling hurt and, perhaps, misunderstood.[154] I had certainly been critical, and publicly critical of him and his brother. I also met with Phillip. Although less strained, it also felt less real, perhaps a measure of the distance we already were from each other, in almost every way.

One or two other relationships were negatively affected by my action, but by far the greatest challenge I faced in the aftermath of the letter was the temptation to feel proud or vindicated. The support was overwhelmingly positive, with people from every level of the diocese confiding in me,

---

included 9 senior clergy (archdeacon or above), 92 clergy, 16 present and former Moore College lecturers (12 of these included in the clergy list), and 175 lay people; with the total number reaching 276. Outside of the Sydney Diocese, respondees included 3 senior clergy, 27 clergy, and 26 lay people. All up 332 people, by my rough, but fairly close reckoning, responded to the letter. All but a handful expressed support for the letter's call.

[153] I had decided to have a break from teaching, to devote myself fully to the new job at Mission Australia. I left Moore College on good terms and continue to be on good terms with its faculty.

[154] I have caught up with Peter again in more recent times, at Peter's initiative. Neither of us holds a grudge against the other. We both desire a renewal and strengthening of fellowship.

some giving strict instructions that I not reveal their identity or share their stories. Very quickly, I began to feel a growing sense of responsibility to do something about what was being told to me. I felt I now had an even bigger responsibility to give voice to those who felt they had no voice, or whose voices had been silenced. I didn't know what to do or how to go about this. Within a month or two of sending the letter, I would be beginning a new and demanding job at Mission Australia. What could I do with so many expressions of heartfelt longing for a better way of being Christian?

Realizing that I was not competent to assess the meaning of these letters, I decided to go looking for some people who might be. I realized there were likely to be legal issues involved. There were sociological and psychological dimensions to what was occurring, as well as theological. There were human resources issues, and a long diocesan history to take into account. The idea emerged that a small band of people with relevant expertise be asked to read through the letters of those willing to have their letters read, and to each write a report. I went looking to find the right people and the right balance of people—with much good advice about who to ask. Five highly qualified and suitably dissimilar people accepted the invitation to join this group: Dr Alan Craddock,[155] Canon Dr Robert Withycombe,[156] Michele Adair,[157] Rev. Dr Bill Salier,[158] and Louise Greentree.[159]

I was thrilled to have so competent and experienced a team. They were not all on the same page theologically, but they did share broadly similar convictions and faith. They were not all Sydney Anglicans, but they knew

---

[155] Alan was a senior lecturer in Psychology at the University of Sydney and a former, part-time lecturer in Pastoral Psychology at Moore Theological College.
[156] Robert was a lecturer in Church History and Historical Theology at Charles Sturt University's School of Theology. He was dean of Students at Moore College in the early seventies.
[157] Michele is a specialist in organizational development and HR.
[158] Bill had recently been appointed vice principal of Moore Theological College and taught in the New Testament and Ministry Departments
[159] Louise was a lawyer and lecturer in the Faculty of Law at UTS. At that time, she was doing Ph.D. studies on conflict resolution processes in the Anglican Church of Australia.

Sydney Anglicanism well, or well enough.[160] The Standing Committee of the diocese had met on 11 December 2006. They too chose a competent mix of representatives to consider the concerns I had raised. What was gratifying at the time was the seriousness with which the letter was treated. Standing Committee already had a busy pre-Christmas agenda, but chose to take time to discuss the letter and its contents. The concerns were deemed serious enough for a sub-committee to be appointed comprising Bishop Glenn Davies, Dr Greg Clarke, Mrs Claire Smith, and Rev. Dr John Woodhouse. I met briefly with this group on 18 December and then again almost eight months later when reports by the other group had been finalized.[161] I also wrote a report in the form of a second Open Letter (Appendix 2). It too was sent to Standing Committee and fed into my discussions with the sub-committee.

We met twice for seven hours in total. They weren't easy meetings by any means. At times, I became quite emotional. I felt the weight of representing people's concerns fairly and accurately. I felt under pressure to justify my own concerns and actions. The group had agreed for me to bring Rev. Geoff Broughton, then rector of St John's Glebe, to be a non-participatory witness. Geoff's presence and wise reflections afterwards were hugely helpful. The meetings were held at the home of John Woodhouse, principal of Moore College. I got the impression that John had taken very personally my criticisms of the diocese and of Phillip and Peter in particular. John was a close friend of both. He attended church at St Andrew's Cathedral where Phillip was dean. He owed his principalship to Peter. I cannot remember him acknowledging the accuracy or fairness of any of the criticisms I had raised. No doubt he agreed with me on at least some points. He simply could not see, or was unwilling to admit, the legitimacy of my call for a change of culture. Probably, he was too close to it, too much a part of it, too closely aligned to those who were creating it.[162]

---

[160] Michele Adair had had the least experience with Sydney Anglicanism, but even this relative inexperience was valuable because she could bring the fresh perspective of someone not already enculturated into ways of being and believing characteristic of Sydney Anglicans.

[162] Some time after the Open Letter process was completed, I was interested and heartened to read an article by John in the Sydney Diocesan Newspaper,

It made me reflect again on how un-objective we all are. We all observe life through coloured glasses, glasses tinted by a host of factors, including personality, culture, theology, philosophy, and sociology. We are sometimes blind to what others see clearly. I struggled throughout each of the seven hours to try to understand where John was coming from, to be as generous as I could to his perspective; to see things from his point of view. I hope he did likewise. The other members of the group I knew much better. Greg Clarke I count as a friend. For as long as I have known him, I have respected Greg as someone able to look at things through other people's eyes. Bishop Glenn Davies I have long admired as a person of generous heart and sharp intellect. I knew him as a colleague at Moore College. On first reading the Open Letter, it struck Glenn as being visceral, and he told me so, though he had to explain what visceral meant.[163] Clare Smith I knew from college days. She may have done a course or two of mine. She is married to Rob Smith, brother of my current pastor, Rev. Dave Smith. I did not feel I was among enemies. I was listened to.

After our two long and sometimes harrowing meetings, the sub-committee co-wrote a report which it presented to the 15 October 2007 meeting of Standing Committee. It came up with two recommendations. The first encouraged the archbishop to take steps to encourage better standards of personal behaviour by clergy and church workers. I wasn't altogether sure what that meant, although it was interesting that it targeted personal

---

Southern Cross, in which he encouraged his readers to express their differences of opinion. He also discouraged the silencing of alternative opinions, and, interestingly, noted one way in which this might happen: 'Disagreement can be silenced through the power of personalities. In the extreme you end up with a cult. One of the marks of a cult is that disagreement with the leadership is not tolerated.' Whether or not John had in mind his friends Phillip and Peter, what he wrote was certainly similar to the concerns of the Open Letter. The article, entitled, 'Healthy Disagreements' was published in the March 2010 edition of *Southern Cross.*

[163] The word visceral derives from the word viscera, which is the soft internal organs of the body. Something is described as visceral if it appears to come from deep within, from one's deep inner feelings.

morality rather than issues of corporate culture.[164] The second recommended an exploration of the adequacy of grievance procedures, again in the areas of pastoral and personal relationships.[165] At the time and since, I have wondered whether both recommendations imply, or could be read as implying, a critique of my own chosen method of expressing grievance. Perhaps that was an intention. Alternatively, these steps may have been seen as a small, but significant step towards giving people permission and encouragement to pursue legitimate grievances.

As the Open Letter process finally ground to a halt, it was hard to judge how effective it was in changing or even putting a dent in the culture I had observed develop. I had no way of knowing. Neither Peter nor Phillip nor John gave even the tiniest of hints that there would be any change of direction, nor that they felt the need for any such change. That was disappointing, though not unexpected. It seemed that the Open Letter was little more than a shot fired over the bow of a ship sailing full throttle in its already chosen direction. These were relatively early days, with optimism still present in the ranks of the sailors. The ship wasn't going to be turning around any time soon.

But another analogy occurred to me some time after writing the letter. A few years ago, South Sydney rugby league team had all but been obliterated. South Sydney was a foundation club of the New South Wales Rugby League. When I arrived from Canada as an eleven-year-old, South Sydney was winning premierships, reviving earlier glory days. Its theme song begins, 'Glory, glory to South Sydney'. But the glory began to fade as new money and new clubs began to erode this proud club's winning heritage, and the

---

[164] The full text of recommendation 1: That Standing Committee encourage the Archbishop to take steps to raise the profile of the standards of personal behaviour and conduct in pastoral relationships required of all clergy and other church workers in the Diocese, outlined in the *Faithfulness in Service* code (Second Edition, 2006), particularly sections 4 and 6.

[165] The full text of recommendation 2: That Standing Committee request the Safe Ministry Board to report (with recommendations) on the adequacy of grievance procedures in the area of pastoral relationships and personal behaviour covered by sections 4 and 6 of Faithfulness in Service (Second Edition, 2006), with reference to procedures outlined in section 3.

club fell onto hard times. Its supporter base was shrinking, crowds were down. Its football team wasn't winning. So low did things get that South Sydney was cut from the premiership with prospects of languishing forever in the second division. This would have happened had not the supporter base rallied, had not two very rich benefactors come along to put the club back onto a sound financial base. High-profile Australian actor, Russell Crowe, teamed up with *Peter Holmes à Court* to build a new culture while simultaneously drawing on the club's long and proud heritage.

The South Sydney rugby league experience was not dissimilar to Peter Jensen's archbishopric. Peter came into his position as CEO and head coach of the diocese with long experience and undoubted skills, particularly as a motivational speaker. He was well-resourced monetarily.[166] He had a vision for the club, a vision to restore it to its former glory, to begin again to instil a winning culture, to bring back the crowds, to increase its supporter base, then sitting at about 2 per cent of Sydney. His audacious vision was to sign up 10 per cent of Sydneysiders to make the club sustainable into the future. He had a great sense of occasion, launching his tenure with a rally and media fanfare. He gathered around him a coaching team of trusted and high-performing friends and family, including his brother, who had excelled as a junior coach. He bypassed, demoted, or transferred coaches considered unorthodox or too risky. The Town Hall was hired out to conduct graduations for new coaches with the confident expectation that graduating classes would get ever bigger. There was, in this, a hint of pride, but the vision was attractive and the new leadership was single-minded. There was a strong sense of history, with people being reminded of the club's long and distinguished heritage, a heritage that had been forged on the anvil of efforts to destroy it or to bad-mouth it, or to bring in new ideas that would certainly undermine it. There was as much need for vigilance and nerve-holding now as at any other time. The club was under threat. It hadn't been performing well. It had become soft and complacent. The new

---

[166] An aggressive investment policy begun in the year after Peter became archbishop swelled the coffers of the Diocesan Endowment Fund with net assets growing to $265 million. The 'club' was already rich as a result of the development and sale of glebe lands supplied to the church by the early colonial government.

coaching staff was being trained to be single-minded, to coax, cajole, and, where necessary, berate the club's underperforming teams.

This vision needed true-believers, lots of them, for it to fly and to flourish. It certainly didn't need one of its former coaches to publically call the vision into question, or to point out that lots of club members, maybe even the majority, weren't on board with it, or that the people of Sydney were unlikely to be attracted by it. Understandably, this would have seemed like disloyalty to the club and its heritage. Perhaps it was, but I wrote the Open Letter because I felt that the club's new management was trying to remain true to one of the less helpful aspects of the club's long history, an aspect that is both defensive and backward looking. There are other and better impulses, including one of similar vintage, to a softer and more open evangelicalism. It seemed to me that giving vent to this earlier impulse would have more chance of being successful in reviving the flagging fortunes of the Sydney Anglican club.

So, as 2007 came towards its end, I wasn't sure whether or to what extent the Open Letter had had an impact. Though optimistic by nature, I was pretty sure it hadn't done much more than to create a splash and soon-to-subside ripple. It didn't begin a movement. Nor was that its purpose. I did become more aware of *Anglicans Together*, a loosely constituted organization of Anglicans in Sydney devoted to a more inclusive and diverse form of Anglicanism than was the norm in Sydney.[167] I warmed to its vision and to its membership. I became a member myself. *Anglicans Together* could well become a strong alternative to the *Anglican Church League*. Perhaps a better way forward would be for all parties to set aside the politics of suspicion and polarization, and seek to promote people of talent, faith, and good will to positions of influence within the diocese. It is a not impossible vision.

---

[167] Anglicans Together was formed just after the formation of REPA, and in partial response. A meeting was called of Sydney Diocesan synod representatives and held at the Chapter House on 10 April 1992. Its purpose was to form an organisation or network of Sydney Anglicans committed to expressing the comprehensive character of the Anglican tradition. One of the aims of the organisation, as articulated at that first meeting, was 'to encourage an open exchange of ideas and views on matters concerning or affecting the Church and its ministry.' See further, *Anglicans Together Newsletter*, Number 44, March 2011, 1-2.

Chapter 8

Vocational Bumps

The roller coaster of emotions we had ridden as a family for the final months of 2006 eventually came to relative rest in 2007. The new year bristled with possibilities. A new phase of our lives had begun. I had always been energized by fresh starts, from my first trans-Pacific voyage in 1960 and for each of the many journeys that would follow. But there was something different about this move. The air into which I was moving seemed clearer, the waters ahead less turbulent.

I had left full-time teaching at Moore College five years earlier to develop a hermeneutic, a way of reading the Scriptures that would be intellectually and personally satisfying. I wanted to bring mind and heart together; to find a way of integrating thought and feeling, theory and practice. By early 2007, I had substantially achieved that goal. I also left Moore College with a desire to re-ignite my faith in the context of grass roots ministry. I had made some progress in this, but still felt I had a way to go. The language of faith I had grown up with, and the pieties that clustered around that way of believing, no longer made sense to me. I needed a new piety, a new way of being Christian.

For most of my life, and certainly for the previous ten years or so, I had deliberately stood at some distance from the God and Christ of my upbringing. My faith had been like a specimen to inspect and to put under the microscope of scholarly investigation. About the only spirituality I possessed was my lifelong quest to know and to understand. This did still energize me, but at a deeper level, my spirit was parched.

Spiritual food wasn't long in coming. On an early Sunday in January 2007, Judy and I drove from our newly rented home in Strathfield to Holy Trinity Anglican Church in Dulwich Hill. Both suburbs are in the inner west of Sydney. We were hoping this might be our new church. On the day we arrived, there was a baptism, which made the service longer than normal. The way church happens at Holy Trinity is an engaging mix of formality and informality. Every aspect of the service has its own integrity and feel. The Lord's Supper or Eucharist is celebrated every Sunday, and so it was on this first Sunday. Nothing at all was shortened to accommodate the baptism, but strangely the service didn't seem to drag. I found myself drawn in to what seemed more like a slice of life than a church service. There were children, lots of them, and a children's song to make them feel included. The music was amazing. Holy Trinity boasted an impressive array of musical talent. The music director was a classical singer. Her husband was a bassoonist with the Sydney Symphony Orchestra,[168] but normally played saxophone at Holy Trinity. Angela, the wife of Dave Smith, has the voice of an angel. She often leads the singing, and did so on our first day there.

Music has a way of ministering to one's heart and soul. If it wasn't on my first Sunday, it often happened that I would find myself quietly in tears, as this or that song spoke to the inner recesses of my sometimes troubled consciousness. What also ministered to me on that first day, and in the days to come, was Dave Smith's preaching. His father, Bruce Smith, was one of Sydney Anglicanism's best preachers. Bruce's ability to paint pictures, to evoke emotion, and to engender insight through words was legendary. His son has his father's gift, though with a more earthy and streetwise flavour. Dave mostly preaches from the Gospel reading for the day, and that too ministered to my needs. Without doubt, it was Jesus who was keeping me in Christian faith, and not only because of his challenging and graceful theology, but also because of his unerring ability to see through and throw off the shackles of any theology or practice that diminished the humanity of those under its sway. Jesus was as good a debunker and destroyer as he was a builder and restorer.

Dave has the ability, week after week, of getting to the heart of the passages he would tackle. And he doesn't preach for long, seldom for more than

---

[168] The church boasts another professional bassoonist.

fifteen minutes. The service moves on into prayer and the sung Eucharist. On our first Sunday, we paused for the baptism and shared the greeting of peace. Judy and I were warmly welcomed, though not with any presumption that we would stay. Newcomers are not gushed over, but are given the space to stay or go. Many do come and go, but from that first Sunday, I wanted to stay. I knew that I would love being part of this church, and I do.

There were some other places where I could begin to find a new spirituality, a new way of being Christian. One of those places was among my new colleagues at Mission Australia. Matching the warm welcome Judy and I felt at Holy Trinity was the warm welcome offered by Mission Australia's chaplains, all seven of them. Early on in our working relationship, we withdrew to a quiet rural location for a two-three-day retreat. The team was all male at that stage, not for ideological reasons, and only temporarily, but apart from gender and a shared Christian faith, the group was highly and refreshingly diverse. There were two Anglicans, with me making three. There was a Baptist, an Independent, formerly Brethren, a Seventh-Day Adventist, a Roman Catholic, a Pentecostal, and a Churches of Christ former pastor. Theologically and liturgically, the group lay at both ends and at various points along the spectrum between fundamentalism and liberalism. One had even flirted with the death of God movement, which made a brief splash on the theological horizon from the mid-1960s.[169] Another had been liberated from his former fundamentalism by the often insightful questioning of the provocative Episcopalian Bishop John Selby Spong.

Had I joined this group twenty, or even ten years earlier, my theological alarm bells would have been ringing wildly, but they didn't ring at all on this weekend. I had become more aware of why people choose to live at various points along the theological spectrum. I myself had inhabited

---

[169] This short-lived, but arguably significant movement drew attention to the increasingly successful reach of non-theistic explanations of the universe and of all that happens within it. It was Nietzsche who coined the phrase 'God is dead.' The question exercising theologians such as Thomas J. J. Altizer, William Hamilton, and Paul Van Buren was: is there any useful place left for explanations of events that invoke the agency of a transcendent being? Naturalistic explanations appear to be more than adequate.

a succession of theological dwellings, mostly very similar, but different enough to cure me of any notion that these places of rest were anything but temporary and provisional. I was now keen to inspect even more of those dwellings, to see what views they offered of realities I knew would always elude the grasp of human conceptualities. I was instantly at home and made to feel at home in this new-to-me team of chaplains.

The retreat was spiritually refreshing. Dominic Arcamone, an ex-Roman Catholic priest, was chef for the weekend, and what an expert chef he was. We ate and played, walked, talked, and prayed together, beginning the delightful process of getting to know each other. What so impressed me about this group, right from the start, was that no one put pressure on anyone else to think or to be any different to the way they were. We all had strong and well thought out views, views we were willing to argue for, even vigorously. But what I walked into was a culture of mutual respect characterised by a willingness to learn from others. This was a culture I had hoped would emerge among Sydney Anglicans.

The Mission Australia I joined was committed to theological diversity. Although only a young organization, having been formed in 2000, its ideological roots are much older and deeper. Mission Australia is an offshoot of the City Mission movement. Beginning with the formation of the Glasgow and London City Missions in 1826 and 1835, City Missions grew up to minister to urban underclasses created in the wake of industrialization. The missioners were mostly religious non-conformists who were passionate about evangelism and compassionate in their approach to ministry. They lived at a time when doctrinal differences mattered, and mattered hugely, but these they were willing to set aside for the sake of the poor and needy. Benjamin Short, who founded the Sydney City Mission in 1862, was deliberate in his creation of a non-sectarian or non-denomination mission.[170] The founding board of the Sydney City Mission had representatives from almost all denominations, with the

---

[170] Charles Chambers, *Coming Together: a dynamic mission; the events that shaped Mission Australia*, (Mission Australia, 2000), 6.

Roman Catholic Church a notable exception. A few more years would need to pass before the Mission became that inclusive, but it did happen.[171]

The CEO of Mission Australia prior to Toby Hall[172] was Patrick McClure. He had been a Roman Catholic priest, and a member of the Franciscan Order, and before joining Mission Australia had worked for the St Vincent de Paul Society. Patrick McClure was a big man, literally, with a big vision for Mission Australia. Under his watch, it became a more inclusive organization with people of all denominations and faiths being recruited to work there. In my first few days and weeks of working at Mission Australia, I encountered that diversity, in all its colourful variety. One of the very first people I met was Chris Jones, who for many people over many years had been the face and voice of the Sydney City Mission and now Mission Australia. Chris is a beautiful Christian woman from a Churches of Christ background. Within a day or two of arriving at the Campbell Street headquarters, in Sydney's CBD, I also met Eric d'Indy, the head of Marketing. Eric's spirituality was warm and generous—with me the frequent beneficiary over coffee.

My office was just around the corner from the Research and Social Policy Unit, a small, but highly talented team. Its head, Dr Maree Leech, was a devout and thoughtful Roman Catholic, as was Anne Hampshire who would shortly replace her. I used to love dropping in for a chat, often around issues of social justice, but also about metaphysics, epistemology, and ethics. One of the teams who I became friends with was a reflective agnostic. I would soon meet Peter Richardson, a person of immense gifts and lively spirituality. He once described himself as a raving Pentecostal. His background was Anglican, and he knew a number of my friends. Peter was as ardent and enthusiastic about his faith as anyone I would meet at

---

[171] I am here indebted to the research of a former colleague at Mission Australia, Digby Hannah, whose beautifully written paper on developing a spirituality for Mission Australia deserves to be published.

[172] Toby Hall was appointed CEO earlier in the same year that I became National Chaplain, 2006.

Mission Australia, but he also was winningly humble in his belief that our human understandings of faith and God are always inadequate and come nowhere near capturing the reality of God.

Within days of arriving at Mission Australia, I received an email of welcome from Steve Fowler. I had known Steve from university days. He had travelled to Indonesia with Judy and me and a group of others to visit Tony and Gaye Doran back in 1975. Steve is a big-hearted, loud-talking enthusiast, and it was great to reconnect with him. He, like Peter Richardson, had been working for many years with Sydney City Mission before it became Mission Australia. Both looked back nostalgically to when the organization was smaller and more obviously Christian.

In growing large so quickly, Mission Australia sacrificed its earlier policy of only employing active or churchgoing Christians. That policy continued for people employed at the upper reaches of the organization, but even at that level, the Christianity of some was little more than skin deep. At the coalface of its services, the staff were as religiously diverse as the populations from which they were drawn. The Board of Mission Australia was keen to retain Mission Australia's Christian character, but how it might do this was unclear. It sensed that the chaplaincy service might be a key to this, and it was.

Not long after my becoming National Chaplain, the organization began a process of re-examining its reason for being. Because of the speed of changes taking place within and outside of the organization, it had become pressingly important to reconsider its mission and values. Meetings were organized in Sydney, with upper management from all over Australia invited to join the discussion. The board also became involved as did the chaplaincy team. The biggest challenge was to find a way of retaining the organization's Christian heritage and ethos while also inspiring and empowering a multi-faith staff. Together, we did a great job, I thought. A new and more inclusive Vision Statement was created.[173] A new set of

---

[173] The new Vision Statement: 'Our vision is to see a fairer Australia by enabling people in need to find pathways to a better life.' The older Vision Statement was converted into a Founding Purpose that could continue to shape and inspire the organization in its efforts: 'Inspired by Jesus Christ, Mission Australia exists to meet human need and to spread the knowledge of the love of God.'

values was embraced that were certainly Christian, but also universal in their ability to inspire.[174]

Realising Chaplaincy's Potential

It was an exciting time to be working at Mission Australia. There seemed so much potential to do good things. I had a wonderful team around me. Chairman Richard Grellman was warmly supportive. He encouraged me to dream and to think big. The organization at that stage was reasonably prosperous, still benefitting from the visionary and expansionary work of Patrick McClure. The chaplaincy team was expanded from 9 to 16, towards an ideal of 1 chaplain for every 200 staff. Each of the States soon had a designated chaplain.[175] Some had more.[176] Helping to make my job of recruiting easier (and harder) was that interest in chaplaincy as a career option was high. I was amazed by the number of applications that began to flood in each time we advertised.[177] The team we ended up with was amazingly talented. Most had a bachelor's degree (or two), eight had at least one master's degree, two had completed doctorates, three had begun doctoral studies. Academic credentials certainly helped, but I was more on the lookout for people who could relate well, who had proven interpersonal skills, who were good at listening and slow to speak. These

---

[174] Eight existing values were replaced by the following five: compassion, integrity, respect, perseverance, and celebration.

[175] Western Australia, South Australia, and Victoria each had one chaplain. They were Bruce Eagles (the current National Chaplain), Nicholas Rundle, and Digby Hannah.

[176] Queensland ended up with three chaplains in Tim Booth, Robin Osborne, and Peter Devenish-Mears. When I first started with Mission Australia, Warren Jackwitz was chaplain to Queensland and Northern Territory. In NSW, Rob Paino, George Anderson, and Dominic Arcamone were joined by Robyn Richardson and Richard Loh. Tasmania was served by husband and wife team Brad Taylor and Jacinta Sinclair. Peter Little became the Northern Territory's first full-time chaplain. The team was strengthened by the addition of a National Office Chaplain in Kate Englebrecht and by talented jack of many trades Rev. Dr Geoffrey Glassock.

[177] For the National Office position, we had 43 applicants, for Victoria, 52, and for Queensland 61.

were the core skills. I was looking for people who could thoughtfully and intelligently commend Christian faith, while respecting those of alternative faiths. I wanted people who knew what they believed, but who were also humble enough to recognize their limitations of knowledge and belief.

While in the process of recruiting chaplains, we put together a Position Description that spelled out the chaplaincy role. Within the Position Description were a number of attitudes we were looking for. The one I enjoyed adding was 'intellectually inquisitive'. There was, for sure, a degree of indulgence in adding this desired characteristic because of its importance to me. However, there were good reasons to include it. To be inquisitive is to be open to new ways of seeing things. Inquisitiveness is a generator of discovery and of new perspectives—some of which prove helpful in our understanding of God and the world.

Related to inquisitiveness is reflectiveness. In wondering about how Mission Australia could retain its Christian ethos while encouraging and inspiring people of all or of no religious tradition, the idea emerged that we chaplains could facilitate this by helping to create a reflective culture. We realized it was not possible, nor did we think it desirable, to promote a particular brand of Christianity to staff. Not only would this violate the founding ethos of the organization,[178] it was likely to be counterproductive in encouraging superficial or lip-service adherence to whichever brand was being promoted. It was also likely to create resentment among those of differing creed or conviction. What was possible was the development of a culture which gave permission, and even encouraged people, to express their beliefs, while respectfully considering the beliefs of others. Within a culture like this, people would also be encouraged to reflect on why they were at Mission Australia, what were the beliefs that inspired and guided them in their endeavours to help others.

Our efforts to develop a reflective culture weren't entirely new. Bill Lawton, my predecessor as National Chaplain, had already begun to explore what it might mean for Mission Australia to be a Christian organization in a

---

[178] The organization's originating emphasis was on need rather than creed.

twenty-first-century world, with a secularized and multi-faith staff.[179] We were able to build on Bill's good work. We began to write papers on the history of Mission Australia and its precursors, on its theology and spirituality, on chaplaincy itself. We sought to embed chaplaincy more thoughtfully into the various business streams of the organization in an early attempt to subject all of the organization's activities to theological and ethical scrutiny.

In time, we thought we might be able to export some of the ideas and practices we were endeavouring to think through. Mission Australia had a Training Institute skilfully being led by David Makin, a person of great gifts and long experience. With David, we began to explore the possibility of training people in workplace chaplaincy. Newly recruited chaplain, Rev. Dr Geoff Glassock, had contacts, as I did, with the Australian College of Theology. He was chairperson of its Ethics Committee. Geoff began to make initial enquiries into how we could turn the idea of chaplaincy training into reality.

It was fun to dream. It was good to be encouraged to dream. There was the sense that things were on the move. This was so both metaphorically and literally. The National Office moved from where it had been for years, moving closer to the centre of Sydney's CBD and into a skyscraper that looked down on St Andrew's Anglican Cathedral and the Town Hall. I could see both from my desk on level 8. It was my job to organize the commissioning of the new headquarters.[180] Improbably, we managed to secure the services of one of Australia's most talented didgeridoo players in Willie Barton. He and Terry Olsen, a talented local dancer, welcomed us to country, reminding us that the land on which our building stood had for generations been cared for by the Gadigal people of the Eora nation.

During my time at Mission Australia, it was my huge privilege to travel all around Australia and, on a number of these trips, to visit Indigenous

---

[179] He had, for example, written a series of booklets, the first two of which, *Open to Change* (2001) and *Actions Speak* (2004), were in circulation when I took over from him.

[180] 11 June 2007.

communities and sacred sites, including the majestic and eerily ancient desert rock of Uluru. A highlight of my time at Mission Australia, and, in fact, of my whole life, was to be present, along with another Chaplain, Robyn Richardson, at the opening of Federal Parliament in 2008, and then to witness the newly elected Prime Minister Kevin Rudd's historic apology to Indigenous Australians. As the first act of his government, Prime Minister Rudd said sorry to Australia's Indigenous population, and, in particular, to members of the Stolen Generations, to the hundreds of Aboriginal children forcefully taken from their families over many generations. This removal was carried out with the horrific intent of erasing their aboriginality and of accelerating genetic assimilation into the Anglo-European mainstream.

This day, Wednesday, 13 February 2008, will forever remain etched in my memory as one of the most moving and wonderful days of my life. I stood beside a man of about my age who was taken from his parents at the age of three. He wasn't, strictly speaking, a member of the Stolen Generations, though he did have Indigenous ancestors. He was removed from a family considered dysfunctional, beginning a lifetime of dislocation and alienation as he was moved from foster family to foster family, and from institution to institution, until all sense of who he was had been obliterated. His experience was sufficiently similar to the experience of those he was standing in solidarity with that he could well and truly understand the pain and grief they were feeling. Tears kept falling down his cheeks, and down mine as well. We stood behind and beside Indigenous families who had come from all parts of Australia to stand together on the lawns of Parliament House. Some, such as my friend and former colleague, Ray Minniecon, were inside the parliament as honoured guests. All were overtaken by emotion as our new prime minister said sorry, not once, not twice, but over and over again to emphasize the genuineness of the words he spoke on behalf of Federal governments past and present. I felt proud to be an Australian that day.

After the apology, I stayed around for a while, soaking up the atmosphere, feeling the euphoria and stirrings of new hope. On my way back to Sydney, I was able to offer a lift to three young people. Two of them were anarchists, the third an orthodox Jew with anarchistic leanings. We chatted non-stop all the way back to Sydney, talking about the apology, talking about life, and the meaning of life. We spoke about our respective spiritualities. They believed that human organizations inevitably corrupt themselves, and corrupt those with power within them. I thought I had a pretty good case to argue against them. I sang the praises of Mission Australia and of the work we were doing as chaplains to utilize for good the resources of an admittedly very human organization. They weren't entirely convinced.

At Mission Australia, we renewed our efforts to contribute to reconciliation with Australia's first peoples. A Statement of Principles had already been forged to guide our work with Aboriginal and Torres Strait Islander Australians. Work soon began on developing a Reconciliation Action Plan, an organisational plan-of-action designed to encourage understanding and respect for Indigenous cultures, along with proactive recruitment of Indigenous staff. Chaplaincy played a key and involved role in this process.

There was much that I loved about being the National Chaplain of Mission Australia. I learned much from those I was privileged to work with. Kate Englebrecht, the National Office chaplain, introduced me to a way of reading the Scriptures that was similar to the one Judy and I had already begun using, under the influence of Paul Ricoeur. I had heard of *Lectio Divina*, but it was instructive and edifying to join Kate and other staff at the National Office for regular examples of its use. *Lectio Divina* is Latin for 'divine reading' and is a traditional practice of reading and prayer that draws one into a reflective and personalizing appropriation of whatever passages are set for the day. The method typically involves four stages or moments. These are (i) *Lectio*, which involves an attentive reading and rereading of the text of Scripture, (ii) *Meditatio*, which is meditating on one or more aspects of the text, (iii) *Oratio*, which is a devotional response to the text that involves opening one's heart in conversation or dialogue with God, and (iv) *Contemplation*, which is a restful and contemplative focus on God.

One thing my own heritage hadn't taught me was the value of silence. I was an activist by nature and training. Evangelicalism isn't without its 'quiet times,' but for me at least, they were often spent in what were essentially intellectual pursuits of trying to understand or master the text of Scripture—with prayer a rushed postscript, normally consisting of a shopping list of requests. I had no developed language of devotion, no sense of there being any approach to God other than through mind or intellect.

But I was open to other ways. My hermeneutic and theology were taking me in the direction of a more mystical or arational approach to God.

Being on a journey helped me to be sensitive to the journeys of others. I was coming to see that many, if not most, people are on journeys of self and God discovery. One of the joys of chaplaincy was walking the three floors of the National Office and engaging in discussion with anyone and everyone, never with any particular agenda, always with an ear to listen to where people were at, and to hear what was important to them. Sometimes issues of spirituality and faith came up. At other times, the conversations were more mundane. I was, and am, energized by people, no matter what the activity we might engage in. I helped to organize a lunchtime touch rugby game which brought me into enjoyable and stress-relieving contact with staff of similar interest. When I left Mission Australia and was working nearby, I would sometimes turn up for a run.

Politics

Not everything about being at Mission Australia was enjoyable. What I wasn't quite prepared for was the politics. A few years earlier, I was at a party with people who, for years, had been working in the corporate world. They'd had many bosses, some good, some not so good—some terrible. I asked one of them to estimate what percentage of managers were good managers, managers he'd be happy to work under. His quick answer was, 'About 7 per cent.' I was a little shocked by his answer and wondered what experiences had made him so pessimistic. But it wasn't too long after coming to work at Mission Australia that I realized he was probably right—good bosses are rarer than most of us would like. Mission Australia is a highly stratified organization. With between 3,500 and 4,000 staff, there are a lot of bosses, and a lot of bossing around. The chaplaincy team was forever hearing about purported cases of poor management, sometimes of bullying, and it wasn't always the bosses who were doing the bullying. As chaplains, we tried hard not to take sides. We knew how important it was to be as impartial as we could be, to suspend judgement, sometimes indefinitely, and to at least attempt to see things from both sides. We weren't always successful. Our instinct, informed by our Christian faith and the example of Jesus, was to side with the underdog and the less powerful, but this would sometimes blind us to the other side of the story, and thereby alienate management. In some ways, we couldn't win. Our even impartial involvement was often considered a threat, certainly when managers were doing wrong, but even when they weren't.

The chaplaincy role was a tough one, and especially so because of the politics—the inevitable jockeying for power and influence which happens within any organization. I was often blind to the politics. I was certainly green, and probably naïve. Others around me were much more experienced, much better at picking the insecurities and ambitions of those who had risen to positions of power in the organization. I had seen politics at work in the church and had some idea of how damaging it could be. But for years, my deliberate tendency had been to think the best of people, and to hope for the best. I also had an inflated belief in my own ability to get on with people, to be able to work through whatever difficulties might come along. I wasn't prepared for just how ruthless and unforgiving politics can be. It was going to be a good lesson for me.

I wasn't totally blind to the politics. From very early days, I began to notice that one after another of my new colleagues on the executive leadership team were being put off. At first, I thought that this was just the inevitable reshuffling and reassembling that happens when a new CEO arrives, the fresh broom that sweeps away the past to create an improved future. But what was puzzling, and more so in retrospect, was that those being replaced were manifestly competent, and, in most cases, hugely experienced within the organization. However, one by one they were put off. Maree Leech and Eric d'Indy went early. Peter Richardson stayed longer, but in time he too was judged no longer suitable, until no one from the previous executive team was left.

One of my biggest regrets from my time at Mission Australia was that I didn't ask more questions, didn't inquire more carefully into the necessity or desirability of these wholesale changes. I have thought a lot about it since. What happens within organizations is that people do get put off, often for good reasons, and with good processes being followed. Moreover, there are always two sides to every story. It is frequently impossible to know whether the decision is right or wrong. Most people don't have all the relevant facts, and must therefore trust that those making the decision are acting ethically and with good business sense. That is why, as chaplains, we tried hard to stand at some distance from disputes involving management and staff. We weren't detectives. That wasn't our job. But standing at a distance could also mean that we unwittingly became complicit in wrongdoing. We would suspend judgement long enough to allow evil to happen right under our noses, while justifying our lack of support for the person being wronged on the normally admirable basis of impartiality. Looking back, I wish I had been more attentive and more supportive of colleagues who were clearly struggling and in anguish at being removed from the organization they had served for so long.

What was interesting and instructive was that those who came onto the team to replace those who were being put off were as flawed and as much a mixture of competence and incompetence as those they replaced. New teams aren't necessarily better teams. They are just different teams, and in this particular case, a less experienced team. What is also interesting about teams and leaders of teams is that their weaknesses and flaws do become more obvious over time. There is almost always a honeymoon period when things are new and fresh. There is the excitement of the new, and I certainly felt that in the first year or so of being at Mission Australia. But over time, the cracks begin to show, and struggles for power and influence begin to create casualties. The gloss of the new is quickly lost and people's true natures come to the fore.

As chaplains, we would often have discussions about managers. And there were some themes that kept coming through. A big one was insecurity. Many of the bosses I encountered were insecure, for all sorts of reasons, including inexperience, or lack of relevant training, or lack of competence in this area or that. Insecurity, or the fear that underlies it, is a potent motivator. It drives people to hide their inadequacies and to seek to bluff their way to positions of power and influence. It demotivates people from recognizing or affirming the talents of others, since those talents have the potential to show them up. The thirst for recognition, in this case, fraudulent recognition, can silence the otherwise normal promptings of conscience as ways are devised to feather their own nests and de-feather others. Great leaders are not afraid of the talents or successes of those they lead. They delight to unleash their potential, are first on the scene to celebrate their achievements.

Closely related to insecurity is the quest for power. I had read, often enough, of the allure of power, but can't say that I'd ever seen it up close. I knew of power's ability to corrupt, and wondered whether I too might be corrupted. I had become the National Chaplain of one of Australia's leading charities. That gave me some power. I was one of only two people reporting directly to the board, via its chairman. The other person was the CEO. That too gave me power, more than I realized at the time, more than I ever deliberately utilized. But power can corrupt. It can corrupt the best of people.

Over time, I received an education in the use and abuse of power. I witnessed the often subtle, but very deliberate grooming of allies in pursuit of greater influence. I saw examples of people compromising their normally high principles to retain new friendships and alignments. I saw flattery and manipulation directed towards those further up the management chain, and the favouring of some, and the isolation and bullying of others, further down. Bullying was common, in part because it is so easy—so easy for those with power, so easy for an in-group to create an out-group. It is a skill we learn in the playground, which is all too commonly utilized in adulthood.

Bullying is an interesting phenomenon. People who have been the victims of bullying can so easily become bullies. Bullying is the misuse of power to get one's way. Managers typically bully when they lose or lack the ability to motivate or inspire. The bully uses the power she has, including institutional power, when legitimate and morally preferable means won't work, or won't work quickly enough. Bullying is not something that can be eradicated from an organization simply by having a policy against bullying. It will always exist. It is as ubiquitous as the insecurities and inadequacies of those given power within our human organizations.

I probably shouldn't have been surprised by the politics, but I was surprised and disappointed. And it wasn't as if I could stay out of the politics. I found myself at odds, a number of times, with the new head of Human Resources. I had realized from early days that HR and chaplaincy do similar work, and, for that reason, needed to work closely and well together. But the growth and success of chaplaincy and the high esteem in which chaplains were held across the organization had the potential to create tensions, and it did, over time.

The first half of 2008 was not one of the easiest half years of my life. In retrospect, it seems I wasn't quite political enough. Some currents were beginning to run, cold currents from my point of view, and I made the mistake of not confronting them more directly than I did. The paradigm that I had brought with me into the job was one of pastoral care, of the often patient and slow work of relationship building and rebuilding. And when some relationships began to be strained, I took the pastoral approach of seeking to rebuild bridges and to be as gracious and forgiving as I could be. That was a good thing to do at the personal level, and I don't regret it, but it didn't prove sufficient in this new context.

As the months went by, and as some of the tensions remained to make my work life challenging and, at times, quite discouraging, I decided the best I could do was to get on with the job of building a first-class chaplaincy team and of encouraging them in the great work they were doing. There was much to do, systems to put in place, opportunities to explore, reflections to give, reports to write, people to care for. It was as full-on a job as I had ever had.

What continued to energize me was the idea that through chaplaincy we had the capacity to embed and articulate a thoughtful and embracive Christianity Mission Australia could become proud of. I was also excited by the possibility of developing and promoting new ways of doing chaplaincy and was continuing to have conversations with other chaplaincy providers, and with a number of theological institutions. We began to plan for an overseas trip to have a close-up look at what was happening elsewhere. I had raised the idea earlier, but it was felt, wisely, that I needed to get up to speed with what was happening at Mission Australia before looking further afield. But the time now seemed right and the board approved a research tour to North America. The South Australian Chaplain, Nicholas Rundle, would accompany me. I was thrilled by the prospect of this trip and was also pleased that it coincided with what appeared to be improving relationships within the executive leadership team.

Throughcare

Going to North America would enable us to survey and sample what was happening in chaplaincy in the United States and Canada, and there were some other potential benefits. Not long after becoming National Chaplain, I was approached by two of the leaders of Kairos Prison Ministry, a largely volunteer organization that runs short courses on the Christian faith in prisons. Although Kairos does offer support to the spouses and family of people in custody, it didn't have a ministry to those leaving gaol, hence their approach to Mission Australia to explore avenues of cooperation and referral. The discussion was low-key and exploratory, but it precipitated further conversations, which began to involve others interested in cooperating in the Throughcare of offenders.

Throughcare is a term that has come to be used to denote an integrated pre—and post-release approach to assisting people transition successfully out of prison and out of crime. Throughcare begins at the point of arrest and/or conviction, and ends, ideally, with offenders no longer offending, because they have been successfully integrated into supportive and fulfilling community life. Research indicates that for this to happen, a complex array of factors needs to be addressed, either simultaneously or in thoughtful sequence. If the problem is drug addiction, this may need to be addressed first, but drug addiction is frequently a symptom of other issues, which also need to be addressed in time. Throughcare takes a longitudinal approach. It seeks to understand the factors that lead to crime in the first place. It considers the impact of involvement in the criminal justice system, including the impact of incarceration. It also seeks to understand the kind of factors which make it less likely that people will re-offend when they return to the community. There is a gathering body of research that indicates that the best way to approach after-prison-care is to take a cooperative and multifaceted approach. Best practice is to work with others in the field, to draw on the expertise of others, to not try to do it all oneself.

It was this realization that brought the two executives from Kairos to a conversation with Mission Australia. Among others soon to join that conversation was Rev. Rod Moore, chaplaincy coordinator with the New South Wales Department of Corrective Services. Rod is an Anglican priest with long experience of working in and outside of prisons. When I first met Rod, he was enthusing about a Throughcare pilot program, part-funded by Correctives Services, called *Home for Good*. The name and the program are modelled on a program running in the American State of Oregon. This very successful program is run by multi-denominational and multi-faith chaplains, and involves a whole of community approach. The program had obvious potential for chaplaincy at Mission Australia, which we began to consider. It also depended on a cooperative and networking approach, which we had begun to discuss with Kairos.

These discussions led in time to creation of a *Throughcare Jigsaw Group*.[181] One of the early conversation points among those involved was whether this group would remain a Christian faith-based and/or faith-informed network,[182] or whether its membership should be extended to include secular and other-faith organizations. We decided, wisely I think, to open up the membership to all organizations working in Throughcare. It was hoped that with so broad a coalition, some gentle pressure could be applied to governments to divert some of the massive budget increasingly being spend on building bigger and better gaols to programs shown to be effective in keeping people out of gaol.

Rod is a visionary. His dream was to enlist the support of high-profile patrons to fly the flag for the network and to attract media attention. Plans were put in place to set up a website[183] to facilitate networking, and to be a source of information on what was happening in Throughcare throughout New South Wales and beyond, with links to research findings and events such as Reintegration Puzzle Conferences organized each year by Professor Joe Graffin of Melbourne's Deakin University. Mission Australia was well placed to play a key role in these developments. Prior to leaving for North America, I was able to help with the organisation of a pleasingly successful networking breakfast with up to thirty-four organizations and institutions represented.[184]

---

[181] The early signatories to a Memorandum of Understanding, setting out the terms of what was designed to be a loose affiliation of organizations and individuals, were Mission Australia, the Chaplaincy Division of the NSW Department of Corrective Services, Sydney Anglican Home Mission Society (Anglicare), Samaritans Foundation, Alpha-Caring for Ex-Offenders, Prison and After-care Support Services, Prison Fellowship Australia, Unchained Ministries, Hillsong CityCare, Kairos Prison Ministry Australia.

[182] 'Faith-informed' is an expression coined to denote organisations like Mission Australia that have a Christian heritage and ethos, but are not staffed solely or even largely by Christians, and that are not focused on promoting Christian faith.

[183] That website now exists: http://throughcarejigsawgroup.org.au

[184] Held on 16 September 2008.

Celebratory Interlude

In the midst of the busy excitement of planning for the North American trip, I was reminded of some politics of a different, but similar kind to what I had been experiencing. I received an unexpected phone call from Patricia Brennan. Patricia was a founding member of the Movement for the Ordination of Women (MOW) in Sydney. Twenty-five years earlier, she and a number of other women and men had stood outside St Andrew's Cathedral to protest against the exclusion of women from positions of leadership within the church. Patricia was phoning to sound me out as a possible speaker at a twenty-five year re-enactment. I was amazed to be asked. Twenty-five years earlier, I was staunchly in favour of Moore College's advocacy of male headship in home and church. I had been completely unimpressed by media images of MOW's landmark protest. I was quick to dismiss Patricia as an angry and misguided feminist. The idea that I would one day be joining her in protest to mark a quarter century of such protests would have seemed fanciful in the extreme.

When Patricia and I met for coffee, I was at first a little reluctant. I wasn't sure I wanted to burn more bridges than I had already burnt by writing my Open Letter. I was also uncertain how my action would be perceived within Mission Australia. The chaplaincy team, not surprisingly, was supportive and encouraging, but others may not have been so keen. It was also a big thing to be asked to do, especially for someone so new to the cause. Was I the right person for the job? Did I have the courage to nail my colours so publicly to the mast? I decided I was and would speak.

Weeks earlier, I had attended my first ever session of Sydney's Anglican Synod, the major legislative body of the diocese. Rev. Chris Albany, rector of St Mark's South Hurstville, had attempted to have Synod reverse its moratorium on debating the ordination of women to the priesthood. Chris felt it was time to at least revisit the topic. I thought I would go along to sit in on the relevant session. It wasn't the most edifying of experiences. The whole process appeared to be carefully choreographed to maintain the dominance of those now in charge of the diocese. This was unsettling, but even more unsettling was the vehemence of the opposition to even discussing this issue. More unsettling still were a number of speeches by female clergy. One of these was to the effect that Synod should just accept the godly scholarship of Sydney's better-known theologians. I was amazed by this, and couldn't help wondering about the many similarly godly and competent scholars from around the world, and even within Sydney's ranks, who had come to entirely different conclusions. It illustrated once again how tribal we human beings are, how dependent we are for what we think on what others around us think. It was also sad illustration of how important it is for the custodians of this line of thinking to be as controlling as they have been. Anything less than tight control is unlikely to prevent a breakout of alternative understandings.

Experiences like this were reason enough for me to speak out on this issue. It was, in fact, a great honour to join Patricia Brennan and many others on the steps of Sydney's Town Hall,[185] just a short walk away from the entrance to the Cathedral, and at the exact day and time that the original protest happened twenty-five years earlier.[186] Once again, there were cameras and lights, with ABC Radio's *Religion Report* later replaying the speeches as part of its report on the event. There were more speeches to come at Chapter House, including some words from Patricia Hayward. Patricia had followed me as president of the St Marks Fellowship at the University of New England back in our university days. She had also been the first ever female president of the Evangelical Union. Patricia didn't think she would ever see the day that I would be speaking in favour of the ordination of women to the priesthood. It just shows that people can and do change their minds. Sydney Anglicans, I am sure, will change their minds as well, if they haven't already, and sooner than most people expect, in my hopeful opinion.

Two days after speaking at the MOW rally, I was booked to leave Sydney for North America. I had earlier rescheduled the trip for this day because of the strong possibility that my rugby league team would be playing in a grand final the day before. They did play. The day after I spoke in favour or the ordination of women to the priesthood, the Manly-Warringah Sea Eagles

---

[185] It was a huge privilege to stand beside Patricia Brennan in what turned out to be her final major protest. Patricia passed away on 7 March 2011, after a six-month battle with pancreatic cancer. Hers was an outstanding life.

[186] The re-enactment happened on Friday night, 4 October 2008.

beat the highly fancied Melbourne Storm 40-0 in the season's decider; the biggest Grand Final winning margin in the history of the game! I watched the game with friends at home and was still smiling the next day when I flew out of Sydney for San Francisco on the first leg of what would turn out to be an exciting and informative chaplaincy research tour.

North American Tour

It is hard to adequately summarize what for me and Nicholas Rundle was a trip of a lifetime. So much was packed into three weeks that it would take me a chapter to tell the story, but a few highlights will suffice. I was flying into an election campaign nearing its climax. Barack Obama had defied the odds to overtake Hillary Clinton as preferred Democratic candidate, and was closing in on the Presidency. Almost everyone I encountered on my journey around North America was talking about the election, and, of course, everyone had an opinion. The United States is anything but united in its politics, and what was especially interesting to me was the nexus between religious belief and politics. I found that people either loved or hated Barack Obama, and not just in the sort of ways that are typical in politics. There were racial and religious undertones that mostly weren't undertones at all, with Obama being labelled a Muslim and/or a communist—in other words not truly American. Those who hated him delighted in including his middle name, Hussein, in descriptions of him, in a none-too-subtle effort to associate him with negative stereotypes.

Three weeks was long enough to feel that I had a fair sampling of North American religious and political life. I was treated to examples of the best and worst of both. What I found disturbing was the often uncritical alignment of Christianity with free market capitalism. America's historic obsession with freedom, freedom of enterprise and freedom of the individual, is the sometimes healthy legacy of the European Enlightenment, and, earlier still, of the Protestant Reformation. However, so one-sided has this emphasis become that corporate and social responsibility has been neglected, sometimes tragically. Complicit in this failure, and illustrative of it, is the tendency among many North American churches, particularly those of more conservative bent, to embrace an individualistic and other-worldly form of the faith. Nicholas Rundle and I had this illustrated for us quite graphically during a visit to Harvard University.

In walking around the campus, we came across The Memorial Church, pastored for many years by one of America's better-known preachers, Professor Peter Gomes. He wasn't there, but a young apprentice was. As we walked into the church, we were greeted by a young African American preacher. He asked if we'd be willing to listen to his ten-minute trial sermon, which was to be critiqued by his mentor, Peter Gomes. We enjoyed the sermon with its African American flavour or style, but this talented and promising preacher almost completely individualised a passage that was all about social justice. The horizontal dimension (our responsibilities to each other and to the world we have stewardship of) was subverted for the vertical, us-God dimension. The sermon ended up being a call for individual repentance, the purpose of which was to avoid hell and be welcomed into heaven. When we chatted to him afterwards (offering a gentle, but encouraging critique), we asked him about tax cuts for the very rich, a legacy of George Bush's Presidency. His hopefully unconsidered response was: 'The millionaires will like it,' the implication being, I think, that this sort of measure was the necessary cost of oiling the economic machine—for the benefit of all. The trouble is that in the United States, the gap between the rich and the poor is huge and had gotten larger under the impact of this way of thinking.

On my very first day in the United States, I was greeted by examples of the sort of poverty that has become commonplace in the United States. I was in San Francisco, one of America's richest and most expensive cities. I learnt that on any given night up to 25,000 people are homeless in San Francisco, with about 60 per cent of them being women and children, many of them being African American. I spoke with two African Americans on that first day. The first was an articulate twenty-nine-year-old selling Barak Obama badges. Here was a young man filled with hope that Obama might be able to make some difference to the entrenched racism and economic inequalities bedevilling the United States in its efforts to be a great nation. The second African American was a homeless man sitting on the sidewalk asking for money. His first name is Kuwante, and when I sat down to chat with him, he began to expound his belief that African Americans, because of their colour (black, and black represents evil), were enemies of God and destined to be the slaves of white people, who rightfully ruled the world. The fact that Barack Obama was about to become president was proof that the end of the world was near. Kuwante had the Bible verses to back up his beliefs, or so he thought,[187] and wouldn't hear my attempted critique, no matter how hard I tried to put a contrary view. The encounter saddened me. Here was as blatant a case as I have witnessed of prejudice and stereotyping being internalized to the spiritual impoverishment of this man who is my brother.

There is no doubt that many are sinned against, not only by economic theories which favour the rich and blame the poor, but also by defective theologies employed to justify them. Nevertheless, I did come across quite a few examples of better theology and of faith willing to roll up its sleeves on behalf of the poor and disadvantaged. A few stand out. One of the really enjoyable fringe benefits of the trip to North America was being able to catch up with members of my family, including my son Damien and his wife Sinyee, then expecting their first child, and Judy's and my first grandchild. They were living in Atlanta, Georgia, city number three on my trip around the United States and Canada. While in Atlanta, I went to church twice, the first time to a suburban, decidedly white and middle-class Presbyterian church. It was big, well-attended, and the sermon for the day was on the evils of pornography. That evening, Damien and I travelled to the impoverished inner city to the Open Door Community, an impressive and inspirational outreach to Atlanta's poor. We sat with, and alongside of, alcoholics and drug addicts, with people who had been welcomed in to Open Door's residential and therapeutic community. This was definitely not middle class, though within the congregation were academics, professionals, and others willing to identify with those living on the edge, or having fallen off the edge of respectable middle-class life. We felt privileged to be there. The singing was lively, the fellowship warm and inclusive, the testimonies moving. This was a place where Jesus would have felt at home. I certainly did. The song book from which we sang was

---

[187] He referred me to the story of Noah's flood, not terribly persuasively given I believed it mythical, and to verses he believed referred to the cursing with darkened skin of the descendants of Ham, one of Noah's sons. Checking up later, I found there is no such reference in the Bible, with the Curse of Ham (more exactly of Canaan—Gen. 9: 20-27) taking on racial overtones through interpretations (contested) of a passage in *The Babylonian Talmud* that refers to Ham being 'smitten in his skin.'

filled with songs drawn from the Civil Rights movement and from African American spirituality. None was individualistic or other-worldly, most expressed a desire to embody Christ-like values in society-transforming ways.

It was special to spend just a few hours at the Open Door Community. Later in the trip, Nicholas and I had the privilege of staying at a quite similar community in New London, Connecticut, on our way to Boston. St Francis House hosts an Urban Ministry Center, self-described as 'an intentional Christian social justice community committed to prayer and social justice.' Drawing on the Catholic Worker Movement,[188] this small community sought to advocate and care for homeless and marginalized people in that city and district. Staying there was one of the highlights of our trip.

A few other highlights stand out. Linking up with Nicholas in New York was one of them. I had come to the United States a little earlier and had already spent days in San Francisco, Houston, and Atlanta. He flew straight to New York. Neither of us had been to New York, and the few days spent there were profitable and exciting. We visited churches and a number of highly impressive organizations including the Interfaith Center of New York, meeting up with its founder and elder statesman, Dean James Morton.[189] One of our projects in North America was to explore the notion of faith-friendly workplaces.[190] Mission Australia was multi-faith, not just multi-denominational, and we were seeking models and inspiration to encourage the development of workplaces where differences of faith were

---

[188] The Catholic Worker movement was founded in 1933 during the Great Depression by Dorothy Day. It is best known for houses of hospitality located in run-down sections of many cities. Catholic Worker Communities, including the Open Door Community in Atlanta, are known for their support of labour unions, human rights, and the development of a nonviolent culture. They are also known as places of prayer.

[189] The Very Reverend James Morton founded the ICNY after retiring (in 1997) from his service as dean of the Cathedral of St. John the Divine, the Seat of the Episcopal Diocese of New York, and has been its president since.

[190] The term 'faith friendly' was given prominence by theologian and researcher Rev. Dr David Miller from Princeton University.

respected, even within contexts of rigorous and honest discussion. We were also looking for better ways for Mission Australia to do its work in a multi-faith Australia. We were keen to observe examples of faith-sensitive work practices, with Nicholas taking a special interest in this aspect of our research tour.

I managed to take a weekend off in New York. Nicholas flew on to Ohio and Indiana, and I had some time to myself. I quickly fell in love with New York City, or at least, those parts of it I saw. I did manage to get all the way down to Queens, thinking that I was headed for the Statue of Liberty, giving me a longer than expected experience of the subway. I did, eventually, get back to the Statue of Liberty, and, from there, to Wall Street and to Ground Zero where for an hour or two I reflected on the scale and sheer terror of an event our family had witnessed from a lounge-room back in Australia. I later walked through Central Park to the site of John Lennon's shooting death. That night, I enjoyed a walk around Broadway and Times Square. On Sunday night, I attended Redeemer Presbyterian church to hear an excellent sermon on the Prodigal Son by its high-profile pastor, Tim Keller.

Strangely, perhaps, one of the most moving experiences of the weekend was going to *Madame Tussauds*. It was then featuring a 9/11 exhibit of the terrorist attack and its aftermath, with a tribute to the emergency services, who themselves took a pounding in seeking to care for all those affected. But what moved me most, unexpectedly, was confronting, not quite in the flesh, but disconcertingly realistically, many of the heroes of my growing up years; people I admired, and, in some cases, was in awe of, people including Nelson Mandela, Martin Luther King, Mahatma Ghandi, Billy Graham, John Kennedy, Mohammed Ali, Michael Jordan, Charlie Chaplin, Jodie Foster, and any number of other celebrities. Some I had seen in person, if only from a distance, as was the case with Billy Graham and Michael Jordan. Others I had read about or had read their biographies. To be able to walk right up to such life-like imitations of these great ones, to even seemingly catch their eyes, was uncannily moving. I found myself becoming lost in the recollections of a lifetime. I could so easily have stayed longer.

On Monday, I was back in the air and on my way to Toronto for a quick stopover. As in Atlanta, and later Calgary and Portland, I was able to catch up with relatives.[191] Another highlight of my two days in Toronto was meeting Mennonite Pastor Harry Nigh, the man who devised the very first Circle of Accountability and Support, a highly successful program to work with convicted sex offenders. Harry reminded me of Tony Doran. He was a small, gentle man, with substance, with depth. He told me the story of how he befriended a mentally delayed, repeat sex offender by the name of Charlie. This was his name. It was no pseudonym. Charlie was 'thrown away' at age four. He was sexually abused when he was 7. His victims were boys in the same age group. St Augustine once wrote that 'all crime is a cry of hunger.' Regardless of how we understand Charlie's actions, they did result for him in terrible remorse and in efforts to self-harm, including eating plastic knives and forks. Harry decided to create a circle of support around Charlie, dubbed 'Charlie's Angels.' The circle was made up of volunteers from Harry's church. When Charlie was released from prison, the police put out a broadcast to alert people. They also distributed photographs of Charlie to schools and childcare centres. Harry's son reported that when photos were distributed to his class, he had piped up, 'I know Charlie. He came to dinner at our place!' It was a socially risky thing for a church to become involved in. The police set up a twenty-four-hour police guard costing $350,000 in just six weeks. The circle met weekly. They were in contact with Charlie every day. Charlie did not reoffend. He lived for a further thirteen years, surrounded by people who loved him, and who he came to love. When they first met him, Charlie had no time for faith, he 'hated' faith, but he came to share the faith of those willing to run the gauntlet of criticism as 'do-gooders' and 'bleeding hearts' to care for him.

Much more could be written about the trip to North America, including reference to two of the most impressive Throughcare initiatives in the United States, the Delancey Street Foundation in San Francisco and the Home for Good program in Portland, Oregon. But that will have to wait until another time and place. Needless to say, I flew back to Australia feeling tired, but energized by all I had seen and learnt. There were, however, some

---

[191] In this case, with my mum's brother Paul, his wife Ruth, my niece, Emma, her husband, Mark, and their three gorgeous sons, Joe, Samuel, and Michael. In Calgary, my next port of call, I caught up with Dorothy, John, and Kate. In Portland, I stayed with my brother, Alan, his wife Donna, and caught up briefly with Joelle, Donald, and Chloe.

feelings of foreboding. Whilst on the trip, I had been involved in one or two very sensitive staffing issues. I handled them well from such a distance, I thought, given their complexity and the personal cost to those involved, but there were signs that not everyone was happy, and, being so far away, it was impossible to know what might be happening in the background.

Bumpy Landing

I came back to a meeting with Toby Hall and Richard Grellman and was told that the board was considering downgrading the role of National Chaplain, with some thought of bringing chaplaincy under the management of HR. This would mean that the dual reporting system would be dismantled, leaving the CEO as the only person with a direct line to the board.[192] It was suggested that I may have some reduced role to play in this impending reality. I could hardly believe what I was hearing. It felt like an ambush and betrayal wrapped into one, especially when the option of me resigning was offered. It was a strange, almost surreal experience. Time seemed to slow down, as in a slow-motion movie sequence. I didn't know what to say—except to ask to speak with Richard one on one. He thought that fair and agreed.

I spoke with Richard, and later with another two members of the board, and was able to give my perspective on what appeared to be happening. I was able to be increasingly frank in saying what I thought were the issues, with some of these becoming clearer as events unfolded. I look back on what turned out to be the hardest few weeks of my life with residual pain. With the benefit of hindsight, I think it was me who let the board down for not sharing my concerns earlier.

I chose not to resign, even when a case was brought against me, a list of reasons for me to resign or be dismissed. I was amazed, even heartened, to read them, because most were old concerns that had long been resolved. Some, when unpacked, were positive rather than negative examples of chaplaincy doing what it should have been doing. None was pursued as

---

[192] There may have been organisational merit in this proposal, though I had not heard a word of its possibility. Moreover, it was obvious, then and since, that agendas other than organisational improvement were at work in the background to this surprising announcement.

a ground for dismissal. What turned out to be the bottom line was that the relationship between the CEO and the National Chaplain had broken down. It certainly had by then.

It hurt me hugely to have to leave Mission Australia. It hurt to have to stop midstream, when, from a chaplaincy point of view, things were going so well, and with such promise. It was hard for my team, most of whom responded magnificently and with warm and loving support. This was a new experience for me. The angst created by the Open Letter process didn't compare. What I didn't realize, but soon learned, with some therapeutic benefit, was that many people, perhaps most, have had experiences like this. Anyone who has spent time in the corporate world, or in organisations of any sort, including the church, is likely to have had a negative brush with politics. It was now my turn. I was soon saying to myself, 'Welcome to the human race, Keith.'

There are probably some good reasons not to write about this experience, or, at least, to delay writing. The impact of it is still slightly raw and recent. Nevertheless, I decided I would write, for a number of reasons. For a start, I could hardly write a book about my life without including what has been one of the more painful experiences of my life to date. I am grateful that God has gifted me with an upbeat and positive nature, but being upbeat and positive isn't always a good thing. A very good friend of mine told me once that my constant positivity wasn't always helpful. I am sure he is right. I suspect that my being so positive isn't just a blessing of nature, it may also be a practised effort to mask or deny emotions I am uncomfortable with or have suppressed.[193] There can be an unreality about upbeatness. Over the years, I have needed to let myself feel hurt or be angry or depressed. I have tried, with some help from Judy, to become more helpfully in touch with my emotions. Working through my experiences at Mission Australia certainly helped me in that process, as has the writing of this chapter.

Coming back from the United States to the traumatic events of November/December 2008 was like walking into an unexpected fight. It was a fight,

---

[193] It could also be a legacy of being third eldest in my family, me coming to take the role of peace maker, perhaps to the detriment of expressing and being in touch with my own feelings.

a fight for my own survival. It felt like I was being picked up by an ocean current and dragged out to sea, or, just as descriptively, picked up by a tsunami and hurled towards an unforgiving shore. No matter how hard I swam or struggled, it made no difference. The struggle became, at its height, a battle of wills, with one or two rearguard actions on my part, including the involvement of legal advice and the possibility of a court case. But by the end of the process, I was bloodied enough to not want to drag my family into any further fight. It was better to stop fighting. It was time to look for another career and start the long process of healing.

I am glad this happened to me. It gave me first-hand experience, for the first time, of being and feeling powerless. It gave me a taste, however shallow and fleeting, of what Indigenous friends of mine have known for generations. In their case, the experience of abuse has been hammered into the very fabric of their culture. My experience, though painful, is nothing compared to what they have experienced. It is nothing at all compared to the experiences of so many of the world's poor and disadvantaged.

I am grateful for the experience, not just for the experience itself, but for what I was forced to learn in its aftermath. Not only was this a new experience of hurt, it was a new experience of being so angry. I was angry, and increasingly so over time. I have never been angrier or angry for so long. Anger can be crippling, and it can easily descend into bitterness or revenge. I struggled with all three for the greater part of 2009. But it was a good struggle to engage in, a good struggle to understand, or to attempt to understand. One of the most helpful books I read during this time was *ACT on Life not on Anger* (2006).[194] It helpfully points out that anger is one of those emotions that can just well up inside you, usually as a result of some trigger or memory that activates it, sometimes unexpectedly. The book counsels not to try to suppress the anger, because then it can create even more problems at the level of the unconscious. It suggests instead that we simply acknowledge and name the feeling, and even its source. By doing this we objectify it, little by little, allowing it to subside on its own over time. Most importantly, we shouldn't act on the emotion. We

---

[194] Georg H. Eifert, Matthew McKay and John P. Forsyth, *ACT on Life not on Anger: the New Acceptance & Commitment Therapy Guide to Problem Anger*, (Oatland, CA: New Harbinger Publications, 2006).

need do no more than acknowledge it, and then get on with what we were doing. The book also discusses forgiveness, which it helpfully describes as a process of letting go; of releasing the one who has done you wrong from any obligation to make amends. You may not feel forgiving, but you can release that person from any expectation that they will say sorry, or be sorry, or seek to be reconciled. I found I could do this, not at first, but over time.

One of the unexpected benefits of being savaged by a political process was that I became much more emotionally attuned to politics and its often brutal outworkings. I was no longer politically naïve. Another benefit was becoming aware of my own complicity in the evil of politics. Politics is about influence. Within any organisation or human grouping, we inevitably influence others, and will need to—for all sorts of good reasons. The challenge is to remain true to our beliefs and core values whilst doing the influencing. That is not so easy to do.

To this day, I am still puzzled by the events of late 2008. But I now no longer need to fully understand. Life has moved on for me and for Mission Australia. Mission Australia continues to do great work, and I am hugely grateful for the two or so years I was there. I am grateful for the good times. I am as grateful for the tough times. I hope they have made me stronger and softer, stronger in being able to more resolutely pursue causes of justice and reconciliation, softer in being better able to empathize with those whose experience of politics has been much harsher than mine.

CHAPTER 9

New Horizons Opening

Christmas and New Year celebrations weren't quite as happy as usual as 2008 transitioned to an uncertain future. This was yet another new beginning, but it lacked the normal excitement, and was muted by still smarting wounds. Some months into 2009, I was visiting my mum, who I knew was feeling for me. In her warm and motherly way, she listened as I revisited recent hurts. I unburdened as I hadn't done since childhood days, when hurts of a lesser kind were readily aired. Part-way into the conversation, the thinly crusted reservoir of built-up emotion burst open in a torrent of tears. They didn't stop until the reservoir had emptied, for then at least.

This was new territory for me without a doubt. To be this hurt for so long was unusual. I needed, and was given, the warm support of family, friends, and former colleagues. Finding a new job was another helpful healer. I had thought about prison chaplaincy. There were one or two options along that line, though not in Sydney. My friend and pastor, Dave Smith, suggested I work with him at Dulwich Hill Anglican. That was tempting, but I was already heavily involved there. I also felt I needed time away from Christian ministry, time at a different sort of coalface. Having just come back from North America, and having learnt more about Throughcare, I wondered about having a go at that sort of work myself. One day in late December, I turned up at the headquarters of Corrective Services NSW to ask about becoming a Probation and Parole Officer. I was aware that Probation and Parole Officers do Throughcare. It is an essential part of their work. It was suggested I ring round the various District Offices and talk with their managers about becoming a case manager, a then good way into Probation and Parole work.

Probation and Parole

That's what I did. I rang around and was invited by the district manager of Sydney's City Office to come in for interview. She seemed to think I might be able to do the job, and by early February, I began what amounted to a fourth career change. Very quickly, I fell in love with the new role. I was blessed by having one of Corrective Services' finest managers and leaders, illustrating once again the craziness of putting an artificial ceiling on the careers of women. My immediate unit leader was a man, a younger man of sharp mind and lively discussion. He was also a talented sportsman, and quickly eliminated my advantage of experience in table tennis. I had helped to organise a table tennis table for the office, enjoying a brief ascendancy at the top of the rankings, before being overtaken by yet another colleague, a man of Islamic faith who quickly became a friend.

My experiences of 2008 prepared me well for my new job of 2009. In so many ways, I wasn't at all suitable for this job. I had lived a privileged life with few upsets and fewer still setbacks. I had two parents who loved and inspired me. I had no personal experience of divorce or of premature loss of a loved one or friend. I had not even once experimented with illicit drugs. I had only ever been drunk once, and that through accidently drinking sherry like it was soft drink. I have never been homeless. I didn't have learning difficulties or a disrupted education. I completed my School and Higher School Certificates, and didn't stop there. I hadn't known depression, not even mild or temporary versions. Nor have I been mentally ill or had disability challenges. And now, every day, I was meeting with and becoming the case manager of people who had taken drugs, whose parents had divorced, or died, or deserted them, whose partners wouldn't speak to them or, if they did, would abuse them, whose children or parents or brothers or sisters had died of overdoses and/or by taking their own lives. Every day I would meet someone struggling to make ends meet, or seeing me because they couldn't resist the urge to take what everyone else seemed to afford so easily; who were hearing voices or being frightened by real or imaginary foes, who were drinking or smoking or shooting up to mask the memories of abuse and neglect, who were homeless, loveless, and lost. What did I know?

But strangely, I did seem to know something. I was able to understand, a little, or at least to listen. There is no greater gift to offer another person than the gift of listening, really listening—with ears, eyes, and heart. I don't know of too many more privileged jobs than that of a Probation and Parole Officer. Our job entails the need to get to know each of our offenders, as we refer to them. No sooner do we meet them than we begin to ask questions, about where they live, and where they have lived, about their parents, siblings, and partners, about what their childhood and growing up years were like, about their cultural and religious background, about their schooling and education, about who their friends were and who they now associate with. We ask questions I wouldn't dare to ask my best friend. We ask about their mental health, what medication they are on, whether they were expelled or suspended from school, or fired from work. We don't just ask them. We get their permission to talk with those who know them best, with parents and partners, siblings and bosses. We have access to their criminal histories, to the comments of judges when they were sentenced. We gain access to reports and feedback from medical and mental health professionals who have also asked questions that most people have no right or experience in asking, all this in the necessary and admirable cause of creating relevant and fine-tuned case plans, all this to maximize the chance of assisting them to not repeat their mistakes and reoffend, thus making the community a safer place.

It is hard to think of an analogous setting where this much knowledge about another person is accumulated in so short a time and with such depth and comprehension. Psychologists and counsellors do some of this of course, and hopefully at greater depth and mostly with more training. We are not counsellors, though we do counselling, inevitably, given that a big part of counselling is listening. The closest thing to an analogy in my own experience is pre-marriage counselling, or preparing to speak at someone's funeral. When I was in parish ministry, I would often be asked to conduct a funeral for people I had never, or hardly ever, met. If I was doing the eulogy, I would need to sit down with the family and talk about the life of the person who had died. More often than not, when I got up to speak, I felt I had at least begun to know the person, with their life and personality laid out for me by the family. In my job with Probation and Parole, I was learning in-depth the life history of people still living, people who could tell their own stories.

This was the best of jobs for me. By nature, I am gregarious and extraverted. I am energized by people and love to hear their stories. This job brought me into contact with an endless stream of interesting and sometimes challenging people. I love people. I am not sure why. At one of my training sessions to become a Probation and Parole Officer, we were inspired by a talk from Ian Pike, chairman of the NSW Parole Board and former Chief Magistrate of NSW. Mr Pike was involved for years in selecting and preparing magistrates for their work of dispensing justice in NSW Courts. He told us that he'd tell each new batch of potential magistrates, 'The only qualification I require is that you like people.' The same thing could be said to each new batch of Probation and Parole Officers. He said it to us. In this respect, at least, I fitted the bill.

There were one or two other things which helped me to start making a fist of this new job. I had life experience. I was a father who had co-navigated the inevitably rocky rapids of five lots of teenage years, with our youngest son not quite out of that stage. Many of my clients were within the range of my sons' ages (18–31). Those who were older and had become parents I could empathize with. Those who were older still were at about my age and were likely to have similar interests. I was then just about to become a grandfather, and did, in April 2009. I also now had my small share of gruelling workplace experiences. One of the questions we ask our clients is, 'Have you been fired?' I could now tick that box.

What also helped to prepare me for this job were my years in pastoral ministry. It is amazing how sheltered the life of a parish priest can be, but parish ministry does inevitably bring you into close and often painful contact with the extremes of human life. There haven't been too many things that have taken me by surprise in my now over three years of dealing with 'offenders'. It was interesting to discover how many of my new colleagues had been ministers or priests in previous lives. One of those who became a good friend at City Office had been a missionary to South America with the Columban Order. Another had been a missionary to Japan, also with the Columbans. Still another had been a parish priest. It wasn't unusual to have so many in the one office.

Perhaps the most surprisingly relevant preparation for this new job was my training and interest in philosophy and theology. I've been amazed by how many philosophical and theological discussions I have had, not just with colleagues, but also with those I supervised. What people don't often realize, and I try to inform them of this, is that the people we see at Probation and Parole, in the community or in gaol, are people from all walks of life, and with every level of education. I've supervised people with larger incomes than me and from more privileged backgrounds than mine. Statistically, of course, those we see do cluster at the disadvantaged end of all populations and face bigger challenges than those of us who haven't yet picked up a criminal record, but that doesn't mean that the big questions of life aren't of interest. Sometimes it is because of these challenges that they are. I would often find myself in theological and philosophical discussion.

One of the first things you learn in becoming a Probation and Parole Officer is how completely ordinary are those we work with, with the same needs, hopes, and desires as the rest of us. What I wasn't prepared for was how extraordinary they are, not just in the challenges they faced, but in their often amazing resilience. I was struck by how hopeful most of my clients are; hopeful that things will get better, that this time round will be the last time round. Such hope is too frequently disappointed, but, time and time again, I found myself being inspired by the ability of people to pick themselves up again and again. Sometimes I was the helping hand to assist them to their feet, but mostly there was still strength in their knees. Easily the saddest moments of my time in this job have been when clients have given up hope. Within a fortnight of beginning the job, a person I hadn't yet met, and had only spoken to on the phone, hanged himself for reasons none of us could quite understand. It seems he had given up hope. The only time I have broken down in tears was just after an interview with a criminalized immigrant to Australia whose mother had rejected him from birth, whose father had later schooled him in the art of drug trafficking. He too seemed to have given up hope. Speaking to him was like speaking into a black hole of despair. I needed the comfort of a friend when I came out of that interview.

Without a doubt, the biggest preparation for this job has been my lifelong Christian faith. One at least partial answer to the question of why I love people is because I have grown up knowing and feeling not only the love of my parents and friends, but also God's love for me and all people. That knowledge has always animated and inspired me, as has the example of Jesus who treated everyone with the same deep respect, who seemed more comfortable with crims, pimps, and prostitutes, with the socially awkward and mentally ill, than he was with the superficially respectable. Being a

Probation and Parole Officer is certainly consistent with my core Christian values.

My friend and former missionary to South America put it well in a note to me one day. The reason he had returned from missionary service was that he was gay and had decided to 'come out' to his family and colleagues, thus ending his career in the church. But his core beliefs remained, influencing his decision to become a Probation and Parole Officer.

In his words,

> As a gay man, I had entry into the world of the poor and oppressed; the anawim[195] of Yahweh. My own journey has led me to a belief that in the smallest act of love given or received is the greatest manifestation of the mystery of our Christian faith. And it still excites me.

One interesting sidelight to this new job was its ability to disabuse me of beliefs I had already begun to shed. One of those beliefs was that persuading people to believe as I did about Jesus and the Christian faith was more important than almost anything else. I had thought that for years. I still believe there is no one on this earth who wouldn't benefit, profoundly and permanently, from an encounter with Jesus, whether devotional or intellectual. I know of no one more impressive, no better candidate for a divine close encounter, no more likely instance of the mystery of God demystified. I have also seen how transformative an encounter with Jesus can be. Numbers of those I supervise have told me of how their faith, new or rediscovered, has helped them meet their many challenges. Churches like Hillsong and the Salvation Army figure often in such stories. Many of my Aboriginal and Torres Strait Islander clients have deep roots in Christian spirituality, deeper still into the ancient spirituality of their peoples. Similarly Pacific Islanders. There is no doubt that faith, and not just Christian faith, has been hugely helpful to people caught up in the criminal justice system.

---

[195] Anawim (pronounced ah-nah-weem) is a Hebrew word meaning, 'the poor who depend on the Lord.' It is used frequently in the Bible, especially the Psalms, and may lie in the background to Jesus' statement 'Blessed are the poor in spirit.'

It has provided them with a moral and spiritual compass—has comforted and inspired them in their efforts to get their lives back on track.

What doesn't make sense to me is the idea that the people I work with need anything more than the faith of a mustard seed to receive the benefits of faith. The idea that they must come to very specific Christian beliefs, such as that Jesus died for them, and that if they don't embrace this and other beliefs, they run the risk of being sent to hell, is deeply problematic. What typically happens when people come into Christian faith is that they are expected to embrace a whole set of new beliefs. The basics of the Christian gospel are soon supplemented by the fine print of whichever doctrinal system is accepted by the church or Christian group they have been converted into.

It is at this point that problems begin to be encountered for probably the majority of those I work with. Most don't go to church, and wouldn't feel comfortable or welcome at church. They are unlikely to come across the sorts of beliefs that would make them acceptable in most churches. Living outside of the persuasional orbit of a faith community, they are unlikely to embrace distinctively Christian (or any other religious) beliefs. Moreover, they are likely to be well warranted in not embracing such beliefs. People have any number of good reasons to not accept even the basics of the Christian gospel. For some, their background makes it sensibly unlikely that they will become Christian. It may be that their parents and friends are from another religious tradition, or are agnostic or atheistic, and they therefore do not feel able or willing to change their beliefs. They are happy to trust the wisdom of their elders.

For some, churchgoing isn't something they or their significant others have ever done. To even countenance that possibility would seem strange. For others, it is their experience of church that has alienated them. They have heard, or had personal experience of sexual and/or physical abuse by priests, youth leaders, and Sunday school teachers, or have looked on helplessly or angrily as church authorities have run for cowardly cover. Or they have been to church and found it unfriendly, or too middle class, or too intellectual, or too prosperity oriented, or just plain boring. Or they just don't know what to think. They left school early without learning to read or write very well, or to analyse or critique. Or they did finish their schooling and went to university and learnt there how odd and antiquated are the beliefs of many Christians, of how completely out of step they are with contemporary attitudes, about women and gays, for example.

Some simply don't have the wherewithal to make informed choices about what to believe. Their lives are pockmarked by the impacts of drugs and alcohol, often resorted to in futile attempts to mask memories of abusive and/or neglectful upbringings, or to avoid facing up to the sometimes dreadful and despicable crimes they have become guilty of. These are people in great need of knowing that someone like God does love them and can forgive them, but they are also often so filled with self-loathing and hatred that they are unlikely ever to avail themselves of the gospel offer. These are the sorts of people Jesus gravitated to and had compassion for in his day, but if the theology of fundamentalism is right, these people are not only very good candidates for hell, because of the awful things many of them have done, they are also likely to leave a lifetime of rejection, grief, and wilful self-destruction to be tipped into an eternity of rejection by their Creator.

There is every good reason to rethink the theologies of fundamentalism.[196] There is every good reason for those I supervise to hold back from embracing a fundamentalist faith, no matter how attractively it is presented to them. Certainly, the fine print needs to be spelled out. Better than that, it needs to be thought out. For the last three or four hundred years, Christians have been preoccupied with matters of belief, with what people should and can believe. This has been a Western preoccupation, and it has skewed

---

[196] With respect to theologies of hell, something is needed other than the usual fundamentalist and/or evangelical obsession with proof texting. I mentioned in chapter 5 the example of John Wenham who, in his book, *Facing Hell, The Story of a Nobody*, rejected the then-dominant doctrine of hell as involving eternal conscious torment. He seeks to justify his rejection of the doctrine by trawling through all the relevant Scriptural texts in order to make room for the possibility that God annihilates those not blessed with salvation. Evangelical elder statesman, John Stott, does similarly. Both he and Wenham feel they need to find a way of rereading texts that appear to support eternal conscious torment. The effort itself is grounded in an unsustainable hermeneutic.

Christianity away from what it does best, which is to be kind, loving, and graceful, being light and salt for the benefit of the world around it. It would do better to re-channel its resources away from trying to talk people into faith into efforts to incarnate a way of living and loving that will adorn what is already a gospel of grace.[197]

Anthony Venn-Brown

The church also needs to rethink its understandings and approach to people it hasn't been so good at loving and being graceful towards, which includes people of homosexual orientation. Not too many months into my new job at City Office, I dropped in to a second-hand book store on my way to work. I noticed a fascinatingly titled book on the stand at the front. It read *A Life of Unlearning* by Anthony Venn-Brown.[198] The title grabbed me. It could so easily have been the title of this book. My own life has been a life of unlearning and relearning. I devoured the book within a few days. It tells the story of Anthony's troubled, even tortured Christian life. Anthony was simultaneously a Christian success story and a failure. He began his Christian life with all the passion and conviction that people coming into Christian faith from the outside normally do. He was captivated by the gospel story of forgiveness and acceptance and by the hope it held out, not just for heaven, but for success in meeting whatever challenges we might face in this life.[199] One big challenge he soon faced was the challenge of his attraction to people of the same gender. When in adolescence his classmates were becoming aroused by the pictures of *Playboy* magazine, he couldn't help noticing the singular lack of effect they had on him. He wasn't 'normal', not in this area of his life at least. For some time, he resisted the idea that he might be homosexual. His parents had no tolerance for such

---

[197] This is not to say that talking about faith is not important. It is. Evangelism remains an important, even defining priority for every Christian church. I talk about my faith more than I have ever done.

[198] Anthony Venn-Brown, *A Life of Unlearning: A Journey to Find the Truth*, (Sydney: New Holland Publishers, 2004). Note that a new and expanded version was published, by the same publisher, in 2007.

[199] Venn-Brown came to Christian faith via Anglican evangelicalism. He spent time in the Baptist denomination before moving into Pentecostalism via the charismatic movement.

an orientation, which they and most others thought unnatural. His church taught, as most churches did at that time,[200] that homosexuality was sinful, sinful because it violated the God-created order of things. It was thought to be a deliberate and defiant rejection of God and his ways.

Anthony therefore refused to give in to the idea that he was homosexual. When the attractions failed to go away, he sought healing, even going to the extent of exorcism to rid himself of this entirely unwelcome aspect of his being, but without success. Even as the struggles intensified, Venn-Brown rose to prominence in Pentecostal circles as an evangelist and conference speaker. He was the originating force behind the formation of Youth Alive, NSW, a spectacularly successful youth organisation organising rallies that attracted as many as 20,000 young people. Anthony had earlier done the hard yards of ministry in small and sometimes struggling rural churches. He had even got married and begun a family, channelling his considerable energy and drive into activities that would give little time or opportunity for him to express his powerful, but still subterranean, sexuality, again without success. Spot-fires broke out. One sexual failure followed another until his life was broken almost completely into two, the public and the private, the outwardly successful and the shameful. Anthony did feel shame, but also, and at great cost to his theology and marriage, he began to feel romance and hints of fulfilment.

Anthony wasn't given the luxury of 'coming out' on his own terms or at a time of his own choosing. His wife, Helen, discovered a letter he'd written to a man he had fallen in love with. She confronted him and brought to a sudden end his double life, producing yet another high-profile 'fallen' Christian leader.[201] Somehow, Helen, Anthony, and their children managed to work their way through this trauma. In time, and with the painful benefit of his experience, Anthony began a ministry to people identifying

---

[200] The early sixties.

[201] Prior to the discovery of the letter, Anthony had all but decided to resign from the ministry, and to do that within twelve months. The letter's discovery, and the public confession and trauma that followed, made a quieter exit impossible.

as gay, lesbian, bisexual, transgender, intersex and queer (GBLTIQ).[202] He has tried his best to make it easier for people to go public and to be truthful about their sexual orientation and history. He has worked especially with Christians, not always happily or easily. Christians have too often been in the front row of those throwing stones, or like St Paul, at the back of the crowd, holding the coats of those doing the throwing, quietly thinking, 'That's exactly what they deserve.'

I decided I'd like to meet Anthony Venn-Brown. His experience seemed so similar to the experiences of lots of people I had now met, including my friend and colleague at work. I got word of a seminar he was running at a church in Glebe and decided I'd turn up. I am glad I did. Anthony shared his story and also his emerging thoughts on how one could be a GBLTIQ person and also a Christian, a coincidence once thought impossible. I wasn't totally persuaded by Anthony's approach. He was thoroughly evangelical in attempting to explain, some would say explain away, passages which appeared to condemn homosexual practice. Lots of good exegetical work has been done to rightly dismiss at least some of these passages, the Sodom and Gomorrah story, for example. It is also true that surprisingly little is said about homosexuality in the Bible. There is no reference to it in the Gospels. Jesus is not reported as saying anything on the subject. However, my educated guess would be that Jesus shared with his Jewish contemporaries, and with his apostles, who did touch on the subject,[203] the belief that sex between men and men or women and women was not acceptable, having been explicitly forbidden in the Jewish Scriptures.

What we don't know from those Scriptures is the reason or reasons such practice was prohibited. We can guess, and all sorts of good guesses have been suggested. One problem I have with the guesses is that they don't quite add up or make sense. One typically offered explanation for the Bible's prohibition of homosexual practice is that such practice violates God's creative intentions. God created Adam and Eve, not Adam and

---

[202] A ministry named *Freedom* 2be which is designed as a network for GBLTIQ people from Christian backgrounds.

[203] In passages such as the following: Romans 1: 26–27; 1 Corinthians 6: 9; 1 Timothy 1: 8–10.

Steve. He laid down the perfect pattern for acceptable sexual relationships by creating human beings male and female, and by his institution and blessing of marriage. Any sex outside of marriage is immoral because it violates God's wise and generous purposes. Homosexuality is wrong on creational grounds. A problem with this way of thinking is that God is the creator not just of the 94–97 per cent of human beings who grow up being attracted to the opposite gender, he is also the creator of gay, lesbian, bi-sexual, and transgender people who make up somewhere between 3 and 6 per cent of every human population.

Even if we grant that social factors may play a role in creating sexual orientation, even if we grant that our knowledge of the causes of homosexual orientation is incomplete, with much research still to do, it still does seem to be the case that there are people who, through no choice of their own, are attracted sexually to people of their own gender. This is the way God has made them. This is the way they are. God's creation isn't perfect in the sense of being monochrome. This is not only so in human populations, but in many animal populations as well. It is therefore not easy to argue, or to argue convincingly, that gay sex is unnatural. It may not be natural to most of us, but that hardly makes it unnatural for those like Anthony Venn-Brown who grew up into a different way of being.

This topic has all sorts of complications, making it difficult for everyone concerned to chart a constructive way forward. These include intersexuality (where children are born with male and female sex organs), Klienfelter's syndrome (a genetic condition in which an individual has XXY chromosomes, rather than typical XY male or XX female chromosomes), and other interesting, though socially painful variations. It is not easy to justify a theology or an ethic which condemns an already small and historically denigrated minority to sexual abstinence, especially by a seemingly cruel appeal to God's perfect creational pattern.

All sorts of subsidiary arguments have been urged to justify lifelong celibacy for those born gay. There are various versions of the social argument. Some argue that our children or youth will be corrupted or made more likely to embrace a promiscuous lifestyle if alternative sexualities are openly tolerated. There may be some truth in this, at least while-ever GBLTIQ people are excluded from the religious and social mainstream, encouraging an understandably rebellious attitude. One could argue, however, that such rebellion against unsustainable and damaging social norms is itself constructive. Young people ought to be joining such revolutions. In any case, emerging evidence suggests that the young are not likely to be 'corrupted' in the direction of changing their sexual orientation or practice because of proximity to homosexual friends, family, or acquaintances. Social values, even changing social values, appear to have minimal impact on the emergence of homosexuality, either to impede it or encourage it, with this being consistent across cultures and over time.[204]

The way forward on this issue is not straightforward or easy. Those of fundamentalist or evangelical, in fact, of any theological orientation, will need to continue to wrestle with what the Scriptures say and mean.[205] Paul's words in Romans 1 are likely to be important. He appears to be talking about people with one disposition acting in ways that are contrary to that disposition, thereby acting unnaturally. Who did he have in mind? Evidence suggests that very few people shift from one orientation to another (going in either direction), with men much less likely to change than women, whose sexuality appears to be more fluid.[206]

Did Paul and the other biblical writers get it wrong, or more modestly, are the reasons for their prohibitions now lost to us given the cultural and historical distance that separates us? Might they have said something different if they had available to them even some of the scientific and sociological evidence that continues to accumulate on these issues? Perhaps so. Contemporary scientific evidence has changed the mind of the church before. It may happen again, and may need to happen. The genius of

---

[204] Glenn Wilson and Qazi Rahman, *Born Gay: the psychobiology of sex orientation*, (London: Peter Owen Publishers, 2005), 23. See also, Simon LeVay, *Gay, Straight, and the Reason Why: The Science of Sexual Orientation*, (Oxford: Oxford University Press, 2011), for a fuller and more up-to-date discussion of relevant scientific studies.

[205] Two recent books that hold promise of promoting further useful discussion are Andrew J. B. Cameron, *Joined-up Life: A Christian account of how ethics works*, (Nottingham: Inter-Varsity Press, 2011), and Fr Nigel Wright (ed), *Five Uneasy Pieces: Essays in Scripture and Sexuality*, (Adelaide: ATF Theology Press, 2011).

[206] See, for example, *Born Gay*, 22–27, 38.

Christianity at its best is its ability to self-reform, to accommodate genuine advances in understanding. All truth is God's truth. If any true belief is considered a threat to any version of Christian theology, so much the worse for that theology.

Having met and talked with Anthony Venn-Brown, I thought it would be good for others to hear his story. I sounded out Dave Smith about the possibility of Anthony coming to our church. He was keen. Early on in his ministry at Dulwich Hill, Dave met and became friends with a gay parishioner who proved wonderfully supportive during some dark days in Dave's life. There is nothing quite like getting to know someone who is gay to disabuse you of your prejudices and fears. There is nothing quite like getting to know a gay person to change your attitude to one of admiration for some of the wonderfully positive benefits of God's creative variety.

Anthony was lined up to come and speak at Holy Trinity one Sunday in July 2009. There was no sense that the congregation at Holy Trinity was expected to agree with Anthony in his efforts to negotiate the exegetical, theological, and ethical rapids that continue to rage around this issue. It was simply a case of wanting to hear his story, and for this to feed in to our own efforts to ride those rapids. Sadly and worryingly, the archdeacon for our area intervened to prohibit Anthony from speaking in church, even if that only entailed being interviewed or sharing his testimony. Puzzlingly, he was allowed to speak after church in the Parish Hall. The only reasons given for this prohibition were that the archbishop had taken a strong stand on homosexuality. Having Venn-Brown speak might be seen as undermining that strong stand. Secondly, Anthony might, if allowed to speak, promote a homosexual lifestyle. Neither reason seemed adequate.

I have long struggled to understand the mindset of those who discourage others from even engaging alternative points of view. I acknowledge the occasional need for censorship and gentle guidance, for children and young people especially. However, for adults, the best way to find out whether one's beliefs are worthy of belief is to carefully and respectfully examine credible alternatives, preferably in their most persuasive form. It is easy to demolish straw men, normally constructed by those who want to knock them down. It is harder to meet and talk with someone who has thought through and become persuaded by an alternative point of view.

Father Elias Leyds

Dulwich Hill Anglican is a place where people are not afraid to hear contrary voices, or to welcome people who think or believe differently. In my time there, two examples stand out. The first happened as a result of one of Holy Trinity's unique ministries, its Fight Club, where people of most ages and all genders learn to box, or just turn up in an effort to get fit. One of the first things you are likely to be asked when you come to church at Holy Trinity for the first time is, 'Would you like to box?' Dave Smith, or Fighting Father Dave, as he is affectionately known, will almost certainly coax you into the ring to do a round or two—unless you have been forewarned, or are strong-willed enough to evade his persuasive skills. I wasn't, and one cracked ribcage later decided I'd stick to touch rugby.

People from around the world have taken an interest in this special ministry forged in Dave's early days at Dulwich Hill. It was used to steer neighbourhood youth away from drugs, crime, and prison, and into better (though still sometimes painful) pursuits. One person who became intrigued by what Dave was doing was Father Elias Leyds, a Dutch monk from the Catholic Order of the Community of St John. When first he came across Dave's website, Elias was in Lithuania and wondering how he might set up something similar for the young people of his neighbourhood.[207] He needed some help, and so organised with Dave to come for a year to observe first-hand how the Fight Club worked.

The year was 2009, and we at Holy Trinity became the beneficiaries of this year-long visit. Elias is a talented theologian and philosopher, with a wonderful ability to connect with ordinary people. He preached from time to time to our benefit, but was more than a guest preacher. He gave valuable help to Dave at the Youth Centre and Fight Club. He organised a visit from pilgrims visiting Sydney for the World Youth Day. To some we were able to offer accommodation—to our enrichment as we got caught up in their enthusiasm for God and Christ. Elias would join us each week in worship while also attending a nearby Catholic Church. Though himself a little shy, you couldn't miss him in the long flowing robes of his Order. Elias

---

[207] He had already organised some one-off boxing events when working as a juvenile prison chaplain in Lithuania.

was Roman Catholic by conviction, in some ways more conservative than those he joined for that year, but we learnt much from him, in part because he approached things from another vantage point, and with the benefit of wide reading and reflection. I don't know of anyone who has subsequently gone off to become a member of the Roman Catholic Church, or to join his Order, nor do I think anyone will, but we still enjoyed the friendship and the growth that comes from being willing to learn from others not quite like ourselves.

Sheikh Mansour Leghaei

Even more stretching, for me certainly, was the process of beginning to learn from people of an entirely different religion, the religion of Islam. Growing up, I had had next to no contact with Muslims. Complicating the process of understanding and appreciation was the fact that any Muslims I did encounter were not only religiously different from me, but also culturally and ethnically different. I was in my forties before I met an Australian-born, ethnically Anglo-Saxon Muslim, and this at a conference put on to educate Anglo-Saxons like me about Islam. I can't now remember the name of the conference, but I do remember being struck by the gentleness and obvious deep piety of those attending. They were very much reaching out to us, wanting to understand, and to be understood. I think there was also some puzzlement that Australians were so irreligious, despite this being, supposedly, a Christian nation.

I knew, and still know, very little about Islam. I've read bits and pieces of articles and books, all helpful for sure, but leaving me with many questions unanswered. More helpful to me than any books or articles has been meeting and learning from people of Islamic belief. When I was at Green Square, I started to get to know an Iranian man who turned up one night to a Carols by Candlelight service at our church, along with his wife and son. They were Sufis, members of the mystical branch of Islam. This man was inquisitive, wanting to know more about Western ways, and how Christianity fitted in, or didn't fit in, to the dominant narratives of Australian life. He was intrigued. I was intrigued by his efforts to understand his own faith and ours. I was attracted to his more mystical and non-literalistic way of reading and understanding the Islamic Scriptures. What also impressed me greatly was the profoundly personal and reverential nature of this man's devotion to Allah, or God.

The only other time I've observed and felt this level of piety and devotion was at a rally in Canberra organized by Dave Smith in support of his friend, Sheikh Mansour Leghaei. Islamic and Christian people from all over Sydney and beyond had descended on Canberra, not unlike its swelling by Indigenous Australians a few years earlier. I couldn't help but see similarities as I and a group of others from Holy Trinity arrived in Canberra to join a growing crowd of mixed faiths, but mostly Muslim, to protest the pending deportation of Sheikh Leghaei.

The story of how Dave Smith came to organise such a rally is worth telling. Not long after his father Bruce passed away, Dave and Angela used their share of the estate to invest in a dirt-bike farm not far from Goulburn in south-western New South Wales. The vision was to create a place of refuge and renewal for troubled youth, such as were dropping in to the Fight Club and Youth Centre. It could also be used for camps and parish house-parties or to get away from the normal busyness of city life. In its early days, when Dave was looking for people to use the farm, a friend of his approached him with news of a group wanting to hire out the farm for a camp. When Dave was told the group was Islamic, he was at first cautious, even fearful, with all sorts of wild thoughts of ideological training camps for young terrorists. He was as ignorant as I had been about Islam, and thoughts of 9/11 came easily to mind. So worried was he by the prospect of this group from The Iman Husain Islamic Centre in Earlwood coming to Binacrombi that he and Angela decided to attend the camp to keep a close watch over what was being taught.

It was a life-changing experience. Dave was amazed at how respectful and conservative the group was. The camp was not unlike camps Dave himself had been to in his growing up years, where speakers would expound and apply aspects of the Christian faith. In this case, it was the Islamic faith and its implications, and especially its implications for life in Australia's highly secularized cultural landscape. Dave was immediately struck by the gentleness and warmth of Shiekh Mansour. A friendship began that weekend which deepened in the days and years that followed. Dave and Mansour started meeting regularly for coffee and became colleagues in a multi-faith round table organised by Marrickville Council. They each benefitted from coming to a better understanding of each other's beliefs. The congregation at Holy Trinity benefitted from this better understanding, with Dave often drawing attention to significant differences and sometimes similarities between Islam and Christianity. This dialogue and friendship was in no way compromising of Dave's or the Sheikh's religious convictions, though it did immeasurably improve their ability to engage with their new Islamic and Christian friends. Stereotypes and misinformation serve no good cause and are inconsistent with the primary virtues of both religions. They are certainly inconsistent with love.

Love and friendship were certainly major motivators when news came through that the Sheikh was likely to be deported. Not long after arriving in Australia, an investigation by ASIO had resulted in two adverse Security Assessments, the full details of which were never disclosed to the Sheikh. Details he was aware of were the result of a poor translation of a document he had with him when he arrived in Australia. That it was a mistranslation was later acknowledged in court. For sixteen years, the Sheikh, his wife, and growing family lived peacefully in Australia. Mansour was a moderate Shia cleric whose ministry had successfully brought together people of diverse ethnic backgrounds. He was the spiritual leader of a congregation which had grown to 1,500 members. For all of his time in Australia, the Sheikh had been an influential voice of moderation at a time when such voices were much needed, especially after 9/11.

For ten years, Sheikh Leghaie fought to have the security assessment revised until in 2007 the High Court decided that rules of procedural fairness and natural justice need not apply in the Sheikh's case, the reason being that he was not yet an Australian citizen. It is hard to imagine a more hurtful or cowardly decision, and in a country that prides itself on a fair go for all. Dismayed by the ruling, Dave Smith unleashed his considerable energies and drive in a shared effort to deflect the Australian Government from its planned actions. I wish I had even half of the energy and sheer doggedness of Dave Smith. He wasn't the only one to become involved, but he was a driving force behind the rally organised for Canberra.

As we gathered on the lawns of Parliament House, within short walking distance of the Parliament, there was some hope that someone from the government might address the rally, if not the immigration minister, Senator Chris Evans, then some other government official. The rally, which happened on Thursday afternoon, 3 June 2010, was peaceful with peaceful intent. Not quite out of sight were riot Police in ominous readiness for any acts of civil disobedience. The crowd which gathered, soon approaching

1,000 strong, was angry, or, if not angry, perplexed by the decision of the government to press ahead with its intention to deport the Sheikh, and with its stony silence when asked to explain its actions. Various speakers at the rally pointed out that even in countries as understandably nervous about acts of terrorism as the United States and Great Britain people would not be deported without explanation. A reason would be given, in terms broad enough to protect national security. That the Australian government would not even do this was puzzling to the point of being outrageous, and certainly unjust.

What struck me about this rally was not the understandable anger, but the relative lack of anger. Here was a community being hurt and disrespected by having its much-loved leader inexplicably taken from them. Here was a community already hurting from insults and accusations that they were terrorists or supported terrorists, whose dress choices were ridiculed, whose loyalty to their country of choice was questioned. What struck me even more than the relative lack of anger was the gracefulness and dignity of those involved in the rally, no one more so than the Sheikh himself. This was no firebrand threatening to erupt in torrents of rage and incitements to jihad, but a man who urged his people to trust and peace. When the rally finally arrived at the edge of Parliament House, with troopers there to prevent any further movement, we non-Muslims witnessed the most amazing thing. Before any of the speeches, before anything was said, the men of the group formed a prayer group, and, facing Mecca, prostrated themselves in prayer. Amidst all the emotion and energy that a crowd this size can create was a moment of calm, a visual and symbolic statement of submission to the will of God, no matter what the results of our efforts. This was hugely impressive.

No one from the government fronted up that day, fearful perhaps of possible political fallout from being seen to be soft on terrorism. I was disappointed. I was disappointed that more Christian leaders weren't courageous enough to come out in support of the Sheikh. It reminded me of the story of the Good Samaritan. Most, it seemed, chose the safer path of walking on the other side of the road, fearful of attracting even a hint of the obvious impurity of being associated with people of another faith. On this day, Dave was Good Samaritan-like. I was proud of him that day, as I often am. Here was someone willing to follow his Master in a very public commitment to justice and the support of the powerless.

Dave gave one of the speeches at the rally. Before it started, and at its conclusion, the gathered crowd broke out into a spontaneous and genuinely meant chant, 'We love you, Father Dave. We love you, Father Dave.' The affection and gratitude was obvious. Others spoke, including Ray Minniecon, who shared with telling empathy the experience of his people who knew well the feeling of not being listened to, and of having their human rights trampled on. A lawyer spoke with feeling and conviction. The Sheikh was last to speak, not passively, and somewhat cheekily in addressing the ears of absent politicians too afraid to front him. But the speech was full of grace and truth.

I was very impressed and moved. I had hardly met the Sheikh. We had corresponded a little by email about our respective theologies, but my life at this time was a little too chaotic to develop anything like the sort of relationship Dave enjoyed. I was, effectively, a bystander, cheering from the sidelines for sure, but not able to do much more. Two months earlier, I had been similarly moved by a quite extraordinary and amazingly gracious visit by the Sheikh and about twenty of his family and friends to Holy Trinity. They joined us for church on Good Friday. It was a Good Friday like none I have ever experienced. The congregation was small, unusually small, but the Sheikh was there.

The service was unashamedly and unapologetically Christian. Things were said in the service about the suffering and death of Jesus, about him being Son of God, in the Athanasian Creed, for example, which contradicted teachings of the Qur'an. None of this was said with intent to offend or convert. We were just doing what we do every year on Good Friday. The furniture was draped in black, the mood was sombre, the music reflective and beautiful. Seven lay preachers, male and female, expounded the seven last sayings of Jesus from the cross. It was, as always, a very special service, all the more special to have our Islamic friends joining us. It brought to my mind the first Good Friday. There weren't only Christians there that day. In fact, there weren't Christians there at all, just puzzled and frightened Jews, along with a few disinterested and duty-hardened Gentiles. On Good Friday the first, the cross was surrounded by doubters and sceptics. Those who were believers only just believed. There were people of other faiths also standing at the foot of the cross of Jesus. How apt for it to happen again all these years later and at Dulwich Hill Anglican.

It was hard at the time to fully appreciate the significance of this Good Friday celebration and of the march (in fact marches) that followed. It is hard even now to make full sense of it. One thing stands out with unambiguous clarity: the resolute courage and compassion of Dave and Angela Smith, and of others caught up in the wake of this very Christian, Islamic, and human quest for justice. I am seeing this from the Christian side, because that is my background and experience. It will be good to hear the same story told by those who know and love the Sheikh. Having him and members of his congregation join us at one of our most sacred Christian celebrations was deeply impressive and humbling.

How else can this be understood? Could it be that these acts of friendship will result in conversions from Christianity to Islam or vice versa? Perhaps, though I think it unlikely. Conversions in either direction don't happen often. They do happen, and are happening in Australian gaols, especially among Indigenous Australians who feel with some justification that Christianity has failed them, who can also identify with the victimization and marginalization of Islamic people. Islam evinces a quiet strength and sincere devotion that is attractive, not just to those made powerless by prison, but to many others as well. Australia lacks soul. It certainly lacks a Christian soul. Muslims appear to be more serious about their religion than most Christians. Islam is a fast-growing religion in contrast to Christianity which is shrinking. There are currently somewhere between 1.2 and 1.6 billion Muslims worldwide, or about 23 per cent of the world's population. Christians make up 32 per cent or just over 2 billion of the world's 6.8 billion people.[208] Those figures apply to those at least notionally

---

[208] An Internet accessed news item dated December 2010 reported that the world's Muslim population is expected to increase by about 35 percent in the next 20 years, rising from 1.6 billion in 2010 to 2.2 billion by 2030. This was according to a report released by the Pew Research Center's Forum on Religion & Public Life. The study is part of the Pew-Templeton Global Religious Futures project, an effort funded by The Pew Charitable Trusts and the John Templeton Foundation to analyze religious change and its impact on societies around the world. Over the next two decades, the worldwide Muslim population is forecast to grow at about twice the rate of the non-Muslim population—an average annual growth rate of 1.5 percent for Muslims compared with 0.7 percent for non-Muslims. If current trends

or nominally Christian. My guess is that those who identify as Muslim are more likely to take their religion seriously than those who tick their census box to say they are Christian.

Will Islam be converted to Christ? I hope so. Coming to a deeper and fuller understanding of the Christ would, I am sure, prove revolutionary. There is certainly encouragement for such engagement in the traditionally respectful attitude Islam has for Jesus.[209] But such a question raises the further interesting question of what Islam would be converting to. Would I want Islam to embrace a fundamentalist version of Christianity? I'm not sure I would. According to David Barrett of the *World Christian Encyclopedia*,[210] Christianity is subdivided into 34,000 separate groupings. Over half of these are independent churches not interested in linking up with others. Most are fundamentalist. Most would expect any converts to fall into line with their way of thinking. An Islamic person would be well-justified in resisting that sort of expectation.

Will the world convert to Islam? I don't think so, and certainly not to fundamentalistic versions of the religion. My understanding of Islam is limited, and so I say the following with some caution, but it seems to me that Islam faces formidable and perhaps unique challenges in breaking itself free from fundamentalism. Any effort to relativise the teachings of the Qur'an encounters the not insignificant obstacle that the words of the Qur'an are believed by many to be the very words of God, with no human agency involved—other than the Prophet Muhammad as privileged recipient of God's revelation. As far as I know, Islam lacks a doctrine of

---

continue, Muslims will make up 26.4 percent of the world's total projected population of 8.3 billion in 2030, up from 23.4 percent of the estimated 2010 world population of 6.9 billion. However, while the global Muslim population is predicted to grow at a faster rate than the non-Muslim population, it is also expected to grow at a slower pace in the next 20 years than it did in the previous two decades.

[209] Devotion to Jesus, following the lead of Muhammad himself, was a key characteristic of the early centuries of Islam.

[210] David B. Barrett, et al., "*World Christian Encyclopedia: A Comparative Survey of Churches and Religions in the Modern World,*" (Oxford: Oxford University Press, 2001).

accommodation, according to which God stoops to employ time-limited concepts and beliefs.²¹¹ Accommodation, along with the variously helpful results of Enlightenment and post-Enlightenment thought, has helped Judaism and Christianity to develop dynamic models of inspiration allowing them to take on board advances in understanding, and to fine-tune their theologies and ethics to take account of new knowledge. It should be noted, however, that in the early years of Islam, there were ferments of scholarship and interpretative reflection that allowed for quite searching questions to be asked about the origins and nature of the Qur'an. Contemporary Islamic scholars are re-asking those questions in efforts to develop more dynamic models of revelation and to help free Islam from the shackles of fundamentalism.²¹²

The need for some such dynamic models is illustrated by the Qur'an's inclusion of the Noah story in its pages. Noah is revered as one of the five greatest prophets through whom God chose to communicate with humankind. There are scattered references to Noah throughout the Qur'an²¹³ and even a chapter bearing his name. An obvious problem, one we have already wrestled with in chapter 6, is that Noah probably never

---

211   There are, however, a number of beliefs that might together form something like an Islamic doctrine of accommodation. These include the distinction often made between the main principles of Islam, which are permanent and trans-cultural, and applications of these principles which vary with time. Also likely to be included in an Islamic theory of accommodation is the Qur'an's encouragement of intellectual pursuits. Muslims are encouraged to study the 'signs' of nature as diligently as they study the 'signs' (or verses—same word *ayāt*) of Scripture, with the acknowledgement that both types of sign are often ambiguous and in need of careful study, often resulting in fresh understandings. See, for example, 3: 7; 16: 11–13, 69; 32: 21–24; 39: 42; 45: 13.

212   For example, the Tunisian intellectual Mohamed Talbi, who has argued for a contemporary and historical reading of the Qur'an, which takes into account historical research into the early history of Islam and its sacred texts. A good further example of progressive Islamic scholarship is the Deer Research Centre—accessed at *www.deenresearchcenter.com*.

213   The following are a sampling of references to Noah in the Qur'an: 17: 3; 37: 75–79, 66: 10.

existed, except as a mythical construct. The details of the story could not possibly be historical. And yet the Qur'an has its version of the story, which, in its essentials, is the same as found in the Jewish and Christian Scriptures, although with some interesting and notable differences.[214] The Qur'an tells the story of Noah differently, with the changed details allowing for the expression of a slightly different theology. This is not at all problematic, if the story is not taken literally. The story is like a parable which can have its details changed to suit whatever good purpose the story teller might choose. But take the story literally or historically and all sorts of problems arise—as we have already seen.

Interpreters of the Qur'an face the same difficulty as do Jewish and Christian exegetes. The Jewish, Christian, and Quranic Scriptures all include Noah in lists of biblical characters. Some of them are historical. Some almost certainly aren't. The Qur'an includes Noah with Abraham, Isaac, Jacob, Elijah, Job, Jonah, David, Jesus, and Mohammed. It describes them all as inspired Islamic prophets. There are very good reasons to doubt the historicity of Noah. There are also good reasons to call into question the historicity of Job and Jonah, and even of Abraham, Isaac, and Jacob. Whether this is so or not, there does seem to be good reason for Islam, like Judaism and Christianity, to revisit its heritage to better make sense of the literature inspiring it.

I have become aware over the years of many Islamic people, and not only its scholars, who are wrestling with the implications of modernity and postmodernity. Such efforts are sometimes ridiculed and dismissed by Islamic fundamentalists, but these efforts ought to be encouraged, in my opinion. That is where the sort of respectful and patient dialogue which began between Sheikh Mansour Leghaei and Father Dave Smith can be

---

[214] For example, those included among Noah's family are not simply those who are biologically related to him, but all those who are righteous and heed his warnings. Of his biological family, one of his sons proves unworthy and is left behind; his wife is also described as unfaithful and, along with Lot's wife, is condemned to enter the fires of hell. It has also been pointed out to me that the Qur'an does not envisage the flood as universal—thus avoiding at least some of the scientific problems raised in chapter 6.

so valuable. Healthy dialogue happens best in a context of friendship and trust—and we have a lot of useful dialoguing yet to do.

For me, this is the next major frontier to be crossed, not just by Islamic and Christian peoples, but by people of all faiths and none. We need to come to a deeper and better understanding of the religious impulse within humankind. What does it mean? Is it there because God has so hard-wired us that we find our ultimate fulfilment in being drawn towards God and in becoming like God? Maybe so. If it is true that God was incarnate in Jesus, and that God can be encountered through an encounter with the human Jesus, then this has implications for our understanding of us and God, one of which is that we can encounter God in other human lives, and not just of the great prophets of religion, but in the ordinary, even troubled human lives I encounter on a daily basis in my current job.

A big challenge for the future of the human race is to think out the implications of these beliefs or possibilities. It no longer makes sense, to me at least, to conclude that an implication of the incarnation is that those who don't quite believe in the way Christians believe will be forever excluded from the presence of God. It similarly makes no sense for Muslims to condemn to hell those whose beliefs and practices are not quite up to scratch.[215] The polarizations of the Qur'an and of the Jewish and Christian Scriptures need to be reread and re-appropriated in ways which don't so

---

[215] Islam appears to be more generous than at least some Christians in its understanding of who will be saved and who will end up in hell. The Qur'an's emphasis is on righteous behaviour as the key determiner of personal destiny, as expressed in the following verses: 'Yes, whoever earns evil and his sin has surrounded him, they are dwellers of the Fire; they will dwell therein forever. And those who believe and do righteous good deeds, they are dwellers of Paradise, they will dwell therein forever.' 2: 81–82. As far as beliefs are concerned, only a small number appear mandatory, including belief in God and the afterlife: 'Indeed, those who believe [Muslims] and those who were guided [Jews], and those who helped Jesus [Christians] and Sabians [followers of John the Baptist]; whoever believes in God and the Last Day and does righteous good deeds shall have their rewards with their Lord, on them shall be no fear, nor shall they grieve.' 2: 62. Polytheists and idolaters will join atheists in hell. The scenario may

readily divide up the human race into the saved and the damned, the acceptable and the unacceptable, the righteous and the unrighteous.[216]

Not that we can dispense with polarizations altogether. We cannot, nor would we want to. Right and wrong, darkness and light, corruption and regeneration, betrayal and reconciliation are opposites that must always guide and warn us. We cannot move beyond these categories, but we can, I hope, find ways to break down the divisions and misunderstandings that bedevil us as a race; ways of being respectful despite our differences, ways of pursuing truth with honesty and courage, ways of loving that will truly incarnate the love of God for all people. How these desirable human efforts will play out eternally, or even within time, I do not know, though I am happy to entrust such things to God.

In telling the story of Sheikh Mansour and Father Dave, I have pretty much brought this book to an end and my life up to date. There are one or two other stories I could tell, but none that would add much to what I have already shared of my journey of faith. There is, however, one final bit of the story I do want to share. It is the story of my mum's death, the loss of the second of the two people this book was written to honour.

---

be more generous and inclusive, though it does still raise its share of fair questions and difficulties.

[216] A long time hero of mine, Billy Graham, appears to have come to similar conclusions in thinking about who will be the beneficiaries of God's love and grace. In a 1997 television interview, Dr Graham was asked by Robert Schuller about the future of Christianity. Graham responded that he didn't think it likely that the world would convert to Christianity. However, in his opinion, this did not thwart the loving purposes of God who could call, and was calling to himself people of all religions and none. In Graham's words, 'He's calling people out of the world for His name, whether they come from the Muslim world, or the Buddhist world, or the Christian world or the non-believing world, they are members of the Body of Christ because they've been called by God. They may not even know the name of Jesus but they know in their hearts that they need something that they don't have, and they turn to the only light that they have, and I think that they are saved, and that they're going to be with us in heaven.'

Just as things were beginning to hot up with the Sheikh's threatened deportation from Sydney,[217] my mother's health began to take a dramatic turn for the worse. For months, she had been saying she no longer felt strong enough or well enough to remain in her small retirement home in Wyee. It had served her and Dad well for many years. It was a family destination of choice. Five years earlier, the whole family had gathered there to farewell my dad, and now Mum was talking about joining him; that her time was running out. We, her children, didn't believe it, didn't want to believe it. Mum's mum had lived to ninety-two, whereas Mum was only eighty-four. We thought she'd live as long, or longer, than her mum. We had convinced ourselves that she also had the longevity gene. It wasn't time for her to go. She hadn't even reached Dad's age at death of eighty-eight. We were in denial, but Mum wasn't.

We managed, in the last few months of her life, to transfer Mum into a room at a nearby nursing home. We were beginning to give it a homely look, had begun to bring her photos and pictures and some furniture across. But she seemed to know that these were not the furnishings she'd need. Heaven was much better endowed. Judy and I were beginning to make almost daily trips up from Sydney to be with her. I had begun writing this book. I had written a draft of the first few chapters and read them to her. It was fun to have Mum as editor, to enjoy her laughter and recollections as I read to her. But I noticed she wasn't completely with me or with her friends who came to see her. I'd sometimes arrive at her bedside and she'd be looking out the window, looking away into the distance. She knew, somehow, that her body was already beginning to shut down, that it wouldn't be long before she'd be gone.

Judy and I were on the phone to my sister Joyce in Melbourne, my sister Dorothy in Calgary, my brother Alan in Portland, keeping them apprised of Mum's fast deteriorating health. It soon became obvious that they would have to join us quickly or they might miss out on seeing her alive. Tickets were purchased, and plans were made to get to Australia as quickly as possible, as it turned out, not quickly enough. On Monday night, 22 March, we received a phone call that Mum had collapsed in her nursing

---

[217] The Sheikh, his wife and 14-year-old daughter left Sydney for Iran on 27 June 2010, leaving three sons behind.

home room and had been rushed to hospital. I was on my way to choir practice at Holy Trinity, and had instead to head north to Wyong. Judy and Jared followed shortly afterwards. Mum passed away quietly in the early hours of 23 March. The night before, Mum was able to tell Judy, Jared, and me that she loved us. I wish my brother and sisters and all our family, including the grandchildren, could have been there to hear those final words, but they know that she thought and felt them.

I am unworthy of my mum in a host of ways. She was the most beautiful of women, inside and out. And what made her so beautiful was her faith, her lifelong, fully fundamentalist faith. She had no trouble believing in Noah and that a big flood had engulfed the world wiping out its inhabitants. Like Dad, she couldn't quite understand why there had to be a hell, or what that might mean for those not of a faith like hers. She was sometimes troubled by aspects of her faith. She wasn't always persuaded by the multiple and detailed theories of her husband, preferring gentle praxis over theory. She was the most loving, gracious, and compassionate person any son could want. All of her children spoke at her funeral. We were bursting with pride and grief.

Chapter 10:

Where to from Here?

As I look back over the years of my life thus far, I do so with a sense of gratitude and wonderment. If it weren't for my son's casual question about whether I would write another book, I doubt whether I would have even thought about embarking on this project, especially since my life's story is still some way off being completed, hopefully. I am still in good health, am still playing touch rugby. I still have much to learn, and all sorts of new discoveries to make. The ocean of knowledge, even of self-knowledge, seems to grow larger and deeper with time, and harder to plumb. But I have never been more content. I have never been more restful. What restlessness remains is the restlessness of not yet being the person I would like to be. It is the restlessness of imperfection and limitation, not just of knowledge, but of love, integrity, and devotion.[218]

This book's title describes my faith as restless. It has been. Fuelling that restlessness has been the relentless onset of questions and puzzles that haven't let me rest as I have tried to answer and resolve them. These first began to trouble me in adolescence and early adulthood. In earlier years, my nurturing in the faith had been so winningly successful that I had no good reason to question the faith of my parents and wider family. I was as happily and contentedly a fundamentalist as any person could be.

---

[218] I feel I need to re-learn, or to learn for the first time ways of expressing my devotion to God and Christ. My mostly intellectual journey needs to transition to a place where heart and spirit join mind in worship.

But questions did begin to intrude, and I could so easily have become an atheist or an agnostic. Preventing me was the discovery of a form of Anglican evangelicalism that appeared to have all the rigour and many of the answers I had begun to look for. I was blessed by meeting some of its finest exemplars, people of impressive intellect, with equally impressive life habits of love, grace, and humility. I was kept in Christian faith longer than many of my earlier friends because of this form of evangelicalism. But over time I have come to see its limitations and blind spots.

What I have become increasingly aware of is the power of paradigms. We all do our thinking, and live our lives, from the vantage point of assumptions and beliefs which make up our worldview—the way we see the world and our life lived within it. A worldview is made up of one's core beliefs and convictions, along with a whole assortment of other beliefs. These are the lenses through which we look at life. They can serve us well or mislead us. They often do both.

For me, the assumptions and beliefs of fundamentalism have turned out to be misleading. Sydney evangelicalism shares many of these beliefs and assumptions, and, to the extent that it does, it too is misleading. The strength of Sydney evangelicalism is its willingness to take on board the well-founded results of contemporary scholarship, while at the same time being reluctant to jump too quickly onto bandwagons that have a habit of crashing or losing their wheels. Evangelicalism is an unstable half-way house between fundamentalisms to its right and liberalisms to its left. There is some strength in this instability. However, the danger, certainly for Sydney evangelicalism, is that in being conservative, it ceases to be open to change and reform. In being defensive, it takes on the tenor or spirit of reactionary fundamentalism. Evangelicalisms of all sorts need a better hermeneutic, one that makes better sense of the Christian Scriptures and of the world we also need to keep trying to understand.

What I also noticed over time was how influential the communities of faith we live in are, and not just religious communities of faith. No matter who we are or what we believe, faith plays a part. We believe things, we trust in things, we assume things, very often without having done much if any scholarly investigation. Even if we have, we are likely to become aware of how hard it is to justify, even to our own level of satisfaction, many of our beliefs. Most of them we just inherit. We pick them up from parents and from the communities which have most influence on us. We all live by faith within communities of faith. We all depend on significant others around us.

That has been my life. It has been a life lived in a succession of communities of faith, the most influential one of all being my family. Along the way, I have discarded some of the beliefs I once had, such as belief in Noah. I don't now think there ever was such a person as Noah, and even if there was, we know next to nothing about him. Not believing in Noah created ripples which ended up being floodwaters strong enough to sweep away earlier ways of reading the Scriptures. These were replaced with a more adaptable model, which now works for me. Hearteningly, it isn't too unlike the model employed by Jesus and his apostles.[219]

I recognise that my own journey of faith has been unsettling for others. It has been for me. But it has also been exciting, and sometimes exhilarating. Each of the communities of faith I have lived in has had a critical element, a willingness to question the status quo and to move on. I have not just inherited beliefs. I have inherited an approach to beliefs, an essentially Enlightenment or even Reformation approach. Even before the Enlightenment, Protestant reformers were critiquing their own religion and encouraging never-ending reformation. The Enlightenment is as much a child of the Reformation as it is of Greek philosophy. My dad was never content to simply accept what was taught him. He would always investigate for himself and encouraged us to do the same. He was happy to have his own views critiqued.

There is some risk involved in being open to have one's opinions criticised and possibly overthrown. It takes courage to admit we may have been wrong. A defining characteristic of Christian fundamentalism was its conviction and fear that if certain of its core beliefs were jettisoned, the whole superstructure of Christian belief would come tumbling down and there would be nothing recognisably left of Christianity. It was an understandable fear, but it has unwittingly created an almost built-in

---

[219] Just as Jesus and apostles were guided by their current experiences and understandings in seeking to understand and appropriate biblical texts, we can follow their lead in doing likewise.

reluctance to face the truth. It has produced the sad spectacle of Christians who have become so concerned with protecting their take on Christianity, their version of its truth, that they cannot see how blind or blinkered they have become.

It is in this sense that Sydney evangelicalism is, or is in danger of becoming, fundamentalist. The admirable impulse to protect the truth has created a culture which has made it less likely that the truth will be known. Sydney evangelicalism needs to change. It needs to lighten up and open up. Unless it does, it will become even more sectarian, and even less likely to win Sydney or the world to its ways. After decades of slight growth, bucking the national trend, Sydney Anglican Churches are shrinking or flatlining. They are certainly not keeping pace with Sydney's population growth.[220] Unless there is a change of heart and direction, this trend won't change.

Change is possible. It does happen, sometimes rapidly, as demonstrated by the collapse of European communism and the dismantling of the Berlin Wall. Change within Sydney and within evangelicalism worldwide is also likely to happen, and may happen quickly. There are promising signs of change.[221] Ironically perhaps, Peter Jensen may himself be a catalyst for

---

[220] Figures available to me indicate that numbers attending Anglican Churches within the Diocese of Sydney have fluctuated both up and down since Peter Jensen became archbishop in 2002, with a low of about 53,000 in 2008. In 2009, there were about 5,000 fewer people attending Anglican Churches in Sydney than in Archbishop Harry Goodhew's final year as archbishop (2001). It is noteworthy that full-time enrolments at Moore College have declined in recent years, occasioning an expansion of part-time study.

[221] Healthy ferment is happening within and beyond evangelicalism. There is the 'emerging church,' and associated 'emerging theology' movements. Older categories of 'liberal' and 'conservative' are being left behind by people who describe themselves as 'post-evangelical' or 'post-liberal.' See, for example, Brian McLaren's *A New Kind of Christianity*, (London: Hodder & Stoughton, 2010) or Marcus J. Borg's *The Heart of Christianity*, (San Francisco: HarperSanFrancisco, 2003). Among evangelicals, the following authors and books are worth dipping into to gain some sense of the issues currently being wrestled with: Peter Enns, *Inspiration and Incarnation: Evangelicals and the Problem of the Old Testament*, (Grand Rapids: Baker

change by taking a more public and decisive stand against Creationism than did his predecessor, Broughton Knox. By embracing a non-literalistic understanding Genesis 1–3, Peter has opened the door to a rereading of Genesis 4–11, and, in fact, to the whole Judaeo-Christian tradition. His opening of the door a little will mean it will be opened wider.

I grew up believing all of the stories of the Bible as straightforwardly factual. Under the influence of modernity's obsession with facts and distaste for fables, legends, and myths, I thought it essential that these stories were both factual and verifiable. It turns out that many of them are not. It may turn out that the Exodus and Conquest stories are not factual, but mythical or legendary.[222] They certainly have not been verified. This would have been an immense problem for me in the early days of my Christian journey.

I have become much more comfortable with stories, whether factual or fictional. They don't lose their value for being fictional. They often become more valuable, more interesting, more amenable to rereading and re-appropriating in the light of where our faith journey has brought us. They also open up new opportunities to understand and appreciate other peoples' stories. This has huge potential for good in places like the Middle East where a literalistic reading of the Jewish Scriptures is creating

---

Academic, 2005), A. T. B. McGowan, *The Divine Inspiration of Scripture: Challenging evangelical perspectives,* (Nottingham: Apollos, 2007); Kenton L. Sparks, *God's Word in Human Words: An Evangelical Appropriation of Critical Biblical Scholarship,* (Grand Rapids: Baker Academic, 2008), William J. Webb, *Slaves, Women and Homosexuals: Exploring the hermeneutics of cultural analysis,* (Downers Grove: Inter-Varsity Press, 2001); Kevin J. Vanhoozer, A. K. M. Adam, Stephen E. Fowl and Francis Watson, *Reading Scripture with the Church: Toward a hermeneutic for theological interpretation,* (Grand Rapids: Baker Academic, 2006).

[222] It is noteworthy that productive efforts are being made to accurately describe biblical history, taking into account fictional elements including myth and legend. V. Philips Long, for example, in *The Art of Biblical History,* (Grand Rapids: Zondervan, 1994), suggests 'fictionalized history' as a useful way of describing biblical history.

such misery for Palestinians now in need of their own Exodus.[223] Stories have power to liberate and enrich. They can also be used to exclude and diminish, depending on how we take them.

As I have walked my own journey of faith, I am aware of lots of fellow travellers. When I have shared my story, as I am doing in this book, I find it resonates and has points of contact with the experiences of many. Others are finding that what they grew up to believe no longer makes sense. Things they once firmly believed they now doubt, though without any clear idea of what the alternatives might be for them. Some squash the doubts and believe more firmly, which is the way of fundamentalisms. Fundamentalisms thrive in times of uncertainty, but they are not the answer. Not only do they create paranoia built on repression, they create easy targets for people like the New Atheists who do us all a service by pointing out the obvious flaws in this style of religion. The world cannot afford the divisiveness and hatred which too often gets stirred up by those who exchange love for God and neighbour for ideological correctness and control.

What is the way forward? Surprisingly perhaps, it is the New Atheists who provide a key to an answer. What has always struck me as I have read through the works of many of the New Atheists is that their enterprise, at its best, is driven by a quest for truth and honesty.[224] They are animated by an ethic which is grounded in the conviction that truth, beauty, and

---

[223] Literalistic Christian and Islamic readings also contribute to what has become a tragic disincentive to embrace any of the world's three major monotheistic religions.

[224] Atheists, whether new or old, are not always as careful with the truth as they should be, as is the case for theists. Able critics of the New Atheists include: Terry Eagleton, *Reason, Faith and Revolution,* (New Haven: Yale University Press, 2009); David Bentley Hart, *Atheist Delusions: the Christian revolution and its fashionable enemies,* (New Haven: Yale University press, 2009); Peter Hitchens, *The Rage Against God: how atheism led me to faith* (London: Continuum, 2010); Alister McGrath, Joanna Collicutt McGrath, *The Dawkins Delusion? Atheist Fundamentalism and the Denial of the Divine,* (London: SPCK, 2007); Keith Ward, *Why there is almost certainly a God: doubting Dawkins* (Oxford: Lion, 2008).

goodness matter. I believe that as well, and it suggests to me, if not to them, that there is at the centre of existence a reality, mysterious and undomesticatable, which is able to unify and give meaning to all—a reality where truth, beauty, and goodness cohere. That reality we know as God.

It is worthy of note that the quest for truth is a pure quest if pursued with purity of heart and motive. None of us is pure, but we recognise purity. It is something we can aspire to. We look to find purity in others, to find people to guide us in our quest for what is good and true. Guides who have led me well are my mum and dad. The best of all guides led them throughout their lives. There is no better guide than the enigmatic Son of man and Son of God from Nazareth. Looking to him, I continue my not yet finished quest, my quest for God.

APPENDICES

Appendix 1: Open Letter to the Anglican Diocese of Sydney. The following letter was submitted for consideration by the Standing Committee of the Diocese of Sydney at its December 11, 2006 meeting. Prior to this, on 30 November 2006, it was sent by e-mail as an Open Letter to people the author considered may be interested. It circulated widely and rapidly. See chapter 7 for the context and background.

I am writing to lay before you some deep concerns I have about the direction in which we appear to be going as a Diocese, to call for a change of heart, and to make some practical suggestions. The concerns are not only mine. They distil countless conversations I have had with many people right across the life of the Diocese; including its leaders and teachers, including many who feel voiceless and powerless.

A vision for the Diocese. If someone were to ask me, 'What sort of a Diocese would you like this Diocese to be?' I would probably reply along these lines: 'I would like to see a more gracious and loving Diocese, within which all people are treated with tender love and respect. I would also, secondly, like to see a more humble Diocese where we all readily acknowledge that we can and must learn from each other. And, finally, I would like to see a Diocese where lively and respectful debate is carried out on the range of issues that face us as a church coming into this 21st century; where other points of view are valued (even when we disagree with them), because they help to sharpen our own thinking—and also because we might learn something from them!

That is the sort of Diocese I would like to see, but sadly that is not what I am seeing emerge. If anything, the trend is in the opposite direction. What has fuelled my concern has been my own experience and the experience of the Parish of

South Sydney over the last 12 months. I am sure that not one of us doubts the importance of love (or, for that matter, humility and openness to enquire after the truth). I am also sure that our Diocesan leaders are motivated by love. However, love is primarily practical and is measured by how well we treat each other, and not just those we agree with or get on with. For a large part of this year, after an early promise of full consultation, the Parish of South Sydney was almost totally sidelined from the process of choosing a new Rector, its appeals ignored, its respectful questions fobbed off (for more details, see appendix). Christian love treats people with respect, but a similar failure to love also happened in the appointment of four new members to the Indigenous Peoples Committee (see below), with its indigenous Chairman, my colleague at South Sydney, not even consulted.

Love has characteristics that simply were not shown in each of these instances, and I suspect that these are not isolated occurrences. I would urge Standing Committee to investigate. Love is also a matter of ethos or spirit. People and churches can be known for their love. Love is a fruit of the Spirit. It ought to characterise us as a Diocese, but, sadly, alarmingly, I simply cannot remember us *ever* being described as loving! I talked with a minister recently who had just come back to Sydney from another Diocese. He was staggered by the critical coldness of some of Sydney Anglicanism's more ardent sons and daughters. This might just be the enthusiasm of youth, but I couldn't help but think of Jesus' words, 'by their fruit you will know them.' If our Christian youth are known less for their 'love, joy, peace and patience', and more for their suspicion, coldness, aggression and self-righteousness, then we have failed them; and the spirit that animates them is not the Spirit of Christ.

I would, secondly, like to see a more humble Diocese. There are all sorts of reasons why we should be humble. We are creatures, not God. We are sinful creatures whose tendency is to distort even the truths we do know. We are profoundly and often negatively shaped by the cultures we grow up in, including our church cultures. We are often blind to our own faults. We over-react to the faults we perceive in others, creating an opposite extreme. We therefore have more than enough reason to be humble, but I am seeing a disturbing lack of humility. Every year during my time in College, students would turn up thinking that they had pretty much learnt everything they needed to know already and were viewing College as a finishing school. More often than not these were students who had come through the Ministry Training Scheme. College does a pretty good job of knocking that sort of arrogance out of students, but often not completely. And why do we have the problem in the first place? Our feeder congregations are clearly failing the Diocese in not teaching and modelling the sort of epistemic humility our Reformed theology ought to demand.

And it is not just in their theological convictions that the sons and daughters of the Diocese are not being humble. I keep hearing stories of students and graduates of Moore College who bull-doze their way into situations because they think they know best; they have the formulas they believe will work best, regardless of the situation, regardless of whose feelings and opinions are disregarded in the process. Of course, there are exceptions to this—many fine exceptions. I have been on nine Moore College Missions and was almost always proud of the team. Often it was just one or two who made a bad name for the rest of us. However, lack of humility is clearly enough of a problem for Sydney Anglicanism to be known for its arrogance.

Arrogance, or even perceived arrogance, would be understandable, though still inexcusable if we Sydney Anglicans had the truth pretty much bottled up; if our understanding and application of the Bible was the best there is in Australia, or even the world. I think sometimes we think and act as if this was the case. It is, in fact, unjustified arrogance. Speaking personally, I have benefited hugely from studying and teaching at Moore College. It is a fine College with many strengths. But there are also weaknesses and blind spots. One of Moore College's great strengths, its Biblical theological approach to drawing out the meaning of Scripture, is not matched by an equally rigorous exploration of the history that lies behind and beyond the text—leading all too often to simplistic and formulaic approaches to preaching and application. The point of saying this is not to criticize Moore College, but to say that we all still have a long way to go in our efforts to understand the Scriptures, not to mention the world and ourselves.

I would, finally, love to see the Diocese become a place where lively and respectful debate was carried out in a context of love, in the pursuit of truth. I don't see this happening, in fact the opposite. There is a disturbing trend towards greater control over and censorship of thought. For example, a questionnaire has recently been trialled with third year ordination candidates asking a series of quite detailed theological questions. Students are assured that some theological diversity is acceptable. However, on certain issues, and these are not specified, 'greater unanimity and clarity of conviction' is required. The effect of these words, in a context where students are also well aware of the (strongly held) opinions of those with power to determine their future, is that dishonesty and fearful compliance is encouraged.

One of the issues canvassed in the questionnaire is whether or not it is acceptable for a woman to preach to mixed audiences of men and women. Phillip Jensen is well known for his view that it is sinful for a woman to preach to men, and also sinful for a man to allow this.[225] This is a position he holds passionately and publicly, as ordination candidates who have attended Ministry Training and Development Days will readily attest. I understand that he believes it to be the *only* acceptable view.[226] Knowledge of such strongly held views (shared by others in MT&D) will inevitably put pressure on students to tick the acceptable box, a pressure that would only increase if answers on other questions are likely to put students out of the mainstream. Such pressure exacerbates an already existing culture of fear that exists within the Diocese.

People are increasingly afraid to voice alternative views; to argue a different case than the dominant line, for fear of being verbally abused and/or socially isolated. People are afraid to go public through fear of being crushed. This is appalling, more characteristic of a cult than of a church. I understand the desire to safeguard the truth. I too am passionate about truth, but the irony is that truth is the first casualty of efforts to stifle healthy and robust debate. It is a sign of lack of confidence in the truth that we attempt to shut down efforts to understand it better, and if the only people we listen to are those who agree with us.

I am worried about the Diocese. I am worried about its future. I am worried about the all engrossing Mission which is producing its own pressures and disappointments. I suspect that one reason that the Mission is not yet thriving as we had hoped it would is because, as a Diocese, we are not sufficiently living in ways that are consistent with the gospel we preach. Not only will God not honour

---

[225] Implied by this view is that Narelle Jarrett, Principal of Mary Andrews College, is sinning when she preaches as she does occasionally at her church. Also implied by this view is that Michael Hill, the retiring vice principal of Moore College, sinned when as a rector of Seaforth he allowed women to preach to men. Also implied by this view is that Phillip's brother, the archbishop, is sinning when he licenses women to preach around the diocese.

[226] I am happy enough for this to be Phillip's personal view. I respect his right to come to it, but I am uncomfortable with Phillip as Head of Ministry Training and Development strongly urging this view to ordination candidates. It undermines the faculty of Moore College where views on this subject are mixed. It puts pressure on students. More than half of this year's fourth year do not believe that it is sinful for a woman to preach to mixed audiences of men and women.

our efforts if we continue to be like this, the people of Sydney who we are seeking to reach are not attracted to this style of Christianity. That certainly is the message I keep hearing in my part of Sydney. In the name of Christ, I am therefore calling for repentance, for a change of heart. I am praying that God will make us more loving, humble and open to truth as together we seek the will and glory of God.

Recommendations:

1. That an enquiry be commissioned to discover whether the concerns expressed in this letter do indeed reflect the views of people and congregations throughout the Diocese;
2. That a HR policy be developed that creates guidelines for the respectful treatment of people and congregations within the Diocese, creating clear lines of accountability so that grievances can be justly resolved and reconciliation achieved;
3. That the administration of the Diocese keep reminding itself of its role as servant of the Parishes; that it adopts a policy of not over-riding a parish's theological and cultural distinctives except in extreme circumstances. It may be that Parishes need to be encouraged to be more assertive of their ecclesiological priority.
4. That the present reluctance to allow non-Sydney and non-Moore College trained people into the Diocese be relaxed (even just a little) to help create a healthier diversity and as a statement of justifiable humility.
5. That Ministry Training and Development be developed in such a way that students and ministers are given permission to differ, and are encouraged to pursue truth in an environment which is supportive of good thinking and scholarship. Within the guidelines of a confessional culture, differences must be allowed; discussion and debate must be encouraged so that a persuasional rather than a coercive or compliant culture develops;
6. That the need for and form of the Questionnaire for 3rd year Ordination candidates be reviewed by a Task Force of suitably qualified and suitably diverse theologians and pastoral leaders.
7. That the Council and Principal of Moore Theological College be encouraged to create and maintain a healthy mix of viewpoints on Faculty. I am often heartened by students who tell me that the Faculty is more diverse and more willing to express divergent points of view than the student body. It would be nice if this greater openness was more general;

Let me finish on a personal note. As you may know, I have recently accepted the position of National Chaplain at Mission Australia. I have started part-time and from next February will be full-time. This is an exciting move for Judy and me. MA wants to reassert its Christian character; to be more decidedly Christian both in its compassionate work and in how the organisation runs. Please pray for me as I contribute to this. Judy and I will be living in Sydney and attending an Anglican Church. I want to continue to work at being more Christ-like myself and to encourage a more Christ-like Diocese. My personal style (born of Christian convictions) is to not burn bridges, but to stubbornly hold onto friendships, even with those with whom I have differences.

I am grateful to you for giving the time to read this.

Yours sincerely,
Rev Dr Keith Mascord

Appendix: South Sydney Parish and the Indigenous Peoples Committee

When John McIntyre accepted the invitation of the Diocese of Gippsland to become its bishop and left Sydney in early February of this year, a suitable replacement needed to be found. The elected Parish Nominators soon discovered that the Parish had lost its right of nomination. However, they were assured that they would be fully consulted in the process of finding a new Rector, which was very generous and encouraging.

Consultation, however, was very limited over a long period of time. This created problems, but worse was yet to come. After months of delay, suddenly a name was suggested: Rev Paul Dew. Paul was given a guided tour of the Parish. There was some haste. Paul had another offer on the table. He met with the Parish Nominators and Parish Wardens; a promising start to what could have been a productive dialogue. However, within two days of this meeting, Rob Forsyth phoned the President of the Nominators to inform him that a letter of invitation would be sent to Paul Dew inviting him to become Rector of the South Sydney. The nominators and wardens had not been asked to give their opinion of Paul's suitability (hardly possible after just one meeting!). Paul himself indicated his inclination to accept the offer, and thus within a few days (after months of delay) the Incumbency of South Sydney had been all but determined, and the promise of full consultation had been broken.

This was disappointing for all sorts of reasons. It was disappointing because the Parish Nominators had been so diligent. They had prayed and called on people to pray, they had resisted negativity; they had tried to be responsible and representative. It was disappointing because this action strained the relationship between Paul and the Parish almost from day one. The impression that Paul had been imposed upon the Parish, that his coming was a *fait accompli*, made it extremely hard for people to embrace Paul as their Pastor, though they have tried very hard (and with increasing success) to do this. It was disappointing because Ray Minniecon, South Sydney's aboriginal pastor, was not consulted as to his opinion about Paul's suitability. Ray was away in Switzerland at an indigenous people's conference for two of the three weeks that Paul had to accept or reject the offer of South Sydney. Moreover, for one of those weeks Paul himself was out of action—in hospital with a burst appendix—making it more difficult for the Parish to get to know him. They hadn't yet heard Paul preach. It was also disappointing because when the Parish Nominators asked Paul to ask the Archbishop for an extension of time (so that both Paul and the Parish could have more time to discern God's will), the Archbishop said no. I also interceded to ask for an extension of time, but received no reply. The president of the Nominators asked for an extension of time. He also received no reply.

How could something like this happen in a Christian organisation devoted to the gospel of the Lord Jesus and to living in ways that are worthy of that gospel? I find that question hard to answer. One could argue, I guess, that we are in a voluntary organisation of churches that gives the Archbishop the right to appoint pastors in certain defined circumstances; such as when its income drops below a certain point. One can well imagine situations where the discretionary power given to the Archbishop by the *Presentation and Exchange Ordinance* might be useful, even necessary, such as when a Parish has become dysfunctional. However, permission given by an ordinance does not, by itself, constitute moral grounds for taking the sort of action that has been taken in this case. The fact that a Parish has lost its right of nomination may actually provide stronger moral grounds for respectful consultation. For example, a congregation may be struggling mightily with the effects of demographic and cultural change; may have been trying its hardest (with great wisdom and appropriateness) to minister the love of Christ in their locality, but with little success. In such a case, to *not* respectfully consult could well be both immoral and un-Christian; as well as a failure of pastoral care.

In the case of South Sydney, it is hard to see any morally justifiable reasons for what was done. The Parish is anything but dysfunctional. It had only just dropped under the local revenue target, and will likely regain it by the end of this year (2006). It is a vibrant and growing Parish. It is unified and inclusive in its love.

The wider community is on side. It is a fantastic Parish, in great shape, which makes its treatment all the more mystifying and disappointing.

What has been even more disappointing than any of the above is that despite this disappointing and unnecessary treatment, the Parish Nominators decided (with some difficulty) to remain godly and to seek reconciliation with the Archbishop (the Biblically mandated thing to do when we are out of fellowship with a brother). They wrote a respectful letter (copies can be made available on request) outlining in detail their reasons for feeling aggrieved, only to receive a letter in reply from Phillip Selden (also available) which did not address even one of the points raised in the letter. This has left the Nominators in even more serious need of reconciliation.

A related example of failure to love in action concerns the Indigenous Peoples Committee. Earlier this year, four new appointments were made to that committee: Deryck Howell, Ken Allen, Greg Anderson and David Woodbridge. What was problematic was not the expertise or otherwise of the appointees, but the manner in which the appointments were made. There was no consultation; none! Its chairperson, Ray Minniecon, wasn't consulted. None of the indigenous people on the committee was consulted about who was to go on to this committee—or off! The Archbishop, under the then current SAIPM ordinance, had the right to make appointments to the committee without consultation. But for there to be no consultation, especially when indigenous people were involved (people with a violent history of marginalization and paternalism), is another disturbing example of failure to love.

Both of the cases mentioned above are serious and in serious need of resolution. However, there is some light emerging at the end of both tunnels. In the aftermath of the decision to appoint new members to the Indigenous Peoples Committee, the new committee, with the exception of Greg Anderson, who had not yet arrived from NT, wrote to the Archbishop (mildly) protesting this failure to consult. The committee hasn't (at this point) heard back from the Archbishop, but the Archbishop has now met with Ray Minniecon and been reconciled with him. Praise God! On the South Sydney Parish front, there has also been a promising first step on the road to reconciliation. At Paul Dew's induction to the Parish on 19 November, a letter was read out from Bishop Robert Forsyth apologizing for the way the Parish had been treated. I am again hoping and praying that the Archbishop will be reconciled both to the Nominators and to the Parish in general. Please pray with me along these lines.

Appendix 2: Second Open Letter. This second letter submitted to the Standing Committee of the Diocese of Sydney for consideration at its 16 October 2007 meeting. It was also made available on a specially constructed web-site.

Dear Archbishop and members of Standing Committee,

As you are aware, a letter sent by me to Standing Committee for consideration at its December 11, 2006 meeting was also sent as an Open Letter to clergy and lay people throughout the Diocese. Many, many people responded to that letter in terms that ought to be of interest and concern to Standing Committee. In this, my second letter, I intend to draw on the concerns and perspectives contained within those responses as I reiterate and elaborate on what I wrote in my first letter.

In trying to understand the significance of these many responses, I invited the following to be my advisers: Dr Alan Craddock, a senior lecturer in Social Psychology and former lecturer in Pastoral Psychology at Moore Theological College, Canon Dr Robert Withycombe, a Canberra-based lecturer in church history and historical theology who in the early 70s was Dean of Students and a lecturer at Moore, Michele Adair, a specialist in organisational development and human resources, Rev. Dr Bill Salier, the recently appointed Vice Principal of Moore College and a teacher in the Ministry and NT Departments, and Louise Greentree, a lecturer in the Faculty of Law at UTS, a lawyer and part-time PhD candidate researching conflict resolution processes in the Anglican Church of Australia. The skills, experience and perspective that these five have brought to this task have been invaluable in helping me (and hopefully you) to better understand our Diocesan life and how we might improve it. They have also each written an independent report.

1. *Are things as bad as the Letter suggests?*

What I called for in my first letter was a more loving, humble and open Diocese. Some who have criticised me for making my call so public have rightly pointed out that we can *always* do better in these areas and that it is not surprising that people have responded so positively to my call. It is like urging parents to do better. Parents will always admit that they could do better, as will Christians!

One could also argue, with some justification, that love does characterize our life together—from the leadership of the Diocese down. I personally have been the beneficiary of love. Peter and Christine, for example, have been wonderfully self-giving in the way they have loved and cared for Judy and myself over the years. Love is hard to quantify, but doubtless there is lots of love around within Sydney Anglicanism, as is also doubtless the case with humility and openness to alternative points of view.

Is it possible that the Open Letter has overstated the problem? That possibility has crossed my mind more than once over the last eight months. However, any such thoughts have been quickly overwhelmed by evidence moving in the other direction. Many people have said that I have understated the problem—and that may also be the case. Let me lay before you some of this evidence.

2. Reasons to think we do have a significant problem:

2.1 The Open Letter process

Such is the nature of internet technology that information can be disseminated rapidly. Anecdotal evidence suggests that the Open Letter has travelled far and wide, and quickly. No sooner had the letter been sent out than responses began to pour in. The letter was sent out in part to ascertain whether the level of concern that I personally felt and had often heard expressed by others was as widespread as I suspected it was.[227]

I am not pretending to have achieved objectivity on this. Pure objectivity, of course, is impossible. However, the responses to the Open Letter suggest, at the very least, that further investigation is called for. Almost all of the letters acknowledged that we do significantly lack in the areas of love, humility and openness to difference, and that, if anything, things are getting worse. Moreover, in letter after letter people claimed to be speaking for many others as well, that their concerns also 'distilled countless conversations.' To date, I have had e-mail and other conversations with 123 clergy people and 194 lay people, including 20 present and former Moore College lecturers.[228] I have received over 300 e-mails with a cumulative word length of 135,000 words, almost all of it supportive of the

---

[227] Note that as I sent the letter out, I encouraged people to send the letter not simply to those who were likely to think similarly, but also to those likely to think differently.

[228] I know of at least another four who haven't made contact with me over the last 8 months, but who have previously expressed concerns along the lines of those expressed in the Open Letter.

Open Letter's thesis and call. Only 2 of the letters argued that we are doing OK in the areas of love, humility and openness to difference. One person thanked me for having the courage to point out the elephant in the room!

2.2   *Evidence emerging from responses to the Open Letter*

- People towards the inner circle of diocesan life are feeling marginalised and powerless.
- People of impeccable evangelical convictions are being told, 'We are not sure we can trust you. We are not sure that you are one of us.' Others are being told, 'You are either with us or you are against us.'
- A common experience by people who don't come from acceptable churches or training paths (such as MTS or MTC) is suspicion, awkwardness and sometimes downright rudeness. People are made to feel that they do not belong, that before they will be accepted they must prove their *bona fides*.
- Some who have transgressed by being open about their even slightly alternative views, or for not sufficiently toeing the party line appear to have been 'punished'; often without explanation, sometimes in ways that have left people deeply hurt. A number of people weren't willing to have their letters read even by the advisory group because of how raw the experience of hurt still was. Some have stopped going to church altogether.
- There has developed an almost palpable culture of fear within the Diocese. I have lost count of how many times people have told me, 'How brave you have been to write that letter!'[229]
- Those just outside of the inner ring feel under suspicion and not really accepted, those further out on the theological and ecclesiological edges of the Diocese are feeling discouraged, beaten, avoided, un-loved—often to the point of cynicism.
- Increasingly, Parishes are having difficulty finding ministers that match their perceived needs and convictions; Parish Nominators are being frustrated time and again by the Diocesan Nominators who are definitely not known for being gracious, humble and open to alternative expressions of Christian faith. Stories have emerged of downright rudeness by members of that group.

---

[229] I myself haven't felt the need to be brave, and have been treated with respect throughout this whole process. However, these comments are consistent with what many others have said about being afraid to speak up for fear of the consequences.

- Sydney Anglicanism's reputation appears to have gotten worse, certainly in Sydney, but also right around the world.
- Moore College trained clergy who work in other Dioceses or overseas have to work hard against the Sydney stereotype of abrasiveness, arrogance and lack of gracious engagement. Sadly, the stereotype keeps on being fed by graduates who won't join Ministers Fraternals (particularly if there are ordained women attending), who avoid contact with their brothers and sisters of different persuasion, churchmanship or denomination, sometimes not even considering them Christian.
- Stories have emerged of evangelical and missionary organisations around the world who are reluctant to take on Moore College trained graduates because of their perceived arrogance and unteachability.

3. Explanation

The evidence such as cited above—drawn from my own experience and from the experience of many others—suggests that the Diocese has a problem, at the very least a pastoral care problem of significant proportions. The challenge for all of us is to understand the nature and causes of the problem. We need to engage in careful diagnosis before any remedies are suggested. My own attempt at a diagnosis follows.

In broad terms, there appears to be something of a culture war (or, less emotively, a tussle) happening. A particular form of Christian culture has emerged to a position of dominance in the Diocese, and appears to be increasing its stranglehold. If my diagnosis is correct, it is this encroaching culture which is creating feelings of alienation, exclusion and powerlessness. What follows is a five-fold description of this emergent culture.

3.1 A fear driven culture

It may, at first sight, appear to be an over-statement to describe this emergent or encroaching culture as 'fear driven.' However, I don't believe this is hyperbole. The fear that I have in mind is the realistic fear of losing or compromising one's faith, or 'the faith'. Conservative, reformed evangelicalism here in Sydney (as in the rest of the world) has faced a series of significant challenges to its existence over the last few hundred years, increasing in intensity and effect over the last 60 years. These perceived and/or real challenges have come in the form of Anglo-Catholicism, modernism, feminism, Pentecostalism and, more recently, post-modernism.

Reformed, conservative evangelicalism has struggled to maintain its character and defining beliefs in the face of these onslaughts.

The Anglican Church League here in Sydney has been committed throughout the more than 90 years of its existence to 'maintain the reformed, protestant and evangelical character of the Anglican Church.' Its present leadership is committed to preserving, in fact, to strengthening the 'reformed, protestant and evangelical' character of Sydney Diocese. The commitment is to preserve and conserve in the face of significant challenges.

It is this commitment which partially explains the fear that is a driving factor in the culture of the Diocese. It is the fear of falling into error, of losing the gospel, of wandering away from the truth. It is an understandable, in fact, a justifiable fear, but it has helped to create a culture that many of us are concerned about.

Evidence of this fear and its effects is seen in the rhetoric of some of our Diocesan leaders. Peter Jensen has more than once explained to audiences his fear that the Diocese might slip into theological liberalism in the belief that we are only ever one generation away from succumbing to this threat.[230] On the ACL web-site, John Chapman notes how New Testament churches, even though founded by the apostles, quickly fell into error, losing the gospel in the process.[231]

The image that comes to mind when thinking of this fear is of a mountain path with progressively steep drops on either side. The only way to avoid danger is to remain in the middle of the path, not letting oneself be enticed even a little way towards the slippery slope. In this scenario, the people who you need to be most afraid of are those who are near you on the path, but who have begun to stray towards the slippery slope. They are the ones most likely to pull you towards that slope from which there is no return. It is the 'soft' evangelicals that are the greatest threat to evangelicalism. That certainly is a common view among those who describe themselves as 'hard' evangelicals.

---

[230] Sharpening this fear has been a book by Fr James T. Burtchaell, *The Dying of the Light* (Grand Rapids: Eerdmans, 1998), which describes the gradual, but irreversible secularization of formerly Christian colleges and universities in the United States, a significant factor in this being the acceptance of 'soft' members who were open to extra-biblical influences; effectively compromised gospel-directed scholarship.

[231] http://www.acl.asn.au/

3.2   *A suspicious culture*

If it is the case that those closest to us are the most dangerous, then we will *need* to be suspicious. We will *need* to always be vigilant, always on the lookout to see whether the person walking with us is truly 'one of us.' We will need to know whether we can trust them; that they won't lead us (or others) towards the slippery slope.

This culture of suspicion manifests itself in various ways, for example, in attitudes to Tom Wright. Tom Wright is one of the world's leading evangelicals, but because of the perception of subtle and therefore dangerous differences of interpretation, he is labelled as unsound or dangerous or a heretic. Even being a Moore College lecturer or student or graduate does not immunise one from suspicion or from being rated 'untrustworthy'.[232] At a deployment meeting for clergy looking for curates, Phillip Jensen was heard to warn the gathered clergy, 'Be careful of the students graduating from Moore College as not all of them think the way we do!'

In letter after letter and conversation after conversation, people have told me of encountering this attitude of suspicion and non-acceptance.[233] Rather than being warmly embraced as brothers and sisters they are kept at arm's length. The sad thing is that pretty much everyone gets this treatment. Those who are closest theologically to those who are driving this culture are being taken aside and told, 'We are not sure we can trust you or that you are one of us.' Those further out

---

[232] A former student of Moore describes his experience: 'I found a general level of competitiveness and "you're out till you're in" that made college a hard and bruising place. A couple of conversations I had fairly early on knocked the wind out me, so to speak. Friends and people I had looked up to . . . were, I was told, "on the outer" and "not to be trusted". When I asked why, it was on the basis of others saying that this should be their approach. I was shocked that the network had such a powerful effect. This wasn't people merely being "not liked". They were considered dangerous, heretical, etc with no basis I could see (they continue in fruitful ministry in the diocese now).'

[233] I keep on hearing stories (and have encountered some of this first-hand) of people being 'warned off' other people and churches; being told not to attend events where 'unacceptable' people are speaking, with unacceptability being quite narrowly defined

are quickly and easily dismissed as unworthy of engagement or respect, often not even considered Christian. I have even heard them described as 'cousins'!

3.3   A politicized culture

Fear and suspicion are the drivers of a highly politicized culture. For many years, the Anglican Church League has been committed to putting its own candidates onto Diocesan committees and into positions of influence in the Diocese. In this endeavour, it has been spectacularly successful. Diocesan committees are now filled with people who are either members of the ACL or ACL approved.[234] But the influence of the ACL now goes further with an ACL approved administration that has the power (and is using it) to appoint whoever it wants to positions of influence.

Synod debate is now dominated by people approved by the ACL, and although it is true that Synod is normally conducted in a good spirit, and is chaired with grace and humour by the Archbishop, it has become an almost entirely compliant body—so much so that many clergy and lay people are choosing to stay away figuring there is no point debating issues that they are sure to lose—if indeed they are even given the opportunity.

The politicisation of the Diocese goes beyond its committees and Synod. Back in the 1990s, REPA developed a strategy of cleansing the boards of other institutions by stealth, so that they would be more acceptable to the dominant Sydney ethos; for example the boards of St Catherine's, Waverley, New College and Robert Menzies College, or of organisations such as AFES and SU.[235]

What is so worrying about this highly politicized character of the now reigning culture is that politics and political means appear to have usurped Christian principles of leadership and relationship. If the outcome is a good gospel outcome, then the means are justified—a form of gospel utilitarianism. The destructive effects of this ethic are seen most obviously in the apparently chronic lack of

---

[234] An estimate from someone who has tried to work this out is that 70 per cent of all contested positions (on Standing Committee for example) are members of the ACL.

[235] The existence and effects of this strategy could easily be documented. I know of numbers of people who heard it articulated.

real consultation with those most affected by decisions being made, including Diocesan officials.[236]

3.4 A monochrome culture

Fear, suspicion and politics are helping to create an increasingly monochrome Diocese. The residual colour and variety of the past is gradually but surely being extinguished. Alternative models of church life are harder to find, and will be in the future if the leadership of the Diocese continues its policy of almost always appointing those it can trust, or whose churchmanship it likes, or whose convictions it approves to parochial and non-parochial positions.

Parish Nominators are instructed to begin their search for a new Rector within the Diocese or, if unavoidable, among those who have come from the Diocese. Only if this search fails, can other evangelicals be considered. Exceptions to this policy apply to existing non-evangelical parishes, but the experience of these parishes when they have sought to find a Rector or curate is that the Diocese has been anything but helpful.[237] Moreover, current Diocesan policy is that if any of these parishes becomes non-viable, an evangelical will be appointed, which, more often than not will mean a Sydney evangelical.

The loss of variety is more serious than simply a strengthening of evangelicalism within the Diocese. It involves the careful guarding of platforms of influence. I remember Peter Bolt once commenting on how few people seem to be allowed to speak at events such as the various Katoomba conventions. His comment: 'It is becoming boring!'[238] Too few people are considered trustworthy enough. The doctrinal credentials of any possible speaker are subject to detailed and narrow scrutiny.

---

[236] In my previous letter, I drew attention to a serious lack of consultation involving the Indigenous Peoples Committee and South Sydney's Parish Nominators. But other examples have kept surfacing, suggesting that this is a problem that needs to be carefully addressed and steps taken to create more respectful procedures.

[237] A comment from a new arrival to the diocese: 'We have not needed to be here even a year to learn that dissenting parishes will find that attempts to gain clergy are vetoed or somehow interfered with.'

[238] Peter still stands by those comments as ongoingly relevant.

Such seems to be the case with MTS—a significant nursery for future Sydney clergy. Earlier this year, I met for breakfast with Col Marshall and Ben Pfahlert. MTS has had an extraordinary life and ministry with over 1,000 men and women having gone through its programmes. Presently, over 200 trainees are connected with MTS in about 80 churches and campuses. The influence and reach of MTS is enormous. Any effort to understand the present state and ethos of the Diocese must take serious account of this influence and reach. In conversation, it emerged that the leaders of MTS have struggled (as have the Faculty of Moore College) with the problem of arrogance and unteachableness among its graduates. It struck me in thinking about this that one of the contributing reasons for this might be that those in the MTS programme are only ever guided and taught by people and churches holding the same or very similar views. If those who address MTS conferences and seminars, and if churches involved with MTS are all of similar conviction, then no matter what is *said* about humility and teachableness this communication is likely to be more than trumped by the meta-communication: 'Only what these teachers and church communities say is acceptable is acceptable. Anything else is not.'

3.5 *An un-self-critical culture*

The culture that has emerged to dominance in the Diocese is highly sensitive to even slight differences in opinion in the belief that even small steps in the wrong direction can have disastrous consequences. As a result, this culture is highly critical of almost every position but its own. From liberalism to post-modernism, from the New Perspective to the Emerging Church movement everything is critiqued. But what I have found to be seriously lacking is robust and non-defensive self-criticism. We (and I include myself) have been blind to our own weaknesses and limitations.

The dominant theology of the Diocese is clearly reactive, but what so often happens with even justifiable reactions is that they become over-reactions. I was amused and saddened recently to hear of a young preacher who was preaching on a passage filled with references to the Holy Spirit and didn't once mention the Holy Spirit (presumably for fear of being thought of as Pentecostal)! The problem with such over-reactive reactions is that the Christianity produced by such reactions is truncated and diminished. Fear of Pentecostal emotion creates emotionally constipated forms of faith. Fear of liberal slipperiness stifles theological creativity and inquisitiveness. Fear of the social gospel leads to socially disengaged, compassion-lacking and environmentally apathetic churches. Fear of feminism creates conditions where women are again repressed and their gifts devalued. Fear of post-modernism and the emerging church movement cements into place modernistic and intellectualist forms of Christianity. All such fear impedes the ability of a church to engage in healthy and on-going reformation of its life and doctrine—in line with the spirit of Luther's adage *ecclesia semper reformanda*.

What I find most disappointing, however, about the presently encroaching culture is that it appears to be unaware of how divisive, unloving and hurtful it is. The fear of one's nearest theological neighbour is fracturing the unity that we have in Christ, a unity that we are enjoined by Scripture to express, strengthen and celebrate. Fear of theological difference and its consequences has produced a dismissive and disrespectful culture where people's feeling and beliefs are being trampled on. This is simply not good enough. I am sure it grieves the Spirit of the Lord Jesus.

4. Conclusion

I mentioned at the beginning of this analysis that 'there appears to be something of a culture war (or, less emotively, a tussle) happening. A particular form of Christian culture has emerged to a position of dominance in the Diocese and appears to be increasing its stranglehold.' I believe that is true. However, I mentioned a war and for there to be a war (or tussle) there must be combatants (or wrestlers). I have come to see that there are indeed combatants or wrestlers—with the struggle as often happening within as between people. The overwhelming theme in almost all of the letters and conversations I have had both before and after the sending of the Open Letter is that people are disturbed by the emergence of this culture. And this includes people within the administration itself. In fact, I can only think of a handful of Christian leaders within the Diocese who are happy (or at least unambiguously happy) with the direction we are taking.

For me, that is a very positive sign. It means that our Diocese is actually filled with people who would like another way—who would like to be encouraged to embrace their brothers and sisters, even those they have differences with; who are ready to acknowledge their own weaknesses and shortcomings of belief and practice; who want to be known for their love (as Jesus said his disciples would be known). A friend of mine recently came back from a conference overseas, and at this conference were Christians of all colours and shades. My friend was blown away by how warmly he was accepted as a Christian brother. His comment, 'They were looking for what unites rather than what divides.' Our Diocese could be like that!

What do I think is the way forward? Strangely enough, I think the way forward is already being taken by increasing numbers of people within the Diocese. The way forward is for all of us to renounce fear, to renounce under-handed, secretive and disrespectful practices; to call to account those who resort to what is unethical (even if legal) thereby dishonouring Christ and causing damage to people. The way forward is for the great majority of people in the Diocese to speak up and say, 'This is *not* what we want! We would like a better way.'

People often ask me what I think about the future of our Diocese. My answer is that I am increasingly optimistic. The culture has already begun to change, or, perhaps more accurately, is resisting efforts to make it more restrictive, punitive and narrow. Join me in praying that God would increasingly fill us with the fruit of his Spirit: love, joy, peace, patience, humility, gentleness, self-control, and that by having this fruit in greater abundance Christ would be honoured and his mission advanced.

INDEX

A

Adair, Michele 163-4, 243
Albany, Chris 187
Allen, Helen 66
Allen, Ken 65, 159, 242
Anderson, Greg 159, 242
Anglican Church League (ACL) 151-3, 247, 249, 256, 259, 286
Anglican Fellowship 152
Anglicans Together 168
apologetics ix, 55 n. 33, 61, 72, 76-7, 97, 129
Arcamone, Dominic 172, 175
Arminius, Jacob 45
atheism 35, 45, 88, 223, 232
Augustine, St, bishop of Hippo 44, 118, 194

B

Babbage, Stuart Barton 128
Barker, Frederic 253
Barrett, David 220
Barry, Alfred 254
Barton, Willie 177
Baxter, Tim 68, 71
Betteridge, Maurice 37, 40, 42, 150
Biblical Theology 54-5, 59, 61-2, 65
Birchley, Keith 54
Blanch, Allan 63
Bolt, Peter 250
Branson, Vic 128
Brennan, Patricia 187-8
Broughton, Geoff 164
Brueggemann, Walter 127 n. 110
bullying 180, 183
But Har Gra 62-5, 107, 158

C

Calvin, John 43-5, 86-7, 118
Carnell, Edward J. 143
Cassian, John 124 n. 105
Celsus 96
Chapman, John 247
Charismatic Movement 29, 67, 207
Chilton, Roger 71-2
Chiswell, Peter 65, 71
Clarke, Greg 164-5
Clifford, W. K. 70
Cohn, Norman 111
Cole, Graham 55-6, 62, 69, 72, 75-6, 131, 155

Craddock, Alan 163, 243, 294
cults, characteristics of 135

D

Darwall, Warren 77
Dasey, Michael 38, 47, 54, 140
Davidson, Phil 71
Davies, D. J. 151
Davies, Glenn 164-5
Dever, William G. 92
Dew, Paul 158, 240, 242
Dewson, Lloyd 68
Dickson, John 78 n. 51, 89
d'Indy, Eric 173, 181
Doran, Gaye 40-2, 174
Doran, Tony 37, 40-2, 54, 56, 58-9, 71, 131, 174
Dudding, Barry 76
Dudding, Jo 76
Dumbrell, Bill 54, 57, 131, 155

E

Englebrecht, Kate 175, 179
Enoch 122
evangelical Anglicanism 36, 43, 56-7, 65, 104
evangelicalism 36-7, 98, 137, 142, 151-4, 168, 246-7, 262-3
evangelism 36, 65, 78, 132, 153-4, 172, 207, 256-60, 283

F

Facing Hell: The Story of a Nobody (Wenham) 101, 206
Farley, Graham 66
Fenton, Albert 4

Forsyth, Robert 76, 109, 151, 158, 161, 240, 242
Fowler, Steve 174
Fraser, Ken 18, 72
fundamentalism 10, 36-7, 142-6, 206, 220-1, 228, 232
Fundamentals: A Testimony to the Truth, The 142

G

Giles, Kevin 37, 43, 262
Glassock, Geoff 177
Gomes, Peter 190
Graffin, Joe 186
Graham, Billy 21-3, 31, 36, 143, 193, 224 n. 216, 257
grammatical-historical method 61 n. 42, 115, 124
Greentree, Louise 163, 243, 263
Grellman, Richard 156-7, 175, 195

H

Hall, Toby 173, 195
Hammond, T. C. 152, 256
Hampshire, Anne 173
Harding, Mark 155
hell 20, 99-101, 103, 121-2, 206 n. 196, 223, 226
hermeneutics 59, 109 n. 82, 169, 180
Hill, Christine 42
Hill, Michael 37, 42, 47, 238 n. 225
homosexuality 128, 130, 207-10
Howell, Deryck 159, 242
Hunter in the Harris, Norm 19-20, 22

I

Indigenous Peoples Committee 236, 240, 242, 250
intersexuality 210
Islam 214-16, 219-22, 223 n. 214

J

Jarrett, Narelle 238 n. 225, 265
Jensen, Michael 144
Jensen, Peter 21, 64, 72, 75, 93-4, 104, 129, 141, 143-4, 146, 160, 162, 167, 230-1, 247
Jensen, Phillip 78-9, 133-4, 136, 138, 140, 153, 155, 157, 238, 248
Jones, Chris 173

K

Kearns, Geoff 25, 39
Keller, Tim 193
Kirk, J. Fergus 6
Klienfelter's syndrome 210
Knox, Broughton 40, 56-7, 63, 93, 231, 258

L

Late Great Planet Earth, The (Lindsey) 29
Lawrence, Graham 64
Lawton, Bill 56, 75, 104, 149, 155-6, 176-7
lectio divina ('divine reading') 179
Leghaei, Sheikh Mansour 214-25
Lewis, C. S. 101, 103
Leyds, Elias 213

liberalism (theological) 143, 145-6, 228
Locke, John 70
Long, V. Philips 91, 92 n. 68, 231 n. 222

M

Marsden, George M. 144
Martyr, Justin 112 n. 84
Maxwell, L. E. 6, 138
McClure, Patrick 173, 175
McIntyre, Jan 148, 150
McIntyre, John xi, 105, 128, 141, 148, 150-1, 240
midrash ('interpretation') 123 n. 103
Minniecon, Ray 141, 150, 158-9, 178, 218, 241-2
Mission Australia 156, 171-82, 184-7, 192, 198
Mohamed Talbi 221 n. 212
monotheism 95
Montgomery, John Warwick 70, 89
Moore, Rod 185
Moore Theological College xi, 50-1, 53-9, 62-5, 75-80, 115, 121, 187, 230, 256, 260, 264
Morton, Dean James 192
Mowll, Howard K. 151-2, 256-7
Muslims 45, 214-15, 219-21, 223

N

Nature of Prejudice, The (Allport) 290
New Atheists 142, 232
Nigh, Harry 194

Noah (Old Testament patriarch) 1, 9, 109-16, 121-2, 191 n. 187, 221-2, 226, 229
Noah's Flood: The Genesis Story in Western Thought (Cohn) 111

O

Obama, Barack 189-90
O'Brien, Peter 56, 72
Olsen, Terry 177
open letter:
    acknowledgment by the press of 263
    copy of first 235
    copy of second 253
    end of 166
    fifth report on 294
    first reading of 165
    first report on 253
    fourth report on 283-7
    origin of 159, 161
    reason for 168
    second report on 263
    third report on 283
Origen (Christian writer) 124 n. 105

P

Packer, J. I. 258
Page, Jenny 25
pesher ('deciphering') 123 n. 103
Peterson, David 72, 76
Pike, Ian 202
Pilgrim's Regress, The (Lewis) 101
Pitman, Walter 112
Plantinga, Alvin ix, 76, 80-8, 101
Porphyry (philosopher) 96
Powell, Ian 71

Prairie Bible Institute (PBI) 5-10, 20, 98
presuppositionalism 61, 97

R

Reformed Evangelical Protestant Association (REPA) 153-5, 249
Rice, Jeremy 71
Richards, Vivian 132
Richardson, Peter 173-4, 181
Richardson, Robyn 175, 178
Ricoeur, Paul 125-6, 179
Rien, Elliot John 2
Robinson, Donald 78
Robinson, Kim 57
Rudd, Kevin 178
Rundle, Nicholas 184, 189, 192-3
Ryan, William 112

S

Salier, Bill 163, 243
Schaeffer, Francis 61, 258
Selden, Phillip 242
sensus divinitatis 86, 88
Shelley, Owen 71
Short, Benjamin 172
Simon, Bill 141
Smith, Angela 170, 215, 219
Smith, Bruce 57, 64, 170, 215
Smith, Claire 164-5
Smith, Dave xi, 64, 165, 170, 199, 212-13, 215-19, 222, 224
Smith, W. S. 255
Spong, John Selby 171
Stanton, Graham 89
Stott, John 206 n. 196, 258
Sumpter, Cathy 68

Sydney Anglicanism   41, 77, 79, 128, 130-2, 142, 146, 151, 154 n. 139, 236-7, 246, 264-5, 276-7

T

Talbot, A. E.   151
Theophilus of Antioch   112 n. 85
Throughcare   184-6, 194, 199
Towner, Doug   25
Tucker, Brian   xi, 77

U

Ussher, James   112 n. 87

V

Van Seters, John   116, 116 n. 94
Van Til, Cornelius   61
Venn-Brown, Anthony   207, 209-10, 212

W

Warranted Christian Belief (Plantinga)   84
Wartheim, R. L.   2
Webb, Barry   56, 75, 131
Wenham, Gordon J.   112
Wenham, John   101, 103, 206 n. 196
White, Alan   48, 50
White, Beth   48-9
Wilberforce, William   36
Withycombe, Robert   163, 243
Women:
  feminism and   261
  ordination of   77, 138, 147 n. 129, 149, 187-8, 281

Women: Biblical teaching   120
Women in Ministry: A Historical and Biblical look at the Role of Women in Christian Leadership (Maxwell)   138
Woodbridge, David   159, 242
Woodhouse, John   164
World Christian Encyclopedia (Barrett)   220
Wright, J. C.   255-6
Wright, Tom   155 n. 145, 248

www.ingramcontent.com/pod-product-compliance
Lightning Source LLC
Chambersburg PA
CBHW050435240426
43661CB00055B/2392